WAR STORIES FROM THE FIELD

—— *by* ——

Joseph Hession
& Kevin Lynch

ISBN 0-935701-91-5

52495>

9 780935 701913

Foghorn
Press
BOOKS BUILDING COMMUNITY™

Foghorn Press, Inc.
555 DeHaro Street #220
San Francisco, CA 94107
(415) 241-9550

Foghorn Press titles are distributed to the book trade by
Publishers Group West, Emeryville, California. To contact
your local representative, call 1-800-788-3123.

To order individual books, please call Foghorn Press
at 1-800-FOGHORN (364-4676).

Library of Congress
Cataloging-in-Publication Data

Hession, Joseph.

War Stories from the Field: a "hit and tell" collection of
the greatest pro football stories ever told
by Joseph Hession and Kevin Lynch, with contributions
from sports writers across the country.

p. cm.
Includes index.
ISBN 0-935701-91-5: $24.95

1. Football players—United States—Anecdotes.
2. National Football League.
I. Lynch, Kevin, 1962-.
II. Title.

GV939.A1H397   1994
796.332'02—dc20

94-29885
CIP

Printed in the United States of America.

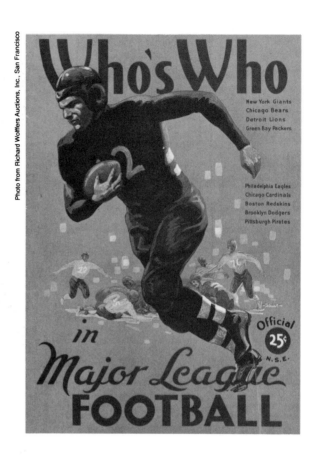

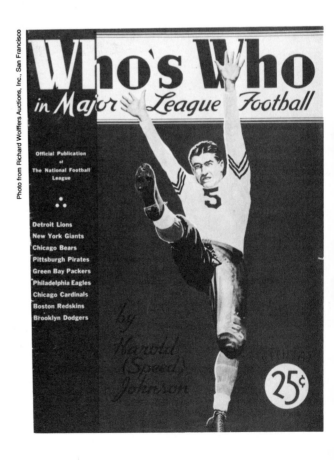

WAR STORIES

FROM THE

FIELD

— by —

Joseph Hession
& Kevin Lynch

Foghorn Press

BOOKS BUILDING COMMUNITY™

BOOK CREDITS

Managing Editor/Book Design: Ann-Marie Brown
Layout/Graphics Coordination: Michele Thomas and Samantha Trautman
Graphics: I. Magnus
Copyediting: Samantha Trautman and Howard Rabinowitz

Special thanks to Bruce Nadler of Great Faces Past and Present, Tim Lynn and especially Clarence Amaral for allowing the Foghorn Press staff to photograph their marvelous collections of football memorabilia.

Thanks also to Peter Hadhazey of the NFL, Frank Krauser and Bruce Bosley of the NFL Alumni, Roger Staubach and Roz Cole of The Staubach Company, and Martin Beeman and Peg O'Donnell of Publishers Group West.

PHOTO CREDITS

Front Cover Photo: Kirk Schlea Photography

Photos by Kingmond Young Photography for Richard Wolffers Auctions, Inc., both of San Francisco: pp. 2 (two magazines), 5 (Super Bowl trophy), 34 (card), 56 (card), 82 (pennant), 101 (pendant), 105 (pennant), 107 (helmet), 119 (program), 121 (Ewbank jacket), 134 (Broncos pendant), 136 (jersey), 139 (helmet), 142 (Stabler helmet), 145 (jersey), 147 (jersey), 159 (Marino helmet), 167 (jersey), 187 (helmet), 198 (jersey), 201 (helmet), 202 (helmet), 203 (helmet), 204 (jersey), 211 (poster), 213 (ring), 218 (football), 229 (card), 231 (helmet), 235 (ring), 268 (helmet), 269 (jersey), 270 (ring), 270 (jersey), 271 (helmet), 272 (jersey)

Photos by AP/Worldwide Photo: pp. 13, 15, 16, 17, 19, 21, 22, 23, 24, 27, 29, 31, 33, 35, 37, 39, 41, 43, 45, 46, 47, 49 (both), 50, 51, 53, 55, 57, 59, 61, 63, 66 (three), 69 (three), 71, 72, 73, 75, 77, 79, 81, 82, 83, 85 (left), 86, 87, 91, 93 (top), 95, 97, 101, 102, 103, 105, 107, 109, 111, 113, 115, 117, 121, 123, 125, 126, 127, 129, 130, 131, 132, 133 (top two photos), 137 (three), 139 (both), 141, 143, 145, 146, 149, 151, 153, 155, 157, 160, 161, 163, 165, 167, 168 (right), 169, 173, 175, 177, 179, 181, 183, 185, 187, 189, 191, 193 (both), 195, 197 (both), 199, 200, 205 (three), 207, 209, 211 (top), 212, 215, 216 (both), 217, 219, 221, 222, 223, 225 (top), 227, 229, 231, 233, 235, 237, 239, 241, 243, 247, 249, 251, 253, 255, 257, 258, 259, 261, 263, 267

Staubach Company: p. 25

Dallas Cowboys: p. 85 (right)

Many sports writers across the country contributed to the stories in this book. In alphabetical order, they are:

Jim Browder, John Bush, Jim Carley, Bob Casterline, Dick Cerasuolo, P.J. Combs, Jimmy Creed, Jim Ducibella, Clare Farnsworth, Jerry Green, Ron Hobson, John Holler, Allen Hoskins, Kevin Kaminski, Bob Labriola, Larry Mayer, Al Pahl, John Rush, Randy Schultz, Dave Spadero, John Steadman, Jerry Strong and Ray Yannucci

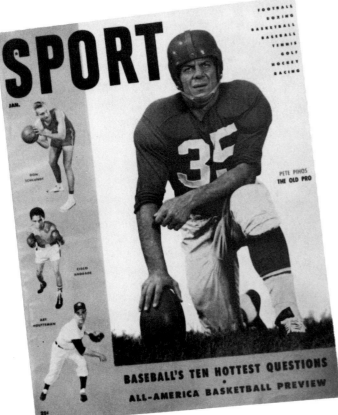

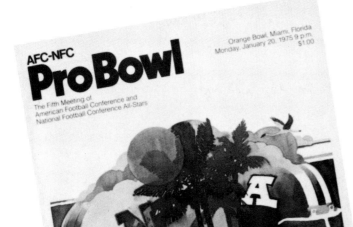

AFC-NFC
Pro Bowl

Orange Bowl, Miami, Florida
Monday, January 20, 1975 9 p.m.
$1.00

The Fifth Meeting of
American Football Conference and
National Football Conference All-Stars

SUPER BOWL V

Price $1.00

WORLD PROFESSIONAL FOOTBALL CHAMPIONSHIP

SEC. ROW/BOX SEAT   ACCT. NO   PRICE

NATIONAL FOOTBALL LEAGUE

1965 WORLD'S CHAMPIONSHIP

SEC. ROW/BOX SEAT

NATIONAL FOOTBALL LEAGUE
1965 WORLD'S CHAMPIONSHIP

BALTIMORE MEMORIAL STADIUM
SUN., JAN. 2, 1966 - 2:05 P.M.

This ticket must not be sold for
more than the price named hereon.
Admission and attendance subject
to Management's right to revoke.

Pete Rozelle
COMMISSIONER

NO REFUND

BALTIMORE MEMORIAL STADIUM . . . SUNDAY JANUARY 2, 1966

NFL SUPER BOWL CHAMPIONS

Super Bowl
Super Bowl III
Super Bowl IV
Super Bowl V
Super Bowl VI
Super Bowl VII
Super Bowl VIII
Super Bowl IX
Super Bowl X
Super Bowl XI
Super Bowl XII
Super Bowl XIII
Super Bowl XIV

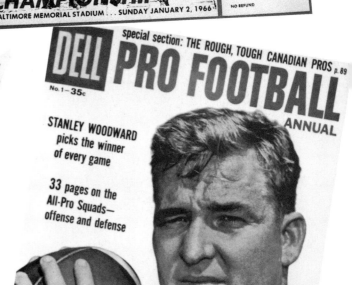

special section: THE ROUGH, TOUGH CANADIAN PROS p. 89

DELL # PRO FOOTBALL ANNUAL

No. 1 – 35c

STANLEY WOODWARD
picks the winner
of every game

33 pages on the
All-Pro Squads—
offense and defense

MAN-EATING LIONS ON THE LOOSE! p. 6

BOBBY LAYNE (above)
TOBIN ROTE (left)

CONTENTS

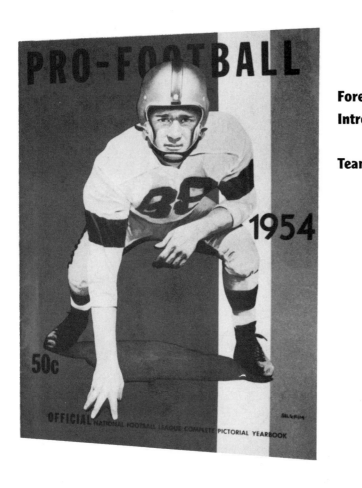

FOREWORD by Roger Staubach

The setting can be a golf tournament, the Pro Football Hall of Fame weekend, a flag football game for charity or a business meeting, but you get more than two pro football players in a room and it won't be too long before the old sea stories start. The most amazing thing is that every down, every hit, every formation, every bad call of every game can be recalled without hesitation.

Pro football is really a fraternity. Within that small club, you go through a lot of different experiences together as teammates and as competitors. You start with training camp, which has a collegiate dormitory-like atmosphere that brings out everything in a person's character, from the crazy to the serious. Then there's practice. And more practice.

Ultimately, it all leads up to the Sunday rivalries. On the field, you can't afford to be a real nice guy. I knew that the players on the other team were out to beat "America's team" and I used that to mentally prepare myself. I knew they didn't like it when I ran out of the pocket, so early in a game I'd run out a few times just to tick them off.

The Dallas Cowboys had a running war with the Washington Redskins in the '70s and they would do anything to get rid of me. Washington's Diron Talbert and coach George Allen were some of the best at trying to distract me with pregame press. Although we were antagonists on the field, we respected each other and eventually became good friends after I retired from football.

When your football career ends, there's nothing better than getting together with old teammates and opponents to rehash the experiences. The Hall of Fame induction ceremonies, when new inductees are brought in and the former inductees attend, provides one of the greatest opportunities to hear about the past. We tell stories. And sometimes you can see the stories begin to escalate.

War Stories From the Field allows the reader entrance into this inner circle. You can hear stories from Hall of Famers like Mike Ditka or classic storytellers like Ray Nitschke, who is always one of the leaders when it comes to reminiscing about games and individuals. NFL players have a number of entertaining stories and you'll find over 200 of them in this book.

Each team has a distinct personality, especially the great teams, and the stories reflect that. The Bears, for example, had the reputation of being the "Monsters of the Midway"—extremely tough. The Steelers were known as an outstanding defensive team that took no prisoners and Jack Lambert, their great linebacker, was the epitome of that attitude. You'd see him across the line of scrimmage with no teeth, glaring at you, and you'd know that this wasn't fun and games.

Dallas was seen as a methodical team, running many formations and plays and being extremely creative. Because Tom Landry was a very serious coach, the Cowboys were perceived as almost sterile, but in reality we had an interesting group of personalities, including players like Thomas Henderson, who had a silver star on his front tooth, Walt Garrison, who was a real cowboy, Ed "Too Tall" Jones, Harvey "Lightning" Martin, Duane Thomas and others.

It all comes back to the stories. Through the stories, you get a glimpse into the game of football itself. It has a bit of everything, from the poetry of life to the brutality of life. When you get in the trenches with the players, you see what it is like out there on the field and what the psychology of the game really is. And it's all right here in this collection.

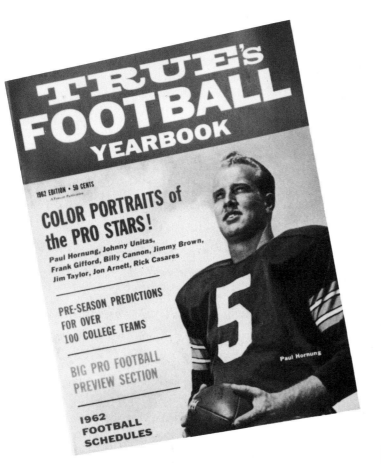

TRUE'S FOOTBALL YEARBOOK

1962 EDITION · 50 CENTS
A Fawcett Publication

COLOR PORTRAITS of the PRO STARS!

Paul Hornung, Johnny Unitas,
Frank Gifford, Billy Cannon, Jimmy Brown,
Jim Taylor, Jon Arnett, Rick Casares

PRE-SEASON PREDICTIONS
FOR OVER
100 COLLEGE TEAMS

BIG PRO FOOTBALL
PREVIEW SECTION

1962
FOOTBALL
SCHEDULES

Paul Hornung

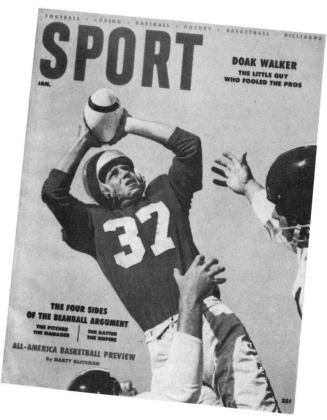

FOOTBALL · BOXING · BASEBALL · HOCKEY · BASKETBALL · BILLIARDS

SPORT

JAN.

DOAK WALKER
THE LITTLE GUY
WHO FOOLED THE PROS

THE FOUR SIDES
OF THE BEANBALL ARGUMENT
THE PITCHER   THE BATTER
THE MANAGER   THE UMPIRE

ALL-AMERICA BASKETBALL PREVIEW
By MARTY GLICKMAN

25¢

SPORTS REVIEW

VOL. 10 · NO. 4 · 1950   PRO FOOTBALL ISSUE   25 CENTS

Pro Football

IN THIS ISSUE
STEVE VAN BUREN STORY ★ 1950 NATIONAL PRO ROUNDUP ★ ACTION PICTURES
WHO ARE THE PRO FOOTBALL COACHES? ★ 1950 TEAM SCHEDULES ★ RECORDS

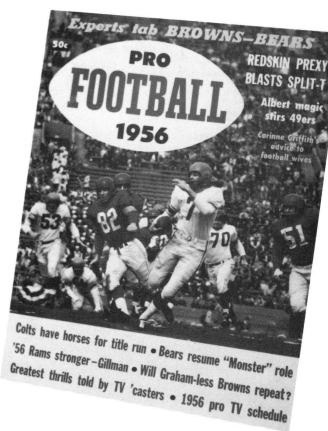

Experts tab BROWNS—BEARS

50c

PRO FOOTBALL 1956

REDSKIN PREXY
BLASTS SPLIT-T

Albert magic
stirs 49ers

Corinne Griffith's
advice to
football wives

Colts have horses for title run • Bears resume "Monster" role
'56 Rams stronger—Gillman • Will Graham-less Browns repeat?
Greatest thrills told by TV 'casters • 1956 pro TV schedule

INTRODUCTION

More than any other sport, professional football lends itself to myth and folklore. After all, football is a game that involves some of the largest human specimens in America. And, like the legendary Paul Bunyan, mighty men seem to be at the root of monumental physical accomplishments that often become bigger than life.

In putting together "War Stories from the Field," we have listened to countless tales from players, coaches, trainers, equipment managers, front office personnel and beat reporters representing every team in the National Football League. The narrators swear the events in many of the stories repeated here happened exactly as recited. Other stories recount some of the most memorable moments in football history and are easily verified.

On the other hand, a few anecdotes seem to mingle factual events with a bit of exaggeration. As we all know, memories become clouded over time and recollections grow vague. But probably more importantly, it seems to be human nature to embellish an exciting incident with a touch of fiction in order to enhance the effect. And, of course, there are some men who enjoy boasting of their physical conquests by adding a little spice to their noteworthy accomplishments.

We felt it was only fair to include a handful of those "enhanced" tales when they seemed to be based on fact and had entertainment value. Even the stories of ancient heroes like Beowulf and King Arthur, handed down orally by professional bards and storytellers, were expanded on and embellished artistically for the benefit of the listener.

In addition, while gathering "War Stories," we occasionally discovered that similar tales were recounted by several different teams. For example, Wayne Walker's turkey prank, which he played on the rest of the Detroit Lions every year at Thanksgiving (see page 99), is now practiced by almost all NFL clubs. And numerous teams recall a time when one of their offensive linemen executed a 'look-out block;' an attempted block where the lineman actually misses his man, then yells 'look out' to the quarterback before he gets creamed.

While most of these narratives have been verified and checked for accuracy, there are a few tales of note that may edge across the thin line that separates history from lore. We hope you enjoy them.

Joseph Hession

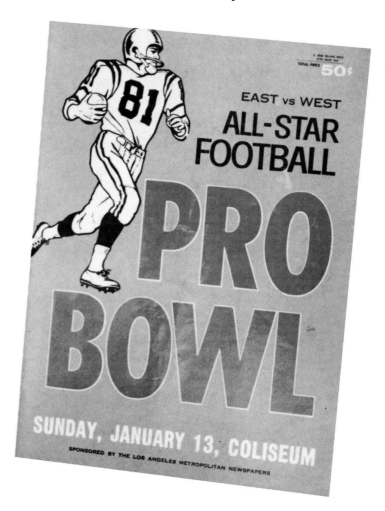

11

Mr. Do-It-All

Early in the 1981 season, St. Louis Cardinals coach Jim Hanifan found himself in a pickle. His receiving corps was so banged up he couldn't find enough pass catchers to put on the field. Hanifan brought the usual parade of free agents and NFL castoffs through camp and was dissatisfied.

Finally, in desperation, he took a look at his own club. Hanifan asked his speedy defensive backs if anyone was willing to give wide receiver a shot. He hoped one had the hands to fill in on a temporary basis.

Third-year strong safety Roy Green was the man who stepped forward. Not only did he have the speed, hands and moves, he'd been studying the Cardinals offense.

"I knew all the plays," Green said. "When the quarterbacks and receivers had meetings, I would listen in. I wanted to know what they were thinking when they tried to get open."

Green got the chance to show his skill sooner than expected. It came just two weeks later in a game against Dallas.

"Coach Hanifan put me in at wide receiver against the Cowboys and I guess no one expected them to really throw to me," Green said.

Quarterback Neil Lomax had other ideas. He heaved a 60-yard pass that Green snatched away from Dallas cornerback Everson Walls at the one-yard line. It set up a touchdown and launched a major career change. Green was not an ordinary pass catcher. Hanifan knew he had himself a deep-threat receiver: an athlete who could turn around games with big plays.

But there was one small problem. Green wasn't ready to give up his role on defense.

In the third week of the 1981 season, Green made NFL history. He caught four passes for 115 yards against the Washington Redskins and had a 58-yard touchdown reception. When the Redskins had the ball on offense, Green simply moved over to his strong safety spot. From there, he intercepted a Joe Theismann pass and found a place for himself in the record book. He became the first player since 1957 to intercept a pass and catch a touchdown pass in the same game.

"I didn't think it was a big deal," Green said. "In high school, I did it. In fact, I never came off the field."

As the 1981 season progressed, Green may have thought he was back in high school. Recognizing his value as a wideout, Hanifan made Green the club's starter. In addition, Green not only returned punts and kickoffs, he was on all kick coverage teams as well. Green's role on defense was diminished, although he still appeared as the nickel back in passing situations.

"I think Roy did everything for us that season but sing the National Anthem," Hanifan said.

Green ended the 1981 season with 33 catches and averaged 21.5 yards per reception.

St. Louis Cardinals receiver Roy Green (81) hauls in a pass against the New York Giants' Perry Williams (23). Green was originally signed as a defensive back. The Cardinals converted him to wide receiver and he became one of the best in football.

ROY GREEN

By 1982, Roy Green was the centerpiece of the Cardinals' high-flying passing game. Playing strictly on offense, Green developed into one of the NFL's most feared receivers, topping the NFC in receptions with 78 in 1983. He was named Wide Receiver of the Year by the NFL Alumni.

The following season, Green led the league with 1,555 yards on 78 catches and 14 touchdowns.

Green went on to catch 559 passes for 8,965 yards and 66 touchdowns during his career. He also had four interceptions during his stint as a safety and shares the NFL record with a 106-yard kickoff return as a rookie.

PLAYING HISTORY:
St. Louis/Phoenix Cardinals
1979-1990
Philadelphia Eagles 1991-1993

13

Heart to Hart

Being in the NFC East, the Cardinals played the Cowboys twice a year during Dallas' glory years. Meeting the Cowboys meant facing their rugged defense, led by free safety Charlie Waters. In one game, Waters was dancing just past the line of scrimmage, faking a blitz and trying to disrupt St. Louis quarterback Jim Hart.

"(Waters) was bouncing all over the place," Hart said. "At one point, I just stopped and looked at him as if to say, 'Will you sit still?' He looked right back at me and mouthed the words, 'I love you.' I completely lost it. My linemen almost stepped on me because after the snap, I forgot it was a pass."

Shut Up and Tackle Me

Without a good offensive line, Jim Hart would have never lasted 18 years in the NFL. Hart considered tackle Dan Dierdorf his personal protector.

"I don't know why Dan Dierdorf isn't in the Hall of Fame," Hart said. "He was so big and fast. Not many people got to me from his side."

One man who tried was Los Angeles Rams defensive end Jack Youngblood, a seven-time Pro Bowl player. He was also one of the most vocal players in the league. But he rarely got through Dierdorf to Hart.

"Jack was always talking during the game," Hart said. "He had this high-pitched voice. He'd always say, 'I'm going to get you. I'm going to get you.'"

Youngblood's voice was always loudest while he was on the line of scrimmage just before the snap. But once the play started, Dierdorf would drive Youngblood toward the sideline and the defensive end's squealing became fainter and fainter to Hart's ears.

"Pretty soon you couldn't hear him anymore," Hart said.

JIM HART joined the Cardinals in 1966 as a free agent out of Southern Illinois University. He inherited the starting quarterback job in 1967, when Charley Johnson was drafted into the army. Hart took over and promptly threw for 3,100 yards. Nearly two decades later, he was still the club's starting quarterback.

Hart excelled in relative obscurity in St. Louis. The Cardinals went to the playoffs just three times during his tenure, each time losing in the first round. But that didn't seem to deter Hart. He was voted to four Pro Bowls and won the NFC Player of the Year award in 1974.

Hart finished his career in 1984 with the Washington Redskins. He passed for 34,665 yards in his career, the sixth highest total of all time. He completed 2,593 of 5,076 pass attempts for 209 touchdowns.

PLAYING HISTORY:

*St. Louis Cardinals 1966-1983
Washington Redskins 1984*

A Wink Under Pressure

Rookie quarterback Neil Lomax broke the St. Louis Cardinals' huddle in a 1981 game and walked slowly toward the line of scrimmage.

He paused behind the center to assess the Dallas Cowboys' defensive alignment. The Dallas safeties had moved toward the line of scrimmage just a bit. Lomax could see a blitz.

"Lomax knew we were coming," former Dallas safety Charlie Waters said. "But he didn't lose it or panic. He looked right at me and gave a little wink. I liked that. I was impressed."

Filling in for injured starter Jim Hart, Lomax oozed confidence, even as a rookie playing in his first NFL game. Waters picked up on it and had to laugh.

"I guess they thought they were going to shake me up a little and throw a blitz at me," Lomax said. "To me, the blitz was just another element to the game. It added to the fun. I was good at reading defenses. I picked it up in college. So I wasn't really rattled."

Lomax fired a 62-yard touchdown pass and showed the poise of a seasoned veteran against the playoff-bound Dallas Cowboys.

Although the Cowboys rallied to beat St. Louis, 30-17, that day, Lomax made an impression on his teammates and opponents with his ability to see the field and his knack for finding open receivers.

"You could see even then that Lomax was going to be a heck of a quarterback," Waters said. "He had all the physical tools. But what impressed me the most was his cool under pressure. We couldn't rattle him."

Neil Lomax (15) joined the St. Louis Cardinals after being the most productive passer in college football history. Lomax passed for 13,220 yards and 106 touchdowns at Portland State. Here, he eludes Redskins defensive end Charles Mann (71).

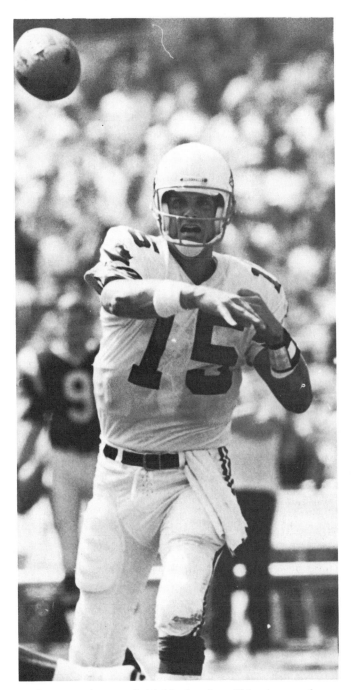

ABOVE: Despite an arthritic hip that slowed him down and forced his premature retirement, quarterback Neil Lomax threw for nearly 23,000 yards for the Cardinals between 1981 and 1988.

NEIL LOMAX

*L*omax guided the Cardinals back to respectability during the 1980s, following the club's dry spell from 1976 to 1982 when they went without a winning season.

In 1984, the Cardinals finished 9-7 and came within a whisker of winning the NFC East Division Championship. It took a last-second field goal by the Washington Redskins to eliminate them. But Lomax almost single-handedly put the Cardinals in the playoffs. He completed 25 of 28 passes in the fourth quarter in a stirring comeback effort.

Lomax finished the 1984 campaign as the league's fourth-ranked passer. He completed 61 percent of his 560 passes for 4,614 yards and 28 touchdowns. Then, in 1987, he topped the NFL in completions and passing yardage. He connected on 275 of 463 passes for 3,387 yards and 24 touchdowns.

Lomax' productivity shouldn't have startled observers. He joined the club in 1981 after the most productive passing career in the history of college football. At Portland State, under coach "Mouse" Davis, Lomax passed for 13,220 yards and 106 touchdowns. Despite his impressive collegiate statistics, Lomax was not selected until the second round of the draft.

During his eight-year career, Lomax completed 1,817 of 3,153 passes for 22,771 yards and 136 touchdowns. Lomax played with the Cardinals from 1981 to 1988.

CARDINALS FACT: The Chicago Cardinals played in the first night game in NFL history on November 6, 1929, in Providence, Rhode Island's Kinsley Park. There, the Cardinals beat the Providence Steam Roller, 16-0. A white football was used so players and fans could see the action.

Need a Hand? Guess Not.

The word "tough" was coined for safety Larry Wilson.

During Larry Wilson's tenure with the St. Louis Cardinals, much of the team's budget was expended on medical supplies to keep him in serviceable condition.

There was not a fracture, laceration, busted tooth, bump, bruise or contusion that could prevent Wilson from lining up in the Red Birds secondary come kickoff time.

"My first year in the league," he said, "I got kind of banged up, so I paid a visit to the trainer. He just gave me a Band-Aid and said, 'Shake it off, kid. You're in the NFL now.' I got the idea."

In the course of one memorable season, the hard-nosed safety played with a pair of broken hands, all the while making his usual triphammer hits. He will always be remembered for a game against the Pittsburgh Steelers. Despite having two broken hands, he persisted in playing—not only playing, but triumphing. Late in the contest, Wilson intercepted a pass to set up the winning touchdown.

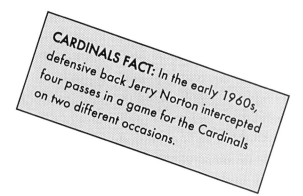

CARDINALS FACT: In the early 1960s, defensive back Jerry Norton intercepted four passes in a game for the Cardinals on two different occasions.

CHICAGO CARDINALS
Coaching Staff

TOM KEANE · BOB NOWASKEY · RAY RICHARDS · CHUCK DRULIS · CHARLEY TRIPPI
HEAD COACH

Keep On Blitzin'

Along with Cardinals defensive coordinator Chuck Drulis, Wilson perfected a daring defensive maneuver which became known as the "safety blitz." On obvious passing downs, he would "cheat up" toward the line of scrimmage and look for a breach in the blocking front. At the snap of the ball, he would burst through the appropriate opening and abruptly confront the quarterback.

"I remember the first time I did it," he said, chuckling. "You should have seen the quarterback's face. His eyes were practically bugging out of his head."

As might be expected, offensive coordinators wasted no time in devising tactics to counter this bit of trickery. Usually, a guard away from the flow of the play would block down behind the scrimmage line, or a big back would be kept in to fill a hole. But Wilson continued to blitz, despite the pain and infirmity involved.

"It still worked pretty well," he said, removing his dentures to reveal a gummy smile. "Besides, it was something I could get my teeth into, so to speak."

LARRY WILSON

$\mathcal{W}$ilson joined the Cardinals in 1960 after graduating from the University of Utah. Initially, the Cardinals tried the six-foot, 190-pounder at cornerback, but he lacked the speed and versatility required to survive at that position. Soon they moved him to free safety where his hard-nosed tactics attained legendary status.

Wilson was also an excellent pass-coverage man. He intercepted 52 passes during his 13-year career and returned them for 800 yards and five touchdowns. In 1966, he led the league with 10 interceptions.

Wilson was named All-Pro six times and played in eight Pro Bowls. After retiring in 1972, he continued to serve the Cardinals as a coach and later in the front office. He was appointed the club's interim head coach at the end of the 1979 season, but declined to continue as head man the following year. In 1978, he was inducted into the Pro Football Hall of Fame, in his first year of eligibility.

CARDINALS FACT: The Chicago Cardinals and the Pittsburgh Steelers merged during the 1944 season because World War II created a shortage of players. They were called "Card-Pitt" and lost all 10 games they played. Fans around the league referred to the club as "the Carpets" because they lay down and let people walk all over them.

CARDINALS FACT: Chicago Cardinals fullback Ernie Nevers set a league record for most points in a game, scoring 40 against the Chicago Bears on Thanksgiving Day, 1929. Nevers scored six touchdowns and added four extra points. He was also the coach of the Cardinals that season.

Nevers was one of the first multi-sport professional athletes. He also pitched for the St. Louis Browns and gave pro basketball a try.

CARDINALS FACT: The Cardinals are the oldest professional football team in America. Chris O'Brien organized the club in 1899. The team got its name after picking up used cardinal red jerseys from the University of Chicago. They were called the Racine Cardinals in those days, until the NFL was formed in 1922 and they relocated to Chicago.

Fair Weather Fans

Ollie Matson returned from the 1952 Olympic Games in Helsinki with a bronze medal in the 400-meter race and a silver in the 1,600-meter relay. He was a national hero.

But Matson's biggest chore still lay ahead. He wanted to make it in the National Football League as a rookie with the Chicago Cardinals.

In just his second week as a professional, he was thrown into the lion's den against the Cardinals' crosstown rivals—the Chicago Bears. The Monsters of the Midway, as the Bears were known in those days, were led by legendary coach George Halas and boasted one of the fiercest defensive units in football. They took on the Cardinals at Comisky Park. For Matson, it was a shocking introduction to the real NFL.

"The Bears had players like Ed Sprinkle and George Connor and Bill George who could really make it rough on a running back," Matson said. "That was a tough group to break in against."

But not as fierce as the Chicago football fans, who were eager to see the ex-Olympian and former All-American halfback from the University of San Francisco put on a good show.

"Early in the game I muffed a punt," Matson

said. "The fans got on me unmercifully and wouldn't let up. I really heard the boos. They were yelling, 'Send him back to San Francisco.'"

Not long afterward, Matson tried to change their opinion. He wanted to atone for his early mistake. He fielded another punt and returned it 94 yards for a touchdown.

The Chicago fans began to soften up a little. The boos slowly turned to light cheers. But they still weren't certain about their rookie.

Matson wasn't through for the day, however. In fact, he was just getting started.

Later in the first half, Matson took a Bears kickoff and scampered 96 yards for another score. The enthusiastic crowd was on its feet now, the applause more vigorous. The fans began to realize they had someone special in their midst.

"After that, I couldn't do anything wrong," Matson said. "It took a while for the fans to warm to me, but once they did they were great to me from that moment on."

To ensure the fans' loyalty, Matson scored a third touchdown on a short run from scrimmage in the second half, accounting for all three Cardinal touchdowns in a 21-10 win over the Bears. As he left the field, he got a boisterous standing ovation. The Chicago fans were finally on his side.

OLLIE MATSON

*I*n his first season with the Cardinals, Matson was named Co-Rookie of the Year and was selected to play in the first of five straight Pro Bowls.

Then, in 1959, Matson was the focal point of a stunning trade that sent him to the Los Angeles Rams for nine players.

Matson was always one of the game's most versatile players. He was equally dangerous as a running back, receiver or kick returner. The 6-foot-2, 220-pound speedster gained 12,844 combined yards during his 14 seasons. He scored 40 rushing touchdowns, 23 on receptions and nine on kick returns.

Matson was elected to the Pro Football Hall of Fame in 1972 in his first year of eligibility.

PLAYING HISTORY:

Chicago Cardinals 1952, 1954-1958   Los Angeles Rams 1959-1962
Detroit Lions 1963   Philadelphia Eagles 1964-1966

CARDINALS FACT: St. Louis Cardinals wide receiver Mike Shumann watched with detached interest as a pair of New York Giants linemen flushed quarterback Jim Hart from the pocket.

As he watched Hart, an 18-year NFL veteran, scrambling for his life, Shumann thought to himself, "He's not going to throw it to me now. I'd get killed."

That's when Hart let fly with a floating pass over the middle. Shumann was dumbfounded, but still stretched to make the catch. As he did, he was blasted by Pro Bowl linebacker Harry Carson. The impact knocked the ball loose and sent Shumann's helmet flying into orbit.

The Cardinals wide receiver landed hard on the Astroturf, but bounced up quickly and began looking for the St. Louis sideline.

"Hey, Harry," Shumann called. "Do me a favor. Just aim me in the direction of our bench, will ya?"

Carson broke out in laughter and sent Shumann toward the Cardinals sideline where he plopped down on the bench next to Hart.

"Hey, Jim," Shumann said. "Why did you throw that pass? You knew I'd get drilled."

"Look, kid, better you than me," Hart replied.

New Kid on the Block

Wide receiver Ken Burrow reported to the Falcons' training camp in 1971 as a wide-eyed rookie and took his place alongside dozens of other draft picks and free agents trying to make an impression on head coach Norm Van Brocklin.

Everyone on the Atlanta Falcons squad knew to watch out for Van Brocklin. He was like General George S. Patton, only a little more brash and unpredictable.

Burrow quickly showed he had the hands to be an effective pass-catcher, but his blocking skills were suspect.

On one play during practice, Burrow's assignment was to throw a crackback block on legendary middle linebacker Tommy Nobis. Burrow knew Nobis was sensitive about his tender knees. So instead of hitting Nobis full steam with a block, he fell to the turf five yards in front of Nobis and rolled into him. It allowed Nobis to protect his delicate knees, but it infuriated Van Brocklin.

"Block him!" Van Brocklin screamed at Burrow. "I want you to put him on his ass!"

A half hour later, the same play was called. This time, Burrow slammed into Nobis and cut him to the turf. Nobis raised up like an angry grizzly bear and attacked the six-foot, 190-pound rookie from San Diego State. Burrow did his best to fend off the attacking beast, but was no match for the All-Pro linebacker.

As the two players went at one another, a smile lit up Van Brocklin's face. He turned to an assistant coach and said, "That Burrow kid is going to be all right. He's going to make it."

"He was just testing me," said Burrow, who won a starting job as a rookie and nabbed 33 passes for 741 yards and six touchdowns. "That's just the way he was."

KEN BURROW caught 152 passes for 2,668 yards and 21 touchdowns during his five seasons with the Falcons. In 1974, he was the club's leading receiver with 34 catches good for 545 yards. Always a deep threat, Burrow averaged nearly 18 yards per reception during his career. He established a club single-game record in 1971 by gaining 190 yards receiving on two different occasions. He played for the Atlanta Falcons from 1971 to 1975.

IN-FLIGHT PATTERN

Falcons coach Norm Van Brocklin was a man who loved confrontation, but a darker side often emerged after his club had lost a football game.

In the early 1970s, the Falcons were usually on the losing end of a long Sunday afternoon. One day, they were trounced by the 49ers in San Francisco. Following the game, long-faced players boarded the plane in silence.

As was tradition, Van Brocklin disappeared into the back of the plane, while the Falcons starters went to the first-class section and pulled the curtain. The rest of the trainers, players and equipment people settled into coach seating. One thing was certain—they all knew to steer clear of Van Brocklin following a defeat.

But after a few in-flight cocktails, Van Brocklin would usually emerge from the back of the plane. By then, he would be particularly vocal and prowl the aircraft searching for anyone who would listen to him complain about the club's ridiculous mistakes.

On this afternoon, Van Brocklin heard a giggle or two from the front of the plane and started in that direction. No one was going to have fun on the plane after a lost game if he could help it.

In the first-class section, a vigorous card game was in progress. Word quickly spread that Van Brocklin was moving that way. Like a group of panicky grade school students, the starting players in first class frantically began hiding cards, poker chips, cold beer and loose change.

By the time the head coach had maneuvered up the aisle and yanked back the curtain, he found the players completely sacked out, some with their faces smashed against the windows, others snoring with wild abandon.

Van Brocklin surveyed the scene, scratched his head and stomped to the back of the plane. After he left, the players broke out the cards again.

It turned out to be the smartest move the Falcons made all day.

BELOW: Atlanta head coach Norm Van Brocklin discusses strategy with guard Royce Smith (64).

Norm Van Brocklin

Norm Van Brocklin was considered one of the greatest quarterbacks to play the game, but he didn't have the same success as a coach. He compiled a 66-97-6 record as head coach of the Minnesota Vikings and later the Atlanta Falcons.

FALCONS FACT: In an effort to shake up the team in 1968 after taking over as head coach, Norm Van Brocklin put five of his starters on waivers and made punter Billy Lothridge, who had just one kidney, a starting safety. Lothridge intercepted three passes and led the league with a 44.3-yard punting average.

Before beginning his coaching career, Van Brocklin was a multi-talented player, who was drafted by the Los Angeles Rams in 1949. During his 12-year playing career, he led the NFL in passing three times and in punting twice.

In 1951, he passed for a record 554 yards in a single game and led the Rams to the NFL title. He clinched the championship game victory over the Cleveland Browns with a 73-yard touchdown pass late in the game.

Early in his career with the Rams, Van Brocklin was forced to share quarterbacking chores with Bob Waterfield. Then, after the 1957 season, he was traded to Philadelphia, where Van Brocklin led the Eagles to the NFL Championship in 1960 and was named the league's Most Valuable Player.

Van Brocklin played in eight Pro Bowls before retiring at the end of the 1960 season. He completed 1,553 passes for 23,611 yards and 173 touchdowns during his career. He also had a 42.9-yard career punting average.

In 1961, he was named head coach of the expansion Minnesota Vikings, then took over head coaching duties for the Atlanta Falcons in 1968. He compiled a 66-97-6 record during his 13 years as an NFL coach. Van Brocklin was selected to the Pro Football Hall of Fame in 1971.

PLAYING & COACHING HISTORY:
Los Angeles Rams 1949-1957
Philadelphia Eagles 1958-1960
Minnesota Vikings 1961-1966 (Head Coach)
Atlanta Falcons 1968-1974 (Head Coach)

STEVE BARTKOWSKI

*T*he Atlanta Falcons needed a miracle as time was running out in a game with the New Orleans Saints late in the 1978 season. Faced with the impossible, Steve Bartkowski delivered.

Trailing 17-6 with 2:23 remaining and the ball at his own 20-yard line, Bartkowski marched the Falcons 80 yards in just over a minute to make the score 17-13.

After holding the Saints on four downs, the Falcons took over again. With 19 seconds left on the clock and the ball on their own 43-yard line, Bartkowski took the snap and heaved a pass over 60 yards in the air, where a cluster of Falcons and New Orleans defenders were congregated. Atlanta wide receiver Wallace Francis deflected the ball into the air and teammate Alfred Jackson nabbed it in the end zone to give Atlanta a miraculous last-second 20-17 victory over New Orleans.

The Atlanta Falcons made quarterback Steve Bartkowski the first player picked in the 1975 NFL draft. During his 12-year NFL career, Bartkowski completed 1,932 of his 3,465 passes for 24,124 yards and 156 touchdowns. He was named to the Pro Bowl twice and was named Falcons Player of the Year in 1980.

Down and Dirty, Pregame Style

In the 1960s, football was a different game. Television money was just trickling in and free agency was 27 years away. Team ownership was still a fledgling venture. So insurance executive Rankin Smith was able to purchase the Atlanta Falcons expansion franchise for a paltry $8 million.

In that initial season, Smith was not quite sure he had made the right investment and he was determined to keep expenses down. He decided to set up training camp at a secluded summer church camp he'd discovered in Black Mountain, North Carolina. But there was a slight problem. There were no football fields, no locker rooms and no shower facilities.

Smith solved the problems by landscaping a large cow pasture, then chalking it off and setting up goal posts. Plumbing was installed in a nearby storage shed to create a shower room. But without proper drainage, the runoff flowed like a river through the shed's front door.

Smith felt the Spartan surroundings not only saved money, but hardened the players for the upcoming season.

After several weeks of practice, the Falcons were ready for their first preseason game. Head coach Norb Hecker's plan was to have a bus transport his club to Asheville, North Carolina, then fly to Atlanta to play the Philadelphia Eagles.

In the late '50s, Hecker had worked in Green Bay as assistant coach to Vince Lombardi and the legendary Packers coach's influence had worn off on him. He ran training camp with the same military sharpness as Lombardi. If a meeting was called at 6:00, players were expected to be in their seats by 5:45. And when the team travelled to games, they were expected to be dressed in their Sunday best.

The Falcons assembled promptly Sunday morning, then watched in amazement as the team buses rolled up. The first two were older model Greyhound buses that were in serviceable condition. But the last one had the roof sheared off as if it had been built for a parade.

After a brief discussion, it was decided that the rookies would ride in the "convertible."

The club departed and buses roared over the partially paved North Carolina roads for nearly an hour. By the time they arrived at the airport, the passengers in the "convertible" looked as if they had stormed Iwo Jima.

Crisp white shirts were black and caked with dirt. Sport coats were wrinkled. Ties were completely gone. The rookies fumbled with their hair, trying to dislodge pebbles and dead insects.

"It looked like they had been through a war," Hecker recalled.

It may have been the only time in NFL history when the players showered before a football game.

But even roses have their share of thorns. Sandwiched between all those seasons of glory, Hecker had his share of prickly seasons as the Atlanta Falcons' head coach from 1966 to 1968.

The Falcons lost their first nine NFL games, then won three of their last five in 1966, finishing with a barely respectable 3-11 record.

Hecker survived as the Falcons skipper until 1968, when he was replaced by Norm Van Brocklin in the fourth game of the campaign.

He compiled a 4-26-1 record as head coach of the Falcons during their inaugural seasons.

PLAYING HISTORY:
Los Angeles Rams 1951-1953
Toronto Argonauts (CFL) 1954
Washington Redskins 1955-1957

COACHING HISTORY:
Atlanta Falcons 1966-1968

NORB HECKER

Some men coach football for a lifetime and never win a title.

Norb Hecker needs nine fingers to show off all the championship rings he's won during his four decades in the NFL.

It started in 1951 when Hecker was a rookie defensive back with the Los Angeles Rams. Behind quarterbacks Norm Van Brocklin and Bob Waterfield, the Rams won the NFL title that year.

In the late 1950s, as an assistant coach with Vince Lombardi and the Green Bay Packers, he captured four more championships.

Then, in 1979, he joined the staff of the San Francisco 49ers as an assistant coach to Bill Walsh. He won four Super Bowl rings with the 49ers.

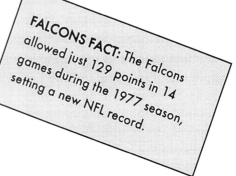

FALCONS FACT: The Falcons allowed just 129 points in 14 games during the 1977 season, setting a new NFL record.

Mind the Feet

In every industry, there are so-called "tricks of the trade." In the NFL, learning these unwritten rules can be a matter of survival.

As a heralded rookie with the expansion Atlanta Falcons in 1966, middle linebacker Tommy Nobis was just beginning to learn pro football's trade secrets. One of the most important things discovered by the Outland Trophy and Maxwell Award winner from the University of Texas was never to anger veterans from other teams.

The easiest way to aggravate a gnarled NFL veteran, Nobis was told, was to take a shot at an area of the body that was suffering from an old injury.

As players advanced in their careers, they invariably developed bumps and bruises that lingered season after season. Some involved surgery. It was best to avoid an opposing player's sore spots. Why give the veterans reason to hold a grudge against you?

Nobis had that unwritten rule on his mind as the Falcons were preparing for their first road trip of the 1966 season and a game against the Philadelphia Eagles. En route to Philadelphia, Nobis was warned by several players to stay away from the battered feet of Eagles tackle Bob Brown.

Brown was a gigantic man. He stood 6-foot-4 and weighed 290 pounds. It was rumored that a hungry grizzly bear was friendlier than an irritated Bob Brown.

Nobis, who was preparing to play in just his second NFL game, took the information and filed it away.

On the Eagles' first series of the game, they ran a sweep. Nobis read it and turned to pursue the play. He took one step and realized he'd made a mistake. There was Brown thundering at him with a full head of steam. Nobis could do nothing to avoid the collision.

Nobis remembers a flash of light at the moment of impact and then his own feet painted against the sky as he fell backward in a heap. After the whistle, Brown reached down and picked the crumpled rookie up off the turf. Then he gave Nobis the standard line.

"Welcome to the NFL," Brown sneered.

Nobis collected his thoughts just long enough to say, "But Bob, I never touched your feet!"

Brown's 290 pounds melted into great peals of laughter. Nobis had been warned, Brown realized. And without knowing it, Nobis had made a friend for life.

FALCONS FACT: All-America and Outland Trophy-winning linebacker Tommy Nobis from the University of Texas was drafted by the NFL's Atlanta Falcons and the Houston Oilers of the AFL in 1965. After the draft, he received a radio message from a pair of astronauts circling the earth. They tried to coax Nobis into signing with Houston. Nobis chose Atlanta and was named Rookie of the Year in 1966.

YOU NEVER KNOW WHAT'LL COME UP

*E*ven players as feared and respected as linebacker Tommy Nobis had their embarrassing moments.

For Nobis, it came in 1968 when the Falcons held training camp in Greensville, South Carolina, just an hour and a half from Atlanta.

The franchise was still in its infancy. In order to promote interest in the Falcons, the camp was open to fans, who were encouraged to drop by for autographs.

One night, Nobis and his teammates hit the town and stayed out a bit later than usual.

"We went out and had a few cold ones," Nobis said. "I let my hair down a little bit more than most."

The next day, practice began at 3:30 in the afternoon. It happened to be the hottest day of camp and about 3,000 fans filed in to watch the club scrimmage. Team owner Rankin Smith was also on hand.

"We had a hard scrimmage up and down the field," Nobis said. "And those cold ones I had the night before started to come up."

With the team owner, head coach Norm Van Brocklin and 3,000 people watching, Nobis bent over in the huddle and vomited.

"The huddle quickly broke and everyone saw it," Nobis said. "I was standing there with half my supper stuck to my facemask. Van Brocklin

yelled, 'Hey, Nobis, have another beer!' Everybody started laughing. He told me to get my tail off the field. But after that there was no way I was going to leave the field. I finished practice, even though it nearly killed me."

ABOVE: Tommy Nobis barks out signals to his teammates during a practice session. Nobis won Rookie of the Year honors in 1966 and became one of the NFL's top middle linebackers. He was selected to play in five Pro Bowls during his first seven seasons. He played for the Atlanta Falcons from 1966 to 1976.

"MUMBO" JUMBLE

During his 18 seasons with the Atlanta Falcons, from 1969 to 1986, Jeff Van Note figures he had at least 18 head-to-head clashes with the Los Angeles Rams Hall of Fame defensive lineman Merlin Olsen.

"A massive man," Van Note remembered. "He had huge hands."

In order to keep the perennial All-Pro in check, Van Note pulled every trick in the book from his center position. He held, clipped, leg whipped, tripped, bit, yelled, cussed and punched in an effort to keep Olsen from making a tackle.

"He never said a word," Van Note remembered. "At the end of each game, win or lose, he'd shake my hand, say politely, 'Nice game,' then walk off the field."

But Olsen, a Phi Beta Kappa scholar and Outland Trophy winner at Utah State, had been taking mental notes during those years. He knew that someday he would get his revenge. He was just waiting for the right time and place.

During the 1970s, Merlin Olsen was all that remained of the Rams' famed "Fearsome Foursome." But he was joined by a pack of young and aggressive defensive linemen that included Jack Youngblood, Fred Dryer and Larry Brooks. Although not as big as the old "Fearsome Foursome," which averaged 6-foot-6 and 275 pounds, they were much quicker. They often took advantage of that speed by running a defensive line stunt they called "The Mumbo."

Olsen's job on the stunt was to take out the center and the right guard, freeing up the Rams defensive end and allowing him to loop around the line to get to the quarterback. It was especially effective in passing situations.

Late in Olsen's career, which ran from 1962 to 1976, the Falcons were hosting the Rams. Although nearly 35 years old, Olsen had played in a record 14 consecutive Pro Bowls. He dominated opponents with brute strength and impeccable technique, but he'd also picked up a few tricks during his long career.

Atlanta faced a third-and-long situation. It was an obvious passing down.

Van Note snapped the ball to quarterback Steve Bartkowski and settled into his blocking stance. Olsen tore into Van Note and then slyly grabbed him and the right guard. It was "The Mumbo."

Van Note, of course, was supposed to break away from Olsen and pick up the charging defensive end. He struggled to break free, but couldn't wriggle out of Olsen's Herculean grasp.

From the corner of his eye, Van Note saw Rams defensive end Larry Brooks steaming toward the quarterback. He plowed into Bartkowski to record a bruising sack.

Van Note was beside himself. He charged up to the referee and pleaded his case.

"Didn't you see that?!" Van Note screamed at the official. "He held me! Hell, he can't do that! Throw a flag!"

Suddenly, the 6-foot-2, 250-pound Van Note felt somebody standing behind him, looking over his shoulder. It was a bemused Olsen, who stood a head higher and outweighed Van Note by 25 pounds.

"Now look who's complaining about holding," Olsen said politely before walking back to the Rams' huddle.

"In the nine or ten years we played against each other, that's the only time he ever said anything to me while the game was still going on," Van Note said. "Back then it just ticked me off. Now I realize how funny it was."

———————— ————————

*Center **JEFF VAN NOTE** reported to the Falcons out of the University of Kentucky in 1969 and spent 18 years as the linchpin of the offensive line. He is the club's all-time leader in games played with 246 and he was the starting center in six Pro Bowls. He played for the Atlanta Falcons from 1969 to 1986.*

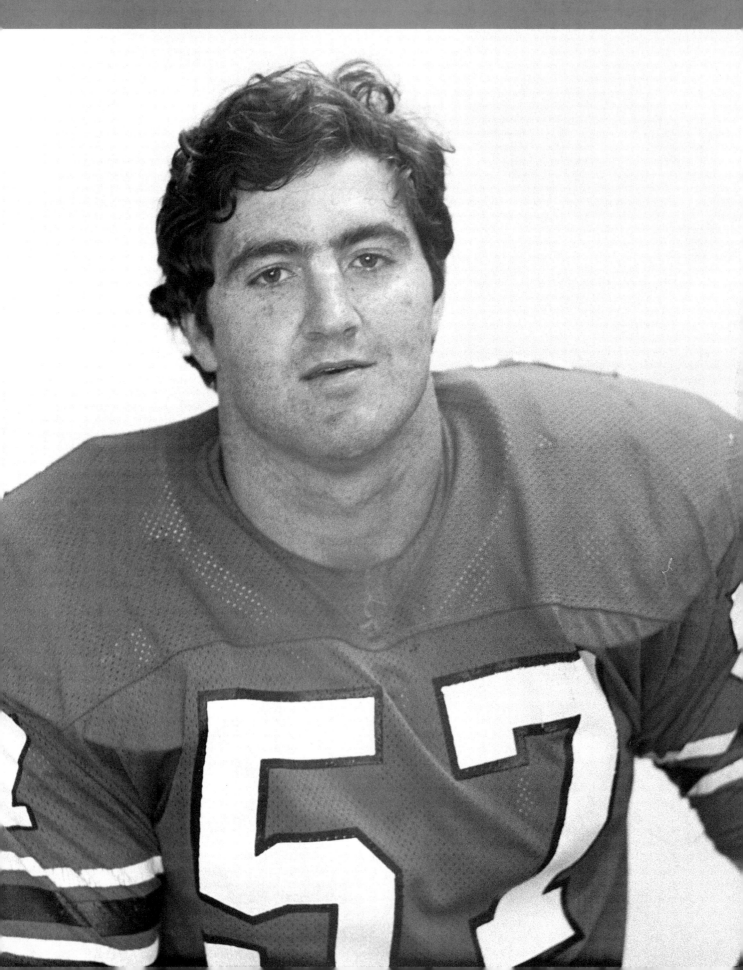

The Sunday Not-So-Funnies

A cartoon appeared in the sports pages of the *San Diego Evening Tribune* on Christmas Day, 1965.

It depicted the huge figure of a pass rusher, wearing number 77, with a striking resemblance to defensive tackle Ernie Ladd of the San Diego Chargers. He was bearing down on a tiny, frightened-looking and freckle-faced quarterback wearing number 15. It was a caricature of the Buffalo Bills' Jack Kemp.

The caption on the cartoon read, "Good Will Toward Men?"

The Buffalo quarterback was a bit upset with the cartoon's "emphasis on my freckles." It was all the motivation Kemp and the rest of the Bills needed the next day when they faced the Chargers at San Diego's Balboa Stadium for the AFL Championship Game. They were defending the crown they won by defeating the Chargers just one year earlier.

Using a double tight-end formation, which was rare at that time, Bills head coach Lou Saban planned from the outset to use Kemp's athleticism to the fullest extent possible.

The coaching staff also surprised the Chargers with a defense which featured three defensive linemen and four linebackers, now commonly known as the "3-4 defense." In 1965, it came as a shock.

Following a scoreless first quarter, Kemp and his Bills broke loose in the second. Kemp threw a 22-yard pass to tight end Paul Costa. Then Kemp hit his other tight end, Ernie Warlock, with an 18-yard strike for a touchdown. The Bills led 7-0.

Buffalo's defense stopped San Diego on its next possession. John Hadl punted the ball back to the Bills' 26-yard line where Butch Byrd caught it. Byrd took off and never looked back, going all the way for another touchdown. By halftime, the Bills led 14-0.

Time and time again, the Bills defense stopped the Chargers. In the second half, Buffalo placekicker Pete Gogolak kicked three field goals. In the end, Buffalo beat San Diego 23-0.

For the day, Kemp was eight of 19, passing for 155 yards and one touchdown. He was voted the game's MVP. A few weeks later, he was awarded the league's MVP award.

For Kemp, who was released by the Chargers on waivers in 1962 after a hand injury, and was later claimed by Buffalo for $100, the 1965 AFL Championship was one to remember.

"We won that game by digging and clawing our way to the win," Kemp said. "I knew we had something to prove that day. Many felt that we won the year before because the Chargers were without Lance Alworth and Keith Lincoln. We proved that 1964 was no fluke."

———————— 🏈 ————————

In 10 pro seasons, **JACK KEMP** completed 1,436 of 3,073 passes for 21,218 yards and 114 touchdowns. He played in the AFL All-Star Game seven times.

Kemp went on to a distinguished political career after retiring in 1969. He was elected to nine terms as a U.S. Congressman from upstate New York, then was selected by President George Bush to serve as a member of his cabinet.

Kemp's son Jeff also played pro football, making them the only father-son combination to play quarterback in the NFL.

PLAYING HISTORY:
Pittsburgh Steelers 1957
Los Angeles Chargers 1960
San Diego Chargers 1961-1962
Buffalo Bills 1962-1967, 1969

OPPOSITE: Jack Kemp is one of only 19 men who played in all 10 seasons of the AFL's existence. He passed for 21,218 yards and 40 touchdowns in his career with the San Diego Chargers and the Buffalo Bills.

JACK KEMP

Breaking 2,000

Several members of the New York Jets defensive unit took a vow prior to their final game of the 1973 season against the Buffalo Bills: O.J. Simpson would not go over the 2,000-yard rushing mark against them.

The Bills had other ideas.

Simpson, the NFL's leading rusher in 1972 with 1,251 yards, began his record-breaking 1973 season with a bang. In the Bills' first league game at New England, O.J. rushed for 250 yards. It was only a precursor of the big things to come.

Behind an offensive line that included Mike Montler, Reggie McKenzie, Dave Foley, Donnie Green and Joe DeLamielleure, Simpson picked up yardage at a record pace through the first half of the season.

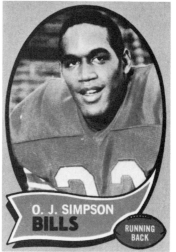

O. J. SIMPSON
BILLS
RUNNING BACK

Photo from Richard Wolffers Auctions, Inc., San Francisco

Just seven games into the year, Simpson had already gained over 1,000 yards, the usual benchmark for running backs. He now had his sights set on former Cleveland Browns star Jim Brown's single-season rushing mark of 1,863 yards, set 10 years earlier.

"I was aware that I was closing in on Jim Brown's record, and then the 2,000-yard mark, because the press always asked me about it," Simpson said. "What was more important to me was winning games. We had a good team and I thought we had a chance to make the playoffs."

With two games left to play, Simpson needed 280 yards to go over 2,000 yards rushing in a single season, a feat similar in

scope to breaking Roger Maris' record of 61 home runs in a season. The New England Patriots and the New York Jets were the two remaining clubs on the schedule.

Simpson took a long step toward topping 2,000 by gaining 219 yards against New England. That left the New York Jets as the only team standing between O.J. and the record books.

The season finale was played on a mud-soaked field in cold, rainy New York. Simpson needed 61 yards to top Jim Brown's single-season rushing mark of 1,863 yards.

Simpson almost met the mark on the club's first drive, picking up 57 yards on the way to a score. The record was finally shattered late in the first quarter on Simpson's six-yard gain.

But Simpson and the Bills had their eyes on the 2,000-yard mark. The Jets defense, led by veteran linebackers Al Atkinson and Ralph Baker, tried to keep Simpson in check on the slick and muddy turf.

Then, midway through the fourth quarter, Simpson took a handoff from quarterback Joe Ferguson, followed the blocks of Mike Montler and Reggie McKenzie, then scooted off left guard for a seven-yard gain. It gave him 200 yards rushing for the game and a season total of 2,003 yards, making him the first man in NFL history to rush for more than 2,000 yards.

"It felt good to break the mark," Simpson said. "I think more than anything I felt a certain amount of relief."

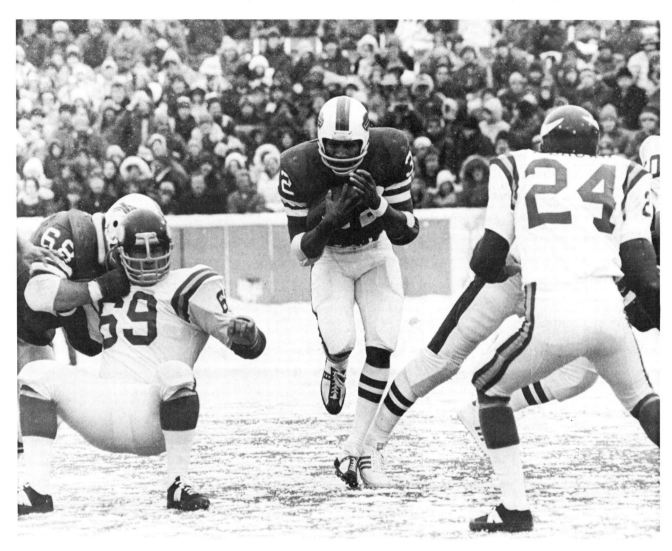

O. J. SIMPSON

After breaking the 2,000-yard record, Simpson was named AFC Player of the Year. The Bills improved to 9-5, their best record since 1966. But it still wasn't enough to bump Buffalo into the playoffs. That would come a year later, in 1974.

Simpson joined the Bills in 1969 as the club's first-round pick after a spectacular college career at USC, where he won the Heisman Trophy. Despite his renown, he was used sparingly in his early years with Buffalo. It wasn't until 1972,

when Lou Saban was named head coach of the Bills, that Simpson's professional career took off.

Saban believed in a strong running game and it was under his offensive system that Simpson's fortunes took a turn for the better. He finally was used as the club's featured running back.

Simpson responded by gaining more than 1,000 yards for five straight years between 1972 and 1976, winning four NFL rushing titles. He was named NFL Player of the Year in 1972, 1973 and 1975.

He was named All-Pro six times.

After nine years in Buffalo, Simpson was traded back home to the San Francisco 49ers for his final two seasons. He finished his 11-year career with 11,236 yards and 61 rushing touchdowns.

Simpson was elected to the Pro Football Hall of Fame in 1985 in his first year of eligibility.

PLAYING HISTORY:
Buffalo Bills 1969-1977
San Francisco 49ers 1978-1979

The Tackle that Turned the Tide

It took just four plays for Buffalo Bills linebacker Mike Stratton to realize he had seen enough of San Diego Chargers star running back Keith Lincoln.

On Lincoln's first carry in the 1964 American Football League Championship Game at Buffalo's War Memorial Stadium, he scooted 38 yards. San Diego needed just four plays to march 80 yards and post a 7-0 lead. Stratton didn't want to see it happen again.

"San Diego had a very explosive offense," said Stratton, a third-year linebacker from the University of Tennessee.

The Chargers' passing attack, under head coach and offensive guru Sid Gillman, was led by quarterback Tobin Rote and his young side-kick, John Hadl. Their favorite target was sensational wide receiver Lance Alworth.

Paul Lowe and Lincoln were the heart of the ground game. Both were quick, slashing runners with the ability to break off a long gain from anywhere on the field.

But there was one way to neutralize it.

"We were pretty confident about how we had just scored," Lincoln said. "But we decided we were going to show Buffalo a new look on offense."

On San Diego's next possession, quarterback Tobin Rote looked for Lincoln as he swung out of the backfield for a pass.

"We called it a delayed double-flare action to the left side," Lincoln said. "I went out of the backfield for a flare pass. Tobin Rote looked downfield first, then looked at me, then looked downfield again before unloading the ball to me.

"I think the minute Rote looked at me a second time a light went on in Mike Stratton's head and he knew immediately I was going to get the ball. On this particular play, Tobin got off a terrible pass. It was thrown like a snowball in a chimney. It seemed as though it would never get to me.

"By the time the ball got to me, Stratton was there, too, and he hit me a good one. It was a solid hit, a clean one, nothing dirty about it. When I went up for the ball, I exposed the sides of my chest and stomach areas. That's where Stratton hit me."

Stratton leveled Lincoln with a crunching tackle that knocked the ball loose and broke one of Lincoln's ribs. The blow unleashed a ripple of excitement through the 41,000 Bills fans on hand and sent Lincoln to the sideline for the rest of the day.

"When the play occurred, I was trying to make sure that I didn't get beat by the San Diego offense," Stratton said. "It had already happened once in the game."

Instead, Stratton's bone-crushing tackle changed the game's momentum. The Buffalo defense came to life and shut down San Diego the rest of the day. The Bills went on to win the game 20-7 and capture their first AFL Championship.

MIKE STRATTON played 11 seasons for the Bills before ending his career, ironically, with San Diego in 1973. He intercepted 21 passes and scored two touchdowns during his 12 years in the NFL.

The Big Interception

Late in the third quarter of the 1991 AFC Championship Game, neither the Buffalo Bills nor the Denver Broncos had managed to put points on the board. Bills linebacker Carlton Bailey could see that the scoreless game was turning into a great defensive battle, one that was likely to turn on a big defensive play.

The Broncos had wasted several scoring chances in the first half. Denver quarterback John Elway faced second-and-10 from his own 19-yard line. In the huddle, he called for a middle screen pass to running back Steve Sewell. Earlier in the first half, the play had worked for 21 yards.

Elway took the snap and dropped back to pass. The Denver offensive linemen deliberately let the opposing defensive players slip off their blocks to put a heavy rush on Elway and leave the middle open for the screen pass.

But it didn't fool the Bills this time. Buffalo nose tackle Jeff Wright stopped his forward penetration and held himself up at the line of scrimmage. As Elway released a soft touch pass over the middle, Wright reached up with his meaty paw and tipped the ball into the air. The football was deflected into the waiting arms of Carlton Bailey, who made the interception at the 11-yard line. The only man standing between Bailey and the end zone was John Elway.

"On the sideline we were screaming, 'Get into the end zone,'" Bills quarterback Jim Kelly said. "The way both defenses were playing, we knew one touchdown might be enough. We needed to score anyway we could."

Bailey didn't need much encouragement. He hauled in the football, side-stepped Elway's attempted tackle and dashed into the end zone. The score put Buffalo in front, 7-0.

"There was no way I was going to be stopped from getting into the end zone," said Bailey, a 6-foot-3, 240-pounder drafted out of North Carolina. "If Elway had caught me and made the tackle, I would have never heard the end of it."

Early in the fourth quarter, Buffalo kicker Scott Norwood added a 44-yard field goal to put the Bills in front 10-0, but Bailey was the only Bill to reach the end zone against Denver. Bailey's first touchdown as a professional proved to be the difference in the AFC Championship Game as Buffalo held on to win 10-7.

The victory sent Buffalo to its second straight Super Bowl appearance. Although the Bills lost to the Washington Redskins in Super Bowl XXVI, Bailey took consolation in knowing it was his interception and touchdown that got the Buffalo Bills to football's biggest game.

CARLTON BAILEY

Bailey was a ninth-round draft pick of the Bills in 1988 after leading the University of North Carolina's defensive unit. Bailey was a standout linebacker with the Buffalo Bills. During his five years with the club, he recorded just two interceptions.

OPPOSITE: The Buffalo Bills' Carlton Bailey runs in for a touchdown during the AFC Championship Game against the Denver Broncos in January of 1992. The Bills went on to beat the Broncos 10-7.

BILLS

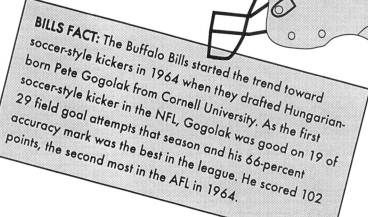

BILLS FACT: The Buffalo Bills started the trend toward soccer-style kickers in 1964 when they drafted Hungarian-born Pete Gogolak from Cornell University. As the first soccer-style kicker in the NFL, Gogolak was good on 19 of 29 field goal attempts that season and his 66-percent accuracy mark was the best in the league. He scored 102 points, the second most in the AFL in 1964.

Here Comes Cookie

*C*arlton "Cookie" Gilchrist was a fullback who ran to the beat of a different drummer. Signed by the Buffalo Bills after spending several years in the Canadian Football League, Gilchrist appeared at the Bills camp in 1962 for his first day of practice in a red Cadillac convertible. On the sides of the car stenciled in gold was the phrase, "Lookie, lookie, here comes Cookie."

Despite his flamboyance, former Buffalo Bills teammates claim Gilchrist had the ability to be the best running back of all time. And in one game Gilchrist proved it, rushing for a pro football record 243 yards and breaking Cleveland Browns' legend Jim Brown's single-game NFL mark of 237 yards.

It happened when the Buffalo Bills travelled to New York to play the Titans in the final game of the 1962 season. It was a contest that meant nothing to New York. The Bills needed a victory to finish with the first winning season in club annals. For Gilchrist, it was an opportunity to become the first AFL player to break the 1,000-yard rushing mark.

"I don't know if any of us ever expected Cookie to have the day he did," said Bills guard Billy Shaw. "There was nothing really riding on the game, except maybe Cookie's chance at getting 1,000 yards."

At 250 pounds, and with the speed and quickness of a frightened deer, Gilchrist was more than a handful for opposing players. But he had toiled in anonymity in the Canadian Football League and, despite his flashy automobile, had received little acknowledgment in Buffalo. For Gilchrist, gaining 1,000 yards meant instant recognition.

"All I ever remember about Cookie was his speed and quickness and his ability to hit," Shaw said. "It was great blocking for him. But if you got in his way, he would hit you and run you over. And I mean he would hit you square in the back. Enough to hurt. You made sure you got out of the way the next time you blocked for him.

"And if that wasn't enough, he would bowl over guys on defense. I think that's what helped him that day in New York. Pure determination. Cookie was the best athlete the Bills had on their team at the time.

"I don't think anybody realized that he had broken any records until the end of the game and the stats were totalled up. But, as usual, the NFL wouldn't recognize the accomplishment because the AFL was considered an inferior league."

COOKIE GILCHRIST'S path to the Buffalo Bills began at a young age. Back in 1954, at the age of 18, Gilchrist signed with the Cleveland Browns right out of high school. Although he didn't make the team, the 6-foot-3, 250-pounder impressed coach Paul Brown with his raw talent.

Nevertheless, the big fullback was determined to play pro football. He headed north to the Canadian Football League and became an all-league performer.

In 1962, Gilchrist signed with the Buffalo Bills. He was nearly 28 years old when he returned to the United States, but for the next four seasons, he was the best running back in the AFL.

Gilchrist became the first AFL player ever to rush for 1,000 yards in a season in 1962, finishing with 1,096. He gained 979 yards and topped the league with 12 touchdowns the next year. In 1964, he was the league's top rusher again, gaining 981 yards, and pacing the Bills to their first AFL championship. And in 1965, playing for Denver, Gilchrist was second in the AFL with 954 yards rushing. Three of those four years, Gilchrist was named to the All-AFL squad.

Gilchrist rushed 1,010 times for 4,293 yards and 37 touch-downs during his six-year AFL career. He also caught 110 passes for 1,135 yards and six touchdowns.

Making History

James Harris' professional football career was more than just a trivia question. It was part of NFL history.

As a member of the Buffalo Bills in 1969, Harris became the first African-American ever to start a pro football season-opening game at quarterback.

The Bills had the worst season in club history in 1968, finishing 1-12-1. They selected Harris out of Grambling State University on the eighth round that year. At Buffalo, he would compete with Jack Kemp, Tom Flores, Dan Darragh and Kay Stephenson for the quarterback job.

"At the time, there were some people who felt that blacks weren't smart enough to play quarterback in the NFL," Harris said. "The pressure I felt in that first camp was just to survive, let alone become the first black starting quarterback.

"I tried not to worry about it. I knew that Coach (John) Rauch liked my ability. But he didn't know if I would make it. And I knew that I was a long shot to make it. In the end, Coach Rauch gave me the chance I needed."

Harris made the club and was named the starter for Buffalo's opening game that season.

"I had to call my own plays," Harris said. "I didn't even know the game plan. I called on Coach Rauch for advice and he told me to simply memorize a few plays and run them, then rely on my arm and just get the ball to the receiver."

Harris' career almost ended before it started. After being chosen in the eighth round of the draft, he was certain there was an element of racism involved in the low selection. He almost decided against turning pro.

"I was the Player of the Year in black college football," Harris recalled. "I had the size and I knew I could produce as a quarterback if given the chance. Other teams had contacted me and said they would draft me earlier in the draft if I would just change my position. I said that was out of the question.

"It was at that point I decided not to play pro football. I felt I had been drafted in the eighth round because I was black, not because I was a quarterback."

Harris went home to sort things out. There, he had discussions with his former coach at Grambling, Eddie Robinson, and with his mother.

"Both Coach Robinson and my mom convinced me to keep going and turn pro," Harris said. "They both said that if I didn't, it might be a long time before an opportunity like this came along again."

To be sure, there were African-American quarterbacks in the professional game before Harris. But never starters. George Taliaferro was a backup quarterback with the NFL's Baltimore Colts, New York Yankees and Dallas Texans in the early 1950s. Willie Thrower was a backup to George Blanda with the Chicago Bears in 1953. And Marlin Briscoe started most of the Denver Broncos games in 1968 after first-stringer Steve Tensi was injured.

But Harris was a true pioneer.

LEFT: James Harris led the Los Angeles Rams to the 1975 NFC Championship Game. In the Pro Bowl that year, he was named the game's MVP after throwing two fourth-quarter touchdown passes.

BILLS FACT: Two of the best running backs in Buffalo history had epicurean nicknames: O.J. Simpson and Cookie Gilchrist.

BILLS FACT: Hall of Famer Tom Landry knows the feeling the Buffalo Bills have endured after losing in four straight Super Bowls. During his early years with the Dallas Cowboys, Landry's club always seemed to play second fiddle to Vince Lombardi's Green Bay Packers. He has a soft spot in his heart for the Bills and coach Marv Levy.

"Although we had quite a bit of success while I was coaching at Dallas," Landry said, "I can feel for Buffalo and what they have been through the last few years. We had our share of times when we couldn't quite win it all. But just getting to the Super Bowl is quite an accomplishment. I know how disappointed they must feel."

BILLS FACT: In 1976, Joe Ferguson had just one of his 151 passes intercepted, a league record.

JAMES HARRIS

After three seasons in Buffalo, Harris signed with the Los Angeles Rams as a free agent. He became the starter midway through the 1974 season and led Los Angeles to the NFC West title in 1974 and 1975.

In 1975, he played in the Pro Bowl and was named MVP after throwing two touchdown passes.

During his 12-year career, Harris completed 607 of 1,149 passes for 8,136 yards and 45 touchdowns.

PLAYING HISTORY:
Buffalo Bills 1969-1971
Los Angeles Rams 1973-1976
San Diego Chargers 1977-1981

Glad You Didn't Have a V-8

On a sweltering Sunday at Wrigley Field, the Chicago Bears overcame a 14-point halftime deficit to beat the Detroit Lions.

The following day, the Chicago newspapers trumpeted the Bears' success. Coach George Halas was hailed for his ingenious offensive adjustments and his invigorating halftime speech.

Sports reporters in the Windy City were unable to ascertain exactly what Halas told his troops during the intermission, but judging by the Bears' second-half performance, they speculated it must have been dynamic.

But former Bears captain and Hall of Fame tackle Stan Jones recalled exactly what happened in the locker room that Sunday afternoon.

The Bears had strict regulations about what could be consumed at halftime in the team's locker room. Oranges, water and ice were the standard fare for halftime consumption. Soft drinks, such as Coca-Cola, Seven-Up and Dr. Pepper, were forbidden.

But just outside the Bears' locker room, the club kept a cooler filled with soda. The ice box was off-limits until the ball game was over, then players could raid it to quench their thirst.

Defensive end Doug Atkins was parched and dehydrated from the long afternoon in the Chicago heat. As the team filed into the locker room at halftime, he decided he was ready for a soft drink, regulations be damned.

To the shock of several players, Atkins opened the cooler and selected for himself an ice cold bottle of Coca-Cola. He brought it into the locker room and was sitting on a stool sipping away when Halas and the rest of the coaching staff entered.

As Halas walked through the locker room, he spotted the 6-foot-8, 275-pound All-Pro defensive end drinking his icy refreshment. He stopped at Atkins' locker and told him to hand it over.

"Atkins told Halas to go to hell," Jones said. "Any time you said something like that to George Halas, you had a confrontation on your hands."

Halas paused, then once again calmly told Atkins to hand over the soda.

Instead, Atkins put the bottle to his lips and took a long, satisfying sip.

Halas asked for the Coke one more time. Again he was rebuffed.

Finally, the 75-year-old Halas reached forward and tried to grab the soda from Atkins' hand. The two men twisted and turned the bottle, trying to gain possession of the forbidden liquid. As the struggle progressed, Atkins was able to wrestle the bottle away from Halas. Then, as Halas continued to struggle for the bottle, Atkins fended him off with one hand while sipping the elixir with the other.

Players and coaches watched dumbfounded, some eating oranges, others holding icepacks to their injuries. Meanwhile, the struggle and ensuing argument continued.

Finally, with the soda nearly finished and the argument still in progress, there was a shout from behind the locker room door.

"Two minutes, Coach," a referee yelled.

The second half was about to begin.

In a hoarse and faltering voice, Halas screamed and cussed at his team, then told them to get back on the field. Chicago scored three second-half touchdowns to pull off a come-from-behind victory.

Afterward, fans and reporters wondered about the magical formula Halas had used to change his club's performance. Little did they know, the coach of the Monsters of the Midway and his All-Pro defensive end spent the entire halftime break fighting over a bottle of soda pop.

...And On The Eighth Day God Created The BEARS

DOUG ATKINS

During his 17 NFL seasons, Atkins earned acclaim as a devastating pass rusher who was particularly dangerous when angered. One of his favorite pass rushing tricks was to throw a lineman at the quarterback.

Atkins played in eight Pro Bowls. In 1982, he was elected to the Pro Football Hall of Fame.

PLAYING HISTORY:
Cleveland Browns 1953-1954
Chicago Bears 1955-1966
New Orleans Saints 1967-1969

Which Side Are You On?

When Dick Butkus held forth at middle linebacker for the Chicago Bears, league opponents frequently altered their offensive schemes to run away from him. They had too much respect for the man who was known throughout the National Football League as the "Marquis de Mean."

As the Green Bay Packers great all-purpose back Paul Hornung once noted, "Butkus played like he really hated you. Like you were someone he had a grudge against from his old neighborhood."

Most NFL veterans felt that Butkus treated members of opposing teams with equal disdain for their life and limb, that his mean streak was spread equitably toward everyone in the league. But a few hapless souls in the wrong uniform came in for special punishment. One such person was longtime Pittsburgh Steelers center Ray Mansfield.

"The guy really bugged me," Butkus admitted, a forbidding frown rutting his broad brow. "Just mention his name and I see two big grimy hands clutching the front of my jersey. He was always holding me, grabbing, hitching, wrestling—a real cheap-shot artist. Only he was pretty cute about it. He hardly ever drew a flag."

Butkus finally caught up with Mansfield in Chicago during the Bears' 1971 season opener against the Steelers.

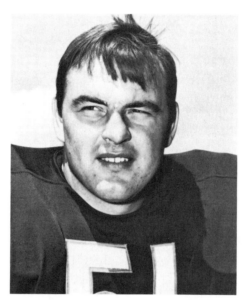

"We opened the 1971 season at home against the Steelers," Butkus said. "It was one of those real physical games and the officials were letting us play ball. Like always, he (Mansfield) held me on practically every snap. And, like always, I just couldn't get a clean shot at him without running the risk of a costly penalty. Then, late in the third period, I got my chance.

"They ran a dive play in a short-yardage situation and we stacked it up," he said. "I came running around the backside and there was Mansfield sticking out of the pile. I gave him a forearm to the back of the head and shouted in his ear. 'There, I got ya, you (expletive).' He rolled around for a while, then staggered to his feet."

But after spending 14 years in the NFL trenches, Mansfield had too much pride to admit suffering pain. He shot an awkward grin at Butkus.

"Mansfield kind of smiled and said, 'I didn't feel a thing, Richie baby,'" Butkus said. "But then he wandered over to the Bears' bench and sat down. (Defensive end) Ed O'Bradovich walked over and said to him, 'You want I should call you a cab, Ray?' I loved it."

It was then that Mansfield realized he was on the wrong bench and sheepishly made his way across the field. But the damage had already been done. Butkus got his revenge.

DICK BUTKUS

*A*fter joining the Bears as a first-round draft pick in 1965, Butkus developed a desire to become the most feared linebacker in football. His opponents would agree that he succeeded. His leadership and passion for the game were key elements to the fierce Bears defensive unit.

Butkus played in eight Pro Bowls during a nine-year span before injuries began to catch up with him. In 1970, he needed surgery to repair a badly damaged knee. It never responded properly and for three years he continued to play as if every game was his last. After the 1973 season, he retired.

During his nine-year NFL career, Butkus registered 47 takeaways—22 interceptions and 25 fumble recoveries. And his style of play is still the standard by which middle linebackers are judged.

In 1979, Butkus was elected to the Pro Football Hall of Fame. He played with the Bears for his entire NFL career, from 1965 to 1973.

BEARS FACT: At 20 years old, Chicago's Dan Fortmann was one of the youngest players ever to wear a uniform in the NFL. He earned a medical degree while playing with the Bears, then retired and became the Los Angeles Rams' team doctor.

BEARS FACT: Dick Plasman, an end who played with the Bears from 1937 to 1942, was the last man to play in the NFL without a helmet. In 1943, the NFL made it mandatory that all players wear protective head gear.

BEARS FACT: The 1933 Chicago Bears were awarded $210.34 each for winning the NFL championship. The 1985 Super Bowl champion Chicago Bears received $36,000 each.

Samurai Linebacker

Linebacker Mike Singletary began laying out opponents early in 1981, during his rookie season with Chicago.

"When I put a good hit on someone, it would excite me for the entire game," said Singletary, the Chicago Bears premier middle linebacker for 13 seasons. "I loved to meet people straight-on. When you hit a guy with the right form, with the helmet right where it's supposed to be, that's thrilling to me."

The 5-foot-11, 235-pound graduate of Baylor University wanted the NFL to know he was a man to be reckoned with. Midway through Singletary's first NFL season, the Bears paid a visit to Kansas City's Arrowhead Stadium. That's when Singletary became personally acquainted with Kansas City's star running back Joe Delaney, who was in the midst of a 1,000-yard rushing season.

Singletary was annoyed with Delaney's gains and he quickly served notice. Delaney ran wide on a sweep and the Bears' "Master of Mayhem" was there to greet him.

"Mike really blasted the poor guy," former Bears safety Doug Plank said. "Delaney made a noise like a vacuum cleaner. You could hear the air being sucked out of his ribs."

Although Delaney eventually regained his breath, he was ineffective for the rest of the game.

"Mike came back to the huddle after that with a little smirk on his face," Fencik said. "But that was common. Whenever he made a big hit, he was happy."

Singletary quickly developed a reputation around the league as one of the game's most intense competitors. The Bears rewarded him with the nickname "Samurai," a reference to Japan's professional warriors of yesteryear. It was a name that seemed to fit.

MOVIE MADNESS

Singletary's intensity was not limited to the playing field. He was an avid watcher of game tapes and took offense if teammates didn't relish the films like he did. Before the 1985 NFC Championship Game with the Los Angeles Rams, Bears defensive lineman Tyrone Keys got a look at Singletary's intensity.

"We were watching a film of Eric Dickerson running for over 200 yards in a game against the Cowboys," Keys said. "It was like a personal highlight film of him. All of a sudden, with us sitting there in the dark, and some guys nodding off, Samurai starts screaming, 'Let's play now! Let's play now!'"

Singletary's outburst ignited a chain reaction of destruction. Defensive tackle Dan Hampton hurled a chair across the room and fellow defensive tackle Steve McMichael toppled the projector with a karate kick.

The carnage continued the next day. Dickerson took a beating and coughed up three fumbles. The All-Pro running back managed only 46 yards rushing on 17 carries and the Bears trounced Los Angeles, 24-0, en route to their first Super Bowl title.

MIKE SINGLETARY

"I just wanted to be the best," Mike Singletary has said. "I wanted to be a complete player, someone who was used on passing downs as well as running downs. I never wanted to come out of a game."

By all accounts, Singletary developed into one of the game's great middle linebackers. To improve on his pass defense skills, he worked long and hard after practice with the Bears wide receiving corps. Chicago's former defensive coordinator, Buddy Ryan, had enough respect for Singletary's pass defense ability to leave his middle linebacker in the game on third-and-long.

In 1984, his fourth NFL season, Singletary was named All-Pro for the first time. For the next eight years, he was a fixture in the Pro Bowl. But it was in 1985 that everything came together for him.

That season the Bears defense, under Buddy Ryan, led the league in fewest points allowed, rushing defense, overall defense, interceptions and takeaway-giveaway ratio. During one six-game stretch, the Bears allowed just 28 points. Singletary was the unmistakable leader of the defensive unit and was voted UPI's Defensive Player of the Year.

Most importantly for Singletary, Chicago went 15-1 and won the Super Bowl. He played for the Chicago Bears from 1981 to 1992.

Couldn't Call 'Em Livestock Anymore

As head coach of the Chicago Bears, Mike Ditka acquired a reputation as a fiery-tempered leader. Game day was akin to war, and like any great military leader, Ditka was a strong believer in the bonds of loyalty.

Among the men who commanded Ditka's devotion were his former head coaches in the NFL, George Halas and Tom Landry. When Ditka's 12-year playing career ended, he carried on as assistant coach with the Dallas Cowboys under Landry. Despite the marked difference in their personalities, they got along remarkably well. Landry enjoys relating a story about Ditka that reflects the Hall of Fame tight end's intense loyalty.

"Mike and I went out to do some hunting on the farm of a friend of mine," Landry said. "When we got there, Mike stayed in the car while I went in the house to let my friend know what we intended to do. My friend had no objections but asked me for a favor. There was an old, sickly mule on the property that he just couldn't bring himself to shoot. He asked me to do it and said we could take all the game we wanted. I reluctantly agreed."

En route to the old mule's grazing area, Landry wrestled mightily with his conscience. Finally he came up with a plot that would put the mule out of its misery.

"I simply couldn't bring myself to do it," he said. "But I had promised my friend I would. Mike could see I was troubled and asked what had happened at the house. I told him the man wouldn't let us hunt on his place because he didn't like the way the Cowboys were playing. Then I said, 'I got half a mind to shoot his mule over there.' Mike jumped up and said, 'I'll do it, coach.' And I said, 'Okay, but make it quick. I'll pull down the road and wait for you.'"

"Mike got out with his shotgun and I drove the car around a bend," Landry continued. "Pretty soon I heard a shot and breathed a sigh of relief. Suddenly there were two more shots and I could see Mike coming toward the car on the run. When he climbed in, I asked him, 'Did you shoot the mule?' Mike said, 'Yeah, and two of the guy's cows. Let's get out of here!' That was Mike."

Ditka's intensity was never more pronounced than in his playing days with the Chicago Bears. Even the master of intimidation, former Bears linebacker Dick Butkus, was no match for Ditka on NFL Sundays.

"I remember the first time I saw Mike in action," Butkus said. "I was a rookie with the Bears in 1965.

The players were leaving the locker room on their way to the field for the team's pregame warmup. Mike was standing at the tunnel door, screaming at the top of his lungs and pounding each guy on the pads as they went out, yelling at them to cream the opposition. But it was an exhibition game. Mike was the only guy I know who got more psyched than me."

MIKE DITKA

Ditka began his pro career as a first-round draft choice of the Chicago Bears in 1961. The rugged tight end proved to be a devastating blocker, but what set him apart from other men that played the position was his ability as a receiver.

In his first season with Chicago, Ditka caught 56 passes for 1,076 yards and was named Rookie of the Year. Two years later, Ditka played a major role as the Chicago Bears won their first NFL Championship in 17 years.

Ditka had his finest season in 1964 when he caught 75 passes, establishing a record for tight ends until the schedule was expanded to 16 games. During Ditka's 12-year career, he caught 427 passes for 5,812 yards and 43 touchdowns, and played in five Pro Bowls.

Ditka ended his playing days in Dallas, then joined the Cowboys coaching staff. After nine years as a Cowboys assistant coach, he was named the Chicago Bears head coach. Under Ditka's tutelage, the Bears climbed back to the NFL's upper echelon. Ditka guided the Bears to victory in Super Bowl XX, the club's first championship since 1963.

In 1988, Ditka became the first tight end to be elected to the Pro Football Hall of Fame.

PLAYING HISTORY:
Chicago Bears 1961-1966
Philadelphia Eagles 1967-1968
Dallas Cowboys 1969-1972

COACHING HISTORY:
Chicago Bears 1982-1992

51

Cool Conspirators

Chicago Bears linebacker coach Bill George was preparing for a game against the Detroit Lions in 1972, but he was gravely concerned about the welfare of his star pupil: middle linebacker Dick Butkus.

Butkus was already a seven-time All-Pro and one of the most feared players in the league. But he had just written a book in which he devoted an entire chapter to the Detroit Lions.

During the 1960s, Chicago had been a perennial whipping boy for the Lions. Butkus hated everything about the Detroit franchise and he vividly expressed that sentiment in his new publication. George, a former All-Pro linebacker and member of the Pro Football Hall of Fame, feared that one of the Lions would seek retribution against Butkus. The star linebacker was already limping on a gimpy knee. George worried that the Lions might try to injure or maim his defensive captain with a cheap shot.

George was concerned enough to call a meeting of the club's linebackers. But he wanted to do it without his All-Pro middle linebacker in the room.

To accomplish his goal without raising Butkus' suspicion, George carefully orchestrated an elaborate plan. He enlisted the cooperation of Bears trainer Fred Caito, who was told to knock on the door during the linebackers' meeting and tell Butkus he had an important phone call.

The scheme didn't go according to plan, however. Butkus' teammates thought it was laughable that one of the game's most intimidating players would need protection. They told Butkus about George's intentions and instructed him to stand outside the door after he was summoned by Caito, rather than going to the telephone.

During the early morning meeting, Caito entered the room as planned and told Butkus there was an important call waiting for him. Butkus left the meeting, then hid behind the door in full earshot of the conspirators. George quickly explained the situation and began soliciting help for his star player. The response was a surprisingly cool one to say the least.

"We all started saying how Dick was a big boy and could take care of himself on the field," said Doug Buffone, a linebacker with the Bears for 14 seasons from 1966 to 1979. "We said that he was making all the money from the book and didn't offer any profits to us, and that we simply weren't interested in the plan.

"George's mouth just dropped and he started turning red. He had been expecting everyone to stick up for Dick. He just went off his rocker. He hit the chalkboard and began pounding his fist.

"By then, we could all hear Dick laughing his head off outside the room. Finally, George caught on to what was happening. It was hysterical."

As it was, Butkus didn't need protection. There were very few players around the league willing to seek revenge against him. He emerged from the game unscathed, although the Bears suffered another humiliating loss to the Lions.

BILL GEORGE

George spent just one season as the Bears linebacker coach but few people were more qualified to instruct players at that position. During the 1950s, it was George who virtually invented the middle linebacker position.

He joined the Bears in 1952 as a middle guard in defensive coach Clark Shaughnessy's five-man line. But by 1954, the Bears altered their defensive scheme to combat the passing game as it became more sophisticated around the league. George was moved off the defensive line and became pro football's first great middle linebacker, playing in eight straight Pro Bowls.

The 1963 Bears finished 11-1-2 and won the NFL Championship on the strength of its defense. George was the leader of the unit which allowed an average of just 10 points per game.

In 1966, George was sent to the Los Angeles Rams after 14 seasons with the Bears. He played one season in Los Angeles before retiring. He intercepted 18 passes during his career.

George was elected to the Pro Football Hall of Fame in 1974.

PLAYING HISTORY:
Chicago Bears 1952-1965
Los Angeles Rams 1966

Bill George spent 14 seasons with the Chicago Bears and is credited with creating the middle linebacker position when he switched from middle guard to linebacker in the early 1950s.

The Unstoppable Juggernaut

After three decades of Super Bowls, few if any teams can match the dominance of the Chicago Bears' march to Super Bowl XX. Quarterback Jim McMahon was the emotional leader behind the club's success.

"I think all of us knew that we had the players who could beat anyone that year," McMahon said. "As the season went on, it just seemed to keep building."

McMahon may be the closest player in modern football to the Detroit Lions' legendary field general Bobby Layne. Although his career has been plagued by injuries, McMahon's confidence and fiery leadership often inspired his teammates to impassioned performances.

That quality was evident midway through the 1985 season in a critical Thursday night game against the Minnesota Vikings.

A series of back, kidney and hand injuries had forced McMahon to miss much of the 1984 season and part of 1985. Against the Vikings, McMahon started the game on the bench where he continued to nurse an injury. But in the third quarter, with the Bears trailing 17-9, he entered the contest and inspired his own brand of magic.

On his first play from scrimmage, he fired a 70-yard touchdown pass to wide receiver Willie Gault. On the Bears' next possession, he needed just one play to toss a 25-yard touchdown pass to Dennis McKinnon. By the time McMahon was finished, he had thrown three scoring passes in all and turned the game into a 33-24 Bears victory.

"That was a heck of a performance," wide receiver Willie Gault said. "The first touchdown got everybody fired up on the sideline, including the defensive players, and then the excitement just fed on itself."

Their confidence built with each weekly victory and manifested itself with a music video—"The Super Bowl Shuffle"—which was released in October.

"People thought we were pretty cocky for doing (the video)," McMahon said. "But at that time we were convinced nobody could beat us. By the time we got to the playoffs, there was no stopping us."

The New York Giants and Los Angeles Rams tried to halt the Bear juggernaut, but Chicago's mighty defense shut down both clubs. New York fell 21-0 and the Rams lost 24-0. The Bears went 15-1 during 1985, losing only in Miami, with McMahon on the sideline again with injuries. Then came New England in the Super Bowl.

They fell hard. After New England took a 3-0 lead on Tony Franklin's 36-yard field goal, the Bears scored 44 unanswered points.

At the Louisiana Superdome for Super Bowl XX, McMahon found the Patriots' secondary to be his own personal playground. In the opening series, he hit Willie Gault with a 43-yard pass that set the trend for the rest of the day. He completed 12 of 20 passes and racked up 256 yards in the air. In addition, he ran for two touchdowns in the game.

The Bears built a 44-3 lead in the third quarter en route to one of the most lopsided wins in Super Bowl history. When it was over, the Patriots limped back to New England as 46-10 losers.

"That Super Bowl game was one where we were all playing in a zone," McMahon said. "We knew we only had one more game to win and we weren't going to let them keep it close."

Although McMahon led the Bears to five straight NFC Central Division titles, the club was unable to equal the Super Bowl success of 1985. McMahon understands that his legacy is tied to that season.

"I've been around the league since then and I've never seen anything like what we had that season," McMahon said. "It was the type of year every player dreams about. I was fortunate to be a part of it."

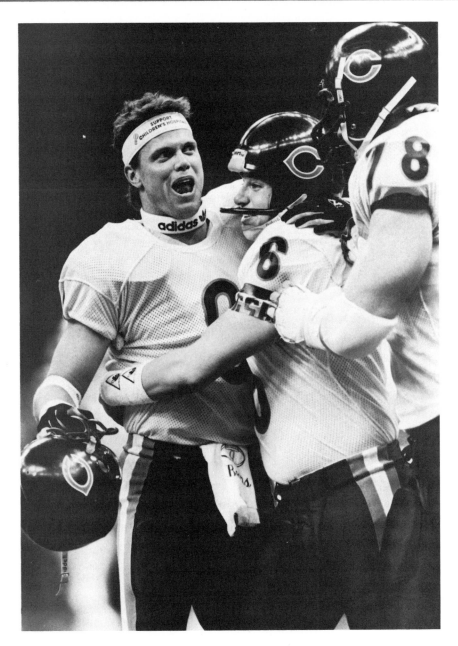

BEARS FACT: Gale Sayers earned a place in the Hall of Fame, despite suffering a pair of knee injuries that limited him to playing only five seasons. He displayed his great running ability against the San Francisco 49ers in 1965 by scoring six touchdowns in a game, tying a league record.

San Francisco's All-Pro linebacker Dave Wilcox recalled chasing Sayers all over the field that day: "I saw Gale Sayers at a banquet after we'd retired," he said. "And when I shook his hand, I said, 'Geez, it's nice to get a hold of you for a change.'

"During that game, I thought the poor guy was going to die of exhaustion," Wilcox joked. "If he could have gotten some oxygen, he would have scored six more touchdowns. He was just fantastic."

Charlie Krueger, a defensive tackle for the 49ers, concurred. "We were playing in the mud at Chicago that day," Krueger said. "I remember looking up at the scoreboard near the end of the game and saw the 61 points the Bears scored and thought, 'This is a hell of a way to treat visitors.'"

JIM McMAHON

McMahon was a two-time All-American at Brigham Young University, where he led the nation in passing yards in 1980 and 1981. The Chicago Bears chose McMahon with their first-round draft choice in 1982, making him the fifth player selected overall. He was named NFC Rookie of the Year by UPI in 1982.

McMahon boasts a .697 winning percentage as a starting quarterback, second only to Joe Montana.

PLAYING HISTORY:
Chicago Bears 1982-1988
San Diego Chargers 1989
Philadelphia Eagles 1990-1992
Minnesota Vikings 1993
Arizona Cardinals 1994-

The Greatest Running Back

During a 13-year career in which he became the NFL's all-time leading rusher, Walter Payton may have been one of the most complete players ever to strap on shoulder pads.

He built a legacy as one of pro football's greatest running backs. His teammates remember him as a man who could run with both power and speed, catch a pass, lay a block and throw a pass.

"Walter was the whole package," former Bears coach Mike Ditka said of his offensive meal ticket. "He did everything we ever asked of him with enthusiasm and excellence."

"Walter took great pride in his all-around ability," Bears tackle Keith Van Horne said. "But becoming a good blocker was important to him because it showed that he wasn't above that. He knew that the linemen who did the blocking helped him get a lot of his yards. By blocking well, he showed that he appreciated our efforts."

Besides being the club's best player, Payton was always its most prolific practical joker. When he reported to training camp as a first-round draft pick in 1975, he demonstrated his athletic skills in clever ways. Payton caught punts behind his back, walked the length of the field on his hands and leaped over a 6-foot-4 assistant coach.

RUNNING BACK
WALTER PAYTON

Photo from Richard Wolffers Auctions, Inc., San Francisco

Leslie Frazier, a cornerback with the Bears from 1981 to 1985, was a frequent victim of Payton's hijinks. One morning during training camp in Platteville, Wisconsin, Frazier got an unexpected wake-up call.

"I'm laying in bed resting and all of a sudden I hear these popping noises like a gun was going off just outside my door," Frazier said. "Guys were running out of the dormitory like the place was on fire. It was only Walter setting firecrackers off in front of everyone's door."

Although he was a big fan of fireworks, Payton didn't need ammunition to create mayhem. A legend on the field, he earned that status off the field as well with his pranks, which ran the gamut from bloodcurdling shrieks in early morning meetings to "goosing" unsuspecting teammates during live television interviews.

"Whenever there was a serious situation, Walter would do something like that to get your attention," Frazier said. "It was just one of his ways of breaking up the monotony of training camp.

"He never really did anything out of line, but when he got close to the line people just figured, 'Well, that's just Walter Payton, the greatest running back ever to play the game.'"

Walter Payton uses a straight arm to break away from Detroit's James Hunter (28). Although Payton is known mostly for his running ability, he also threw seven touchdown passes during his career.

WALTER PAYTON

Payton was named All-Pro five times and chosen as NFL Player of the Year in 1976 and 1977. In 1993, he was named to the Pro Football Hall of Fame.

Besides rushing for over 16,700 yards, Payton had 492 receptions during his career and threw eight scoring passes. His first six completions were all for touchdowns. He had the most 100-yard rushing games in NFL history (77), the most rushing touchdowns (110), the most 1,000-yard rushing seasons (10) and the most combined net yards (21,803). To top it off, he was known around the league as a ferocious blocker.

The Bears nabbed the 5-foot-10, 200-pound Payton out of Jackson State with their first-round draft pick in 1975, the fourth overall selection. Payton played his entire career with the Bears, from 1975 to 1987.

A Close Call—Too Close

Unfortunately for the Bengals, the difference between losing Super Bowl XXIII and walking away with a victory over the San Francisco 49ers was a matter of exactly 34 seconds.

It had been a game of field goals through nearly three quarters of play when San Francisco kicker Mike Cofer tied the game at 6-6 with a 32-yard boot.

When Bengals running back Stanford Jennings broke loose and streaked 93 yards for a touchdown, giving the Bengals a 13-6 lead over the San Francisco 49ers with less than a minute left in the third quarter of Super Bowl XXIII, wide receiver Tim McGee did a little jig on the sideline. He was sure the Bengals were on their way to a championship.

But the game was just getting started. San Francisco quarterback Joe Montana was only warming up. As the pressure mounted, he started to catch fire. Montana quickly tied the game after hooking up with Jerry Rice on a 14-yard touchdown pass.

The Bengals wouldn't give up. They marched downfield and Jim Breech did it again, kicking his third field goal of the game to give the Bengals a 16-13 edge.

The clock slowly and meticulously ticked away and McGee felt comfortable that the Bengals' three-point lead would hold up. With just under three minutes to go, he couldn't help but feel a victory in his hands.

But no grasp was tight enough to prevent Montana and the 49ers from taking that win away. They drove 92 yards in 11 plays and Montana hit wide receiver John Taylor for the game-winning touchdown with 34 seconds left.

"When Stanford was running the ball across the goal line, I thought, 'Finally, I've gotten to play in a Super Bowl and win it, too,'" McGee said. "I was happier than I've ever been. Then to see Joe Montana take the ball down the field like that was like suffering a slow death. He just kept picking away at our defense, over and over. They got all the way down the field and their moment came. I didn't even get to see the touchdown because I closed my eyes and hung my head. I had a feeling of what was about to happen and it did happen. It was the worst agony of defeat you could imagine."

McGee was heartbroken by the loss, but there was one consolation. The Bengals were a young squad. He felt they would have numerous opportunities to get back to the Super Bowl. The next time they would win it.

"I was only in my third season when we made it to the Super Bowl," McGee said. "I thought the playoffs would be a regular thing for us. Now, I guess it has turned out to be the most important learning experience I've had in my career—that you can't take anything for granted. You might be good one year, but it doesn't mean you're going to be good the next year, or even ever again."

McGee's dream turned out to be a mirage. The Bengals went 29-53 in the four seasons after their Super Bowl appearance, finishing last in the AFC Central Division three times.

TIM McGEE

ABOVE: Cincinnati Bengals wide receiver Tim McGee (85) hauls in a pass while Philadelphia's Andre Waters (20) and Wes Hopkins (48) move in to make the tackle.

During the Bengals' 1988 drive to the Super Bowl, McGee was an integral part of the offense. He grabbed 36 passes for 686 yards and six touchdowns. In Super Bowl XXIII, he had two receptions for 23 yards.

The following season McGee was the club's leading receiver. He caught 65 passes for 1,211 yards and eight touchdowns. He has been the club's big play receiver ever since. McGee started playing for the Bengals in 1986.

Best of Times, Worst of Times

For most NFL players, career highlights and low points are diverse and unrelated. Cincinnati Bengals nose tackle Tim Krumrie experienced the most memorable and disappointing moments of his career in the same game, only minutes apart.

News accounts say the Bengals lost to the San Francisco 49ers in Super Bowl XXIII because of quarterback Joe Montana's heroics in the game's final three minutes. Another explanation, however, suggests the outcome was influenced heavily by a single first-quarter play.

It was a simple off-tackle play on San Francisco's second possession. Montana handed off to running back Roger Craig, who bulldozed through the left side of the Cincinnati defense. Tim Krumrie beat a block from center Randy Cross to pursue Craig. But when Krumrie moved left, his momentum caused him to twist and his left foot was caught in the turf. The pressure of his 274-pound frame broke the leg below the knee. He took another step and broke it again.

The official diagnosis was a broken fibula and tibia. The tibia—the shin bone—was cracked in three places. Krumrie, the Bengals' top tackler and inspirational leader, was taken off the field on a stretcher.

"I broke my leg after playing only seven defensive downs," Krumrie said. "It happened on the second or third play of San Francisco's second series. Nobody hit me or cut me. It was clean. That was the most disappointing moment of my career."

It occurred just minutes after Krumrie's most memorable moment—having his name announced as the starting nose tackle in the Super Bowl while sprinting onto the field at Miami's Joe Robbie Stadium.

"Here I was in the biggest game of my life with 80,000 people screaming in the stands and who knows how many more millions watching," Krumrie said. "Every football player at any level—high school, college or pro—everybody wants to play in a Super Bowl. It's the biggest football game there is and the entire world sees it. The excitement that was going through my mind and body is indescribable. I wish everybody could feel it at least once in their life. It would change how they look at things. That game—what I did play—I'll remember the rest of my life."

Krumrie may have missed playing the remainder of the game, but he didn't miss seeing its conclusion. Krumrie refused medication and transportation to the hospital until the start of the fourth quarter to provide his teammates with an emotional boost. He watched most of the game from the Bengals' locker room, then saw the last five minutes in the hospital shortly after an emergency helicopter dropped him off.

Backup lineman David Grant played well in his absence, but no one knows exactly how much Cincinnati suffered when Krumrie went down. The Bengals went on to lose 20-16, when Montana hit wide receiver John Taylor for a 10-yard touchdown with 34 seconds left.

TIM KRUMRIE

Krumrie was drafted out of the University of Wisconsin in the 10th round by the Bengals in 1983. By midseason of his rookie year, Krumrie was the club's starting nose tackle and by 1985 was named All-Pro. Krumrie is consistently among the Bengals' team leaders in tackles and has been selected to four Pro Bowls.

RIGHT: Cincinnati Bengals nose tackle Tim Krumrie (69) tries to elude a Buffalo Bills lineman in the 1988 AFC Championship Game won by the Bengals. Early in Super Bowl XXIII against the San Francisco 49ers, Krumrie broke his left leg in two places.

BENGALS FACT: During their inaugural season in 1968, the Bengals played their home games at the University of Cincinnati's Nippert Stadium.

BENGALS FACT: Franchise owner and head coach Paul Brown decided to name his club the Bengals as a tribute to Cincinnati's American Football League team of the late 1930s and early 1940s, which was also called the Bengals.

BENGALS FACT: Two of the Bengals' quickest and most agile running backs have had unlikely nick-names: "Booby" Clark and "Ickey" Woods.

BENGALS FACT: Against Houston in 1983, Ken Anderson completed a then-NFL-record 20 straight passes.

Sweet Victory

Dave Shula had little reason to be pleased with his first two seasons as the Cincinnati Bengals head coach. The Bengals, who were struggling through a rebuilding process in 1992 and 1993, won only eight of their first 32 games under his command, a .250 winning percentage. One of those victories, however, did afford Shula a small feeling of vindication.

In its second regular season contest of 1992, Cincinnati recorded a 24-21 overtime victory over the Los Angeles Raiders at Riverfront Stadium. Shula's first victory as an NFL head coach came a week earlier in the season opener against the Seattle Seahawks at the Kingdome. But this second win carried much more personal weight.

Shula, the son of Miami Dolphins head coach Don Shula, began his NFL career in 1981 as a wide receiver with the Baltimore Colts. The Princeton graduate spent most of his time as a special teams player that season, returning punts and kickoffs. He quickly saw his future was not as a player but as a coach. After playing just one season with the Colts, he followed his father into the coaching ranks.

Shula got his start as an assistant coach with the Miami Dolphins in 1982. After serving as a member of the Dolphins' coaching staff for seven seasons, he moved on to the Dallas Cowboys in 1989 and then to Cincinnati in 1992.

The Raiders always seemed to be a thorn in the side of Shula-coached teams. The Miami Dolphins possessed a 5-16-1 overall record against the Raiders through the 1993 season, and posted a 1-3 record against them while Dave Shula was an assistant with the club. So beating the Raiders was an added bonus.

"It had special significance to me because of all the years I spent in Miami," Shula said. "The Raiders were the one team that beat the Dolphins more than anybody else throughout the years. They were a good team in 1992 and we were just getting started. It gave us a chance to go 2-0 and win our home opener. Winning in that kind of a dramatic fashion was exciting."

Dramatic it was. The Bengals scored a touchdown in each of the first three quarters to take a 21-14 lead, but the Raiders were never a team to lie down and die. Los Angeles quarterback Jay Schroeder riddled the Bengals defense in the second half. He completed 25 of 40 passes for 380 yards and two touchdowns in the game. But it was Raiders running back Marcus Allen's one-yard plunge with 1:50 to play that sent the game into overtime.

Cincinnati's chances began to look bleak when the Raiders won the overtime coin toss and elected to receive the ball. But the Bengals kick coverage team forced a fumble on the kickoff and recovered on Los Angeles' 21-yard line. Two plays later, Shula moved in for the win. He sent in Cincinnati kicker Jim Breech, who delivered the game-winning 34-yard field goal to spoil the Raiders' overtime bid. As the ball split the uprights, Shula closed his eyes, tilted his head back and raised his fists toward the sky in triumph.

"I just said a quick little prayer," Shula said. "Basically, I said, 'Thanks.' Jay Schroeder had a great day throwing the ball against us, but we ran the ball well, wore them down and kicked their butts physically. It turned out in our favor."

To add to Shula's satisfaction, the Bengals posted a 16-10 victory over the Raiders the following season.

DAVE SHULA

The Bengals have had more lows than highs during Shula's inaugural years at the helm. After a 3-13 season in 1993, the Bengals' luck appears to be changing. It began when the club used its first-round draft pick in 1994, number one overall, to select Ohio State defensive tackle Dan Wilkinson. By all accounts, Wilkinson was college football's most dominant lineman. He is expected to continue his excellent on-field performance with the Bengals.

"Things are looking up for us now," Shula said. "We had a strong draft and a number of important veterans are returning to the team. I see a bright future ahead."

PLAYING HISTORY:
Baltimore Colts 1981

COACHING HISTORY:
Cincinnati Bengals 1992-

Cincinnati Bengals coach David Shula talks strategy with quarterback Boomer Esiason. Shula was named head coach in 1992. The club has struggled through a rebuilding process during his first two seasons.

Catch of the Century

The Raiders had a 17-7 edge over Cincinnati in the third quarter of the contest when Bo Jackson started a sweep to the left side. The Bengals had seen the play before. In a meeting between the two clubs a year earlier, Jackson sprang for a 92-yard touchdown run on the same play. This time the Cincinnati defense, including cornerback Rod Jones, adjusted accordingly. So did Jackson.

Seeing the left side sealed off, Jackson reversed his field and headed back to the right side. He used his speed to get outside, then sprinted into the open field. It looked like a sure touchdown.

"He actually reversed to what was originally my side of the field," Bengals cornerback Rod Jones said. "When I ran back to my side, (quarterback) Jay Schroeder threw a block on me. I had to avoid that block. When I avoided it, that put me directly behind Bo."

All that remained was a foot race to the end zone.

"When he broke free, all I was thinking about was catching him. That entire week (preparing for the Raiders) the coaches were telling us how fast he was. They said if we didn't contain him and he broke free, we couldn't catch him. When he broke free, I kept saying to myself, 'Catch him! Catch him! Catch him!' And that's what happened."

Jackson dashed 88 yards before Jones caught him and made a diving tackle at the one-yard line.

Even though Los Angeles crossed the goal line two plays later, it didn't lessen Jones' accomplishment.

"All I remember is being tired," Jones said. "I didn't think it was a big deal until after the game, really. In the locker room there must have been 30 or 40 reporters surrounding me and asking me, 'How did it feel to catch Bo Jackson?' Then I was thinking, 'Wow, this must be a big deal.' I had more press around me than the quarterback did.

"I guess it was spectacular for the people to see because they didn't expect it. But it really wasn't that spectacular for me because it's something I was expected to do.

"What I'll remember is walking off the field after that game when I felt somebody tap me on the back. I turned around and it was Bo. He said, 'Rod, why did you run me down like that?' I told him, 'I'm just doing my job, Bo. Just doing my job.'

"I guess I'll always be remembered as the man who caught Bo Jackson."

ROD JONES

Cornerback Rod Jones and running back Bo Jackson entered professional football together in 1986 as first-round draft picks of the Tampa Bay Buccaneers.

But Jones and Jackson never played together for the Buccaneers. Jackson elected to play major league baseball with the Kansas City Royals and skipped the 1986 NFL season. In 1987, he signed with Los Angeles and went on to become one of the decade's most celebrated athletes by excelling in both pro football and major league baseball at a combined level never before reached.

Although Jones' career never reached the legendary status of Jackson's, like Bo he was blessed with exceptional speed. He ran the 100-meter dash, the 400-meter relay and the 600-meter relay at Southern Methodist University.

Jones, pro football's 25th overall draft choice from SMU, played four seasons at Tampa Bay before being traded to the Cincinnati Bengals in September 1990.

PLAYING HISTORY:
Tampa Bay Buccaneers 1986-1989
Cincinnati Bengals 1990-

HALL BARTLETT PRODUCTIONS, INC. presents

featuring JAMES MILLICAN · JAMES BROWN
Written and Produced by HALL BARTLETT · Directed by FRANCIS LYON
A REPUBLIC PRESENTATION

CRAZYLEGS

starring ELROY "CRAZYLEGS" HIRSCH · LLOYD NOLAN · JOAN VOHS

THE LOS ANGELES WORLD CHAMPION RAMS — TOM FEARS · DICK "Night Train" LANE · DEACON DAN TOWLER
NORMAN VAN BROCKLIN · BOB WATERFIELD · PAUL "Tank" YOUNGER

HUGH McELHENNY says "My favorite bread is...

Quality BLUE SEAL Bread

The bread with the TWO seals of quality

...hoose the bread of a great ...mpion—the bread that has ...d the Good Housekeep... ...Guaranty Seal and the ...al of Quality. New, fresh,

and flavorful Blue Seal Bread is now available at your food store. Insist on Blue Seal White, Wheat, and Variety Breads —the freshest breads in town.

Copyright 1954, Interstate Bakeries Corp.

Guaranteed by Good Housekeeping

Honors heaped on "Hurryin' Hugh"
All & UP All American 1951
East West Game
Player 1952
Rookie of Year NFL 1952
Player 1952
Sport May 5 —Player of
Year 1952

Elroy Hirsch poses in a movie still for a film about his life, called "Crazylegs." Hirsch acquired the nickname because of the way his legs kicked up awkwardly as he ran from defenders.

Before the days of million dollar shoe endorsements, NFL stars earned a few extra dollars plugging household products. San Francisco 49ers running back Hugh McElhenny makes a pitch for his favorite bread.

1960 YEARBOOK
NATIONAL FOOTBALL LEAGUE

BALTIMORE
CHICAGO
SAN FRANCISCO
LOS ANGELES
GREEN BAY
DETROIT
DALLAS
NEW YORK
CLEVELAND
PITTSBURGH
PHILADELPHIA
ST. LOUIS
WASHINGTON

50¢

This NFL yearbook from 1960 reflects a time when the league boasted just 13 teams.

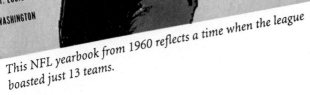

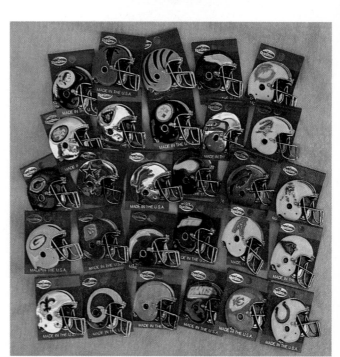

The Fog Bowl: Bears' free safety Maurice Douglass (37) runs out of the haze to be congratulated by his teammates after intercepting a Randall Cunningham pass late in the fourth quarter.

Eagles' quarterback Randall Cunningham emerges from the fog to throw a pass.

Lights illuminate Soldier Field—barely—during the NFC playoff game between the Chicago Bears and the Philadelphia Eagles on New Year's Eve, 1988. The Bears defeated the Eagles 20-12 in what became known as The Fog Bowl.

SUPER BOWL XX

$5.00

NFL The Official Super Bowl XX Game Program

Chicago Bears vs.
New England Patriots

XX

SUPER BOWL
AFC vs NFC

AFC vs. NFC for the NFL Championship and the Vince Lombardi Trophy   Sunday, January

The Vince Lombardi Trophy, awarded annually to the Super Bowl champion, is prominently displayed on the cover of this Super Bowl XX program.

In 1977, Gale Sayers became the youngest player ever elected to the Hall of Fame at age 34.

THE SUPER BOWL SHUFFLE*
THE CHICAGO BEARS SHUFFLIN' CREW

*A substantial portion of the proceeds from this record will be donated to help feed Chicago's neediest families.

Confidence in action: The Chicago Bears recorded a tune called the Super Bowl Shuffle even before making it to the playoffs in 1985.

67

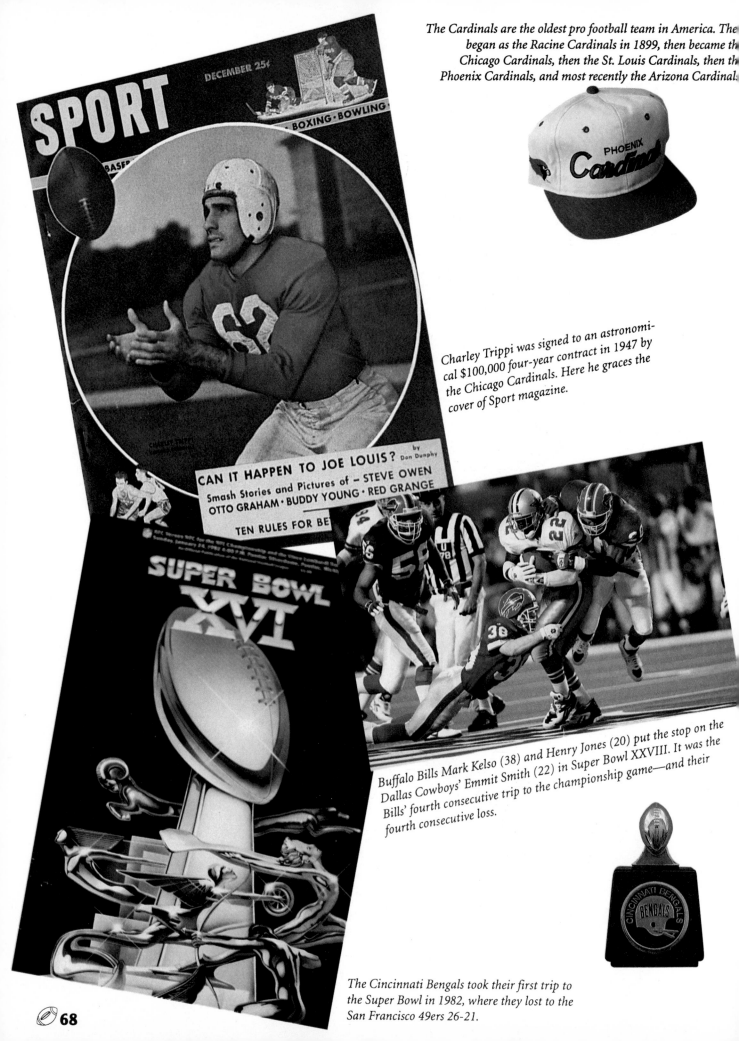

SPORT

DECEMBER 25¢

BOXING · BOWLING

CAN IT HAPPEN TO JOE LOUIS? by Don Dunphy

Smash Stories and Pictures of — STEVE OWEN
OTTO GRAHAM · BUDDY YOUNG · RED GRANGE

TEN RULES FOR BE

SUPER BOWL XVI

PHOENIX *Cardinals*

The Cardinals are the oldest pro football team in America. The began as the Racine Cardinals in 1899, then became th Chicago Cardinals, then the St. Louis Cardinals, then th Phoenix Cardinals, and most recently the Arizona Cardinal.

Charley Trippi was signed to an astronomi-cal $100,000 four-year contract in 1947 by the Chicago Cardinals. Here he graces the cover of Sport magazine.

Buffalo Bills Mark Kelso (38) and Henry Jones (20) put the stop on the Dallas Cowboys' Emmit Smith (22) in Super Bowl XXVIII. It was the Bills' fourth consecutive trip to the championship game—and their fourth consecutive loss.

The Cincinnati Bengals took their first trip to the Super Bowl in 1982, where they lost to the San Francisco 49ers 26-21.

68

Jack Kemp (15) and Daryle Lamonica (12) gave the Buffalo Bills two excellent quarterbacks in 1964. Kemp won the starting job and led the Bills to the AFL title in 1964 and 1965. Lamonica moved on to the Oakland Raiders in 1967 and directed them to the first Super Bowl.

Official Program . . .

Price 25¢
INC. TAX

Los Angeles
RAMS
vs.
Chicago
CARDINALS

LOS ANGELES MEMORIAL COLISEUM
SUNDAY, DECEMBER 4, 1949

Johnny Unitas is considered by many to be the best quarterback in NFL history. He set a league record by throwing at least one touchdown pass in 47 straight games. He threw 290 scoring passes in his 18-year career.

Green Bay coach Vince Lombardi is hoisted to the shoulders of star running backs Jim Taylor (31) and Paul Hornung (5) after the Packers beat Cleveland 23-12 to win the 1965 NFL title.

Bait and Tackle

There were times that Cleveland Browns defensive tackle Jerry Sherk wished he'd never met Kansas City Chiefs center Jack Rudnay. At least not on a football field.

Their odd relationship began at the Pro Bowl in 1974 where they were introduced for the first time. They became fixtures in the game during the late 1970s, teaming up to lead the AFC to victory on several other occasions. But it was during the regular season, when they went head-to-head with one another, that problems arose.

"I found out at the Pro Bowl that he was kind of a character," Sherk said. "From then on, whenever we played each other, we tried to make the other guy laugh in order to break his concentration."

Inevitably, Rudnay came out on top.

The Browns and Chiefs played in Kansas City two years after that initial Pro Bowl meeting. During the first quarter, the Browns' defense, with Sherk as a defensive tackle, played an even front. The alignment prohibited Sherk and Rudnay from lining up directly in front of one another.

Finally, an uneven formation was called and Sherk shifted from his defensive tackle spot so he was directly in front of Rudnay. He knew Rudnay would pull something.

"He was less than a foot away from me," Sherk said. "And you have to see this guy to appreciate him. If he's facing north, his nose is facing due west. That's because he broke his nose and never got it reset.

"Anyway, he stares at me through his face-mask. The quarterback is going through the signals, so Rudnay can't speak too loudly. But, in a clear, subtle voice, he says, 'The Popeel Pocket Fisherman. Still only $19.95.' Then the ball's snapped and he puts his helmet right in my chest."

The Popeel Pocket Fisherman was a product advertised on late-night television, but the absurdity of the comment caused Sherk to break into laughter. While he chuckled, Rudnay blew him off the line of scrimmage and the Kansas City fullback rambled past Sherk for 15 yards.

Rudnay scrambled back to the huddle unfazed and ready to go again. But Sherk could not regain his composure.

"I couldn't get it together for the rest of the day," Sherk recalled with a laugh.

Kansas City walloped the Browns by three touchdowns and Sherk was dejected as he made his way back to the locker room. As Sherk prepared to shower, he noticed a package stuffed into his locker. It was a Popeel Pocket Fisherman. The gift brought a smile to the defensive lineman's face.

"I still don't know what it is," Sherk said. "It was something you could fit in your pocket. It was a rod and a reel I think, maybe a couple of fishing lures, too. I'm sure I left it in Kansas City."

JERRY SHERK

Although Jack Rudnay used humor to take advantage of Sherk, it wasn't often that a center got the best of him. The 6-foot-4, 255-pounder from Oklahoma State managed to keep his game together for 12 seasons with the Browns.

Sherk was selected by the Browns in the second round of the 1970 draft and stepped right into Cleveland's starting unit. He was selected AFC Defensive Player of the Year in 1976 and played in the Pro Bowl four straight seasons from 1974 through 1977. Jerry Sherk played with the Cleveland Browns from 1970 to 1981.

LEFT: Cleveland defensive tackle Jerry Sherk was named AFC Defensive Player of the Year in 1976 and was a four-time Pro Bowl selection.

BROWNS FACT: Art McBride, the original owner of the Cleveland Browns, also ran several Cleveland-area taxicab companies in the 1940s. When it came time to trim the Browns' roster to 33 men to start the season, McBride took care of the players cut from the squad by giving them jobs as taxi drivers. During the course of the season, injured Cleveland players would immediately be replaced by a member of McBride's "taxi squad." The term soon became commonplace in the NFL to refer to players on the reserve list.

BELOW: Cleveland Browns team photo, 1960

Scents of Humor

*B*efore the advent of league rules to stimulate the passing game, football was dominated by teams with hard-charging running attacks. No one ran the ball like Cleveland Browns' running back Jim Brown.

There were only a few who could tackle a smooth and powerful back like Brown unaided. New York Giants middle linebacker Sam Huff was one of them. He is still remembered as one of the most ferocious middle linebackers in NFL history. Known for his fearlessness and cocky swagger, Huff liked to establish his dominance early in a game.

Playing on two of the best teams of the era, Brown and Huff clashed often. Brown recalled an encounter that was typical of their stormy on-field relationship.

"The Browns and the Giants were playing at Municipal Stadium in Cleveland," Brown said. "I don't remember the year, but we were both in the title hunt. Twice in a row I carried the ball and each time I got stopped for short yardage. After the last run, we're unpiling and Sam sticks his face right in mine and says, 'You stink.'"

Brown ignored the remark and silently handed the ball back to the referee before returning to the huddle. Quarterback Milt Plum began calling the next play.

Jim Brown (32) leaps through the Philadelphia Eagles line and into the end zone for one of the 126 touchdowns he scored in his career, a league record. Attempting to stop the Cleveland Browns fullback are Jerry Wilson (88), Jim Carr (21), Jess Richardson (72), Marion Campbell (78) and Don Owens (70).

"I want the ball," Brown interrupted. "I'm going up the middle."

Plum called Brown's number and broke the huddle. Brown took Plum's handoff and thundered through the line. Huff squared his shoulders. Brown stuck his helmet in Huff's chest and blew him backward. Huff landed on his back. Brown planted one foot on the linebacker's midsection and darted into the secondary. He rambled 50 yards for a touchdown.

After handing the ball silently to the referee, Brown looked back to midfield. Teammates were helping Huff struggle to his feet. At that moment, Brown got in the final dig. He yelled to Huff, "Hey Sam! How do I smell from there?"

Fullback Jim Brown (32) was the most dominating running back in the NFL during his nine years with the Cleveland Browns from 1957 to 1965. He won eight rushing titles in nine seasons.

JIM BROWN

*B*rown was the most dominating figure in the NFL between 1957 and 1966 after being drafted out of Syracuse University in the first round. As a rookie, he won the league rushing title and was named Rookie of the Year and Player of the Year.

Although he played just nine seasons, Brown is considered by many to be the greatest running back of all time. He was a unanimous All-Pro pick eight times and won eight rushing titles. He rushed for over 1,000 yards in seven different seasons. Twice he was named the NFL's Most Valuable Player.

Brown was just 30 years old when he stepped away from pro football in 1966 at the peak of his career. In nine seasons, he never missed a game and left behind a legacy that will be hard to match.

He rushed for 12,312 yards during his career, averaged 5.2 yards per carry and is the fourth leading ball carrier of all time. Brown's 126 touchdowns were an NFL record until Jerry Rice broke it in 1994. His single-season rushing record of 1,863 yards stood for 10 years until O.J. Simpson broke it in 1973.

In 1971, Brown was inducted into the Pro Football Hall of Fame.

Sorry, Wrong Team

Cleveland Stadium was rocking with 74,000 people on their feet. The Browns were down 16-14, but driving in the dying moments of a 1973 game against the hated Pittsburgh Steelers.

Rookie running back Greg Pruitt had just put Cleveland in scoring position after taking a 42-yard pass from quarterback Mike Phipps. In the huddle, Phipps was calling his number again.

Pruitt took the handoff from Phipps and sprinted toward the left sideline on a sweep. He found a seam, then darted upfield, going 18 yards for the winning score.

After the game, elated Browns fans poured onto the field. Pruitt found himself surrounded by newfound admirers.

"It's okay when 200 or 300 people slap you on the back as you leave," Pruitt remarked. "But when it gets to be 10,000, it can get a little scary."

Pruitt swam through the throng and was directed toward the baseball dugout. He made his way down the dugout steps to a tunnel which led to the locker room. Once safely inside, Pruitt hesitated and looked out into the crowd.

"I thought, 'This is my moment,'" Pruitt said.

He drank it all in, the cheering fans, the two touchdowns. Then he gathered his thoughts and anticipated questions from the media.

"I knew there would be a huge crowd around my locker," Pruitt said. "I was sitting there imagining what I was going to say."

Finally, Pruitt was ready to face the cameras and the media barrage. He charged up the walkway and burst into the locker room. There he found Steelers coach Chuck Noll screaming at his dejected football squad.

"Whoops. Sorry, Coach," Pruitt said, as he quietly shut the door and backed out.

In the bedlam of the moment, Pruitt had been ushered toward the wrong tunnel. The Browns locker room was on the other side of the field. He peeked out of the dugout and saw nothing but crazed Browns fans still swaying in revelry.

"I had to wait for 20 to 25 minutes until they cleared out," Pruitt admitted. "This was my big moment and by the time I got to my own locker all the media was gone."

Fortunately it wasn't the last time the media came calling for Pruitt after one of his big games. It was just another rookie mistake he chalked up to experience.

Running Back, Running Nose

In a 1978 game against the Steelers, Pruitt raced for over 100 yards against Pittsburgh. He was the only back to gain over 100 yards against them all season.

"I had a head cold that day," Pruitt said. "I was fine, except my nose just wouldn't stop running."

Early in the game quarterback Brian Sipe audibled to a run play that featured Pruitt.

"I had stuff coming out of my nose and dripping to the ground," Pruitt recalled. His sinuses were also draining onto his uniform jersey.

After taking the handoff, Pruitt was met by five or six Steelers, who clawed at his jersey while making the tackle. As they began to unpile, the tacklers soon realized the origin of the sticky fluid now on their arms and hands. Pruitt was uniformly cussed out by his opponents.

"They tackled me very carefully after that," he said.

OPPOSITE: Cleveland running back Greg Pruitt (34) dashes into the end zone against the Kansas City Chiefs in 1975. Although the Browns won just three games that season, Pruitt gained 1,067 yards and averaged nearly five yards per carry.

GREG PRUITT

Pruitt joined the Browns as a second-round draft pick in 1973. Despite being the runner-up to Heisman Trophy winner Johnny Rodgers in 1972, Pruitt was tagged as a kick return man when he first reported to the club.

In 1975, Forrest Gregg was named head coach of the Browns and Pruitt's role changed dramatically. The former Oklahoma Sooner star gained over 1,000 yards in each of the next three seasons and had a fourth season

of 960 yards.

Pruitt's 12-year career ended in 1984 with the Los Angeles Raiders. He gained 5,672 yards, scored 27 rushing touchdowns and averaged 4.7 yards per carry in the NFL. He also caught 328 passes for 3,069 yards and another 18 scores.

PLAYING HISTORY:
Cleveland Browns 1973-1981
Los Angeles Raiders
1982-1984

BROWNS FACT: Cleveland Browns running back Greg Pruitt once used his diminutive size to slither through the grasp of Kansas City Chiefs mammoth defensive end Buck Buchanan for an extra three yards, infuriating the future Hall of Famer. As they unpiled, the 6-foot-7, 275-pound Buchanan looked down at the 5-foot-9 Pruitt and glared.

"You do that again, little man, and I'm going to bite your head off," Buchanan grumbled.

"You do that and you'll have more brains in your belly than you have in your head," Pruitt replied.

Close to Greatness...Really Close

Getting ready for a football game at old Tigers Stadium in Detroit was like dressing in a shoe box. But rookie wide receiver Paul Warfield hardly noticed. It was the first game of the 1964 preseason and Warfield was wide-eyed as he slipped on his Cleveland Browns jersey for the first time.

Warfield jogged out of the tunnel and felt his cleats sink into the dirt of the sparsely sodded field. He looked up at the rusting girders that held the great rafters aloft. He saw the smattering of Detroit Lions fans settle into the wooden seats just before pregame warmups. Before long, the national anthem was sung and the game began.

On the Browns' opening drive, Warfield took his place in the Cleveland huddle. He placed his hands on his knees and leaned forward to listen to quarterback Frank Ryan call the play. Suddenly, he felt a presence beside him in the huddle. Ryan's voice faded into the background as a startling revelation fell like a curtain across Warfield's consciousness.

"Growing up in northeast Ohio, I had been a Browns fan all my life," Warfield said. "Just eight months earlier, I was watching the Browns on television at my college dorm at Ohio State with 20 other guys. We were all cheering for the Browns. I remember thinking what it would be like to be in their huddle. And now I was in the huddle. And standing next to me was the greatest runner of all time. Number 32. Jim Brown."

Warfield recovered from his slack-jawed awe and quickly blossomed into one of the league's top wideouts. During his rookie season, he led the club in receiving with 52 catches, good for 920 yards and nine touchdowns.

It was just the beginning of a remarkable 13-year NFL career that eventually landed Warfield in the Hall of Fame alongside his idol Jim Brown.

BROWNS FACT: During 10 seasons with the Cleveland Browns from 1946 to 1955, quarterback Otto Graham directed his club to 10 divisional or league championships.

PAUL WARFIELD

For five seasons, from 1964 to 1969, Warfield performed spectacularly as Cleveland's big-play wide receiver. In 1970, he was traded to the Miami Dolphins. There he teamed with quarterback Bob Griese and averaged over 21 yards per reception as Miami compiled a perfect 17-0 season in 1972 and won Super Bowls VII and VIII.

After playing in the World Football League in 1975, Warfield returned to the Browns in 1976 and 1977 for his final two seasons.

Although he played for run-oriented teams throughout his career, Warfield made 427 catches for 8,565 yards. Warfield's 85 touchdown catches is sixth best of all time and his 20.1-yard average per catch is fifth best in NFL history.

In 1983, Warfield was elected to the Pro Football Hall of Fame in his first year of eligibility.

PLAYING HISTORY:
Cleveland Browns 1964-1969
Miami Dolphins 1970-1974
Memphis Southmen (WFL) 1975
Cleveland Browns 1976-1977

BROWNS FACT: Cleveland Browns trainer Leo Murphy watched star running back Marion Motley get popped at the goal line, then remain on his hands and knees during a game in the late 1940s. He immediately thought the worst: Motley had probably suffered a crippling injury. But then he noticed several other players down.

"We were playing the Pittsburgh Steelers," said Murphy, who spent 39 years in the Browns locker room before retiring in 1989. "I look toward the end zone and there are six guys crawling around near the goal line, three Steelers and three of our guys. I'm thinking what the hell's going on here?"

Murphy raced on the field. "I said, 'Are you alright?' and one guy said, 'Yeah. We're looking for Motley's gold tooth.'"

LEFT: Cleveland Browns flanker back Paul Warfield in the locker room at Yankee Stadium, after the Browns beat the New York Giants 52-20 in a December 1964 game.

The Best Game He Ever Forgot

Troy Aikman had completed 14 of 18 passes for 177 yards and two touchdowns in leading the Dallas Cowboys to a commanding 28-7 lead over the San Francisco 49ers in the 1993 NFC Championship Game at Texas Stadium.

It was one of Aikman's greatest games. And he doesn't remember 99 percent of it.

An accidental knee to the head on his second play of the third quarter robbed Aikman's memory of all but one play of that game—an incomplete pass to Alvin Harper.

Slamming into 49ers defensive tackle Dana Stubblefield's knee left Aikman with a concussion. However, he didn't leave the game after the hit. Acting on instincts alone, Aikman handed the ball to Emmitt Smith on the ensuing third-and-21 play.

When the punting unit came on the field, Aikman walked off to the sideline where he encountered center Mark Stepnoski, who was on crutches following a knee injury and surgery weeks earlier. Aikman appeared surprised at his center's condition.

"Hey, what happened to you?" Aikman asked Stepnoski.

It didn't take a medical degree for Stepnoski to realize that Aikman needed help.

"I told him, 'Don't worry about me, I'm fine,'" said Stepnoski, who summoned trainer Kevin O'Neill.

When smelling salts and oxygen failed to clear the cobwebs in Aikman's brain, Dr. J. R. Zamorano began asking Aikman questions.

"He couldn't remember if he was the Most Valuable Player in the Super Bowl last year," Zamorano recalled. "He couldn't remember the score, the date of the game or who we played."

It would be a hard Super Bowl performance to forget, since Aikman completed 22 of 30 passes for 273 yards and four touchdowns, and was named MVP in the Cowboys' 52-17 rout of the Buffalo Bills. So Zamorano tried a different line of questioning. He asked Aikman about the upcoming Super Bowl.

"When I asked him where the 1993 Super Bowl would be played, he said, 'Henryetta,'" Zamorano said.

Aikman had named his hometown of Henryetta, Oklahoma, instead of Atlanta, Georgia as the site of Super Bowl XXVIII. That's when the doc knew it was time to send the Cowboys quarterback to the hospital.

Dallas was able to hang on even without Aikman in the lineup. Backup quarterback Bernie Kosar came on in relief and threw a crucial touchdown pass as Dallas defeated the San Francisco 49ers and advanced to the Super Bowl.

Meanwhile, the folks in Aikman's hometown took advantage of the situation for a little publicity. They sold tickets for a Super Bowl game in Henryetta, just in case Aikman did show up.

Aikman recovered from his concussion in time to lead the Cowboys to a second straight Super Bowl victory over the Buffalo Bills. He regained his memory almost completely, but still needed the magic of videotape to recall his 1993 NFC Championship Game performance.

TROY AIKMAN

$\mathcal{S}$ince the former UCLA star was chosen by the Cowboys in the 1989 draft, Aikman has developed into one of the game's top quarterbacks. He competed with Steve Walsh for the Dallas quarterback job in his rookie season, but Walsh was traded prior to 1990, clearing the way for Aikman.

Aikman made steady progress, then blossomed midway through the 1990 season and guided the Cowboys to four straight wins before suffering a shoulder separation.

In 1991, Aikman led the league in completion percentage, connecting on 65 percent of 363 passes. The Cowboys improved to 11-5 and a spot in the playoffs for the first time since 1985. Aikman has played for the Cowboys continuously since 1989.

It's Alive!

Despite the Miami Dolphins' lofty 8-2 record, few people viewed their 1993 Thanksgiving Day encounter with the defending Super Bowl champion Dallas Cowboys as a battle of the league's elite. For the Dolphins, it was more of a survival test.

With starting quarterback Dan Marino and backup Scott Mitchell sidelined to injury, Miami's fortunes rested on the arm of the league's oldest player, 39-year-old Steve DeBerg.

Considering DeBerg had a little over two weeks of experience with the Dolphins' complicated offensive scheme, it appeared Miami would need a miracle to continue its improbable run of success.

Against a surreal backdrop—the first game-day snowfall ever at Texas Stadium—a miracle is exactly what the Dolphins got, courtesy of a blunder by Dallas defensive lineman Leon Lett.

Trailing 14-13 with 2:16 remaining, DeBerg engineered a brilliant drive through the slush. It was a field better suited for 'skateball,' according to Dallas running back Emmitt Smith. After converting two third-downs and one fourth-down situation, DeBerg drove Miami to the Dallas 24.

With 15 seconds remaining, Miami kicker Pete Stoyanovich lined up for a potential game-winning 41-yard field goal. It was no chip shot. In the first quarter, from a similar distance, Stoyanovich had slipped on the sleet-covered artificial turf and crashed onto his behind.

This time, Dallas defensive lineman Jimmy Jones blocked the low line-drive attempt, send-ing the ball spinning downfield. The Cowboys would have a first-and-10 and the game would be over.

While a small group of Dolphins followed the ball, Dallas players on the field and the sideline began celebrating.

Everyone except for Lett. Inexplicably, the huge lineman plowed through the circle of Dolphins and slid into the football.

Like a group of blood-thirsty piranhas, Miami attacked the loose, and suddenly live, football.

"We're running downfield after the kick and I'm thinking we need to push one of their guys into the ball or something," said Miami center Jeff Dellenbach, who finally recovered the football at the Dallas one-yard line.

"All of a sudden, Lett comes flying out of nowhere and we hear this 'THUMP.' Boom! Now, it's a live ball. The only bad thing was that I should have scored a touchdown. I'm laying on the ball in the end zone and no one had touched me yet."

"Obviously, it will go down as one of the great NFL bloopers," Dallas safety James Wash-ington said.

Lett was already a charter member of the blooper club. At Super Bowl XXVII earlier in the year, Lett picked up a fumble with nothing but clear sailing ahead. But Lett began to celebrate a little too soon and Buffalo's Don Beebe caught him from behind and knocked the ball out of his hands and through the end zone.

That mishap merely cost the Cowboys six points in a game it won 52-17. This one cost the Cowboys a game.

"We get paid a lot of money," Dallas cornerback Kevin Smith said. "Leon is supposed to know the rules. I knew the rule and so did nine other guys. He didn't."

Meanwhile, as officials spent several minutes determining possession and placement of the ball, Stoyanovich and holder Doug Pederson tried to clear a spot for a second field goal attempt.

Two things, however, hindered the pair's efforts. First, the line of scrimmage changed three times before the officials finally spotted the ball at the Dallas one. The second hindrance was Dallas fullback Daryl Johnston.

"Johnston kept kicking snow back into the area we were trying to brush clear," Pederson said. "Pete and I were getting tired from cleaning all the snow and ice away."

But not tired enough that Stoyanovich couldn't nail a 19-yarder with no time left to secure the wacky win for Miami.

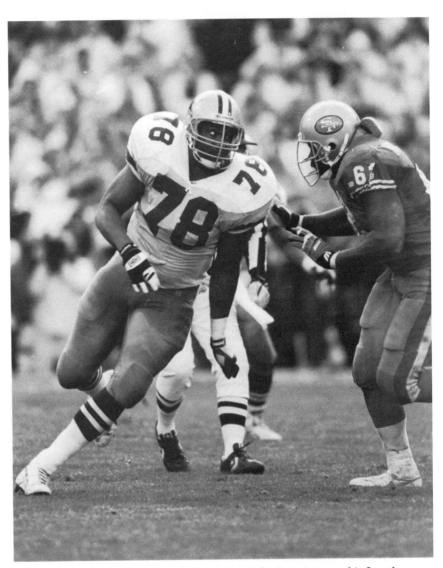

Dallas' Leon Lett (78) is known as much for his defensive miscues as his fine play on the Cowboys' defensive line. Here, he tries to elude San Francisco 49ers Pro Bowl guard Guy McIntyre (62) during the 1992 NFC Championship Game.

COWBOYS FACT: The Cowboys have a long history of outstanding running backs. The first Dallas back to rush for 1,000 yards in a season was Calvin Hill in 1972.

LEON LETT

The 6-foot-6, 290-pound Lett was an all-league player at tiny Emporia State College in Emporia, Kansas before signing with the Cowboys as a rookie in 1991.

COWBOYS FACT: Tony Dorsett has the NFL's longest run from scrimmage, a 99-yard touchdown dash against the Minnesota Vikings in 1983.

COWBOYS FACT: Ed "Too Tall" Jones, a 6-foot-9, 275-pound defensive end, retired from the Cowboys in 1979 to begin a pro boxing career. After winning six straight heavyweight fights, he returned to the Cowboys for the 1980 season.

RIGHT: Dallas quarterback Roger Staubach shows his jubilation after firing a touchdown pass to Butch Johnson in Super Bowl XII, won by the Cowboys 27-10.

Photo from Richard Wolfers Auctions, Inc., San Francisco

DON'T CALL HIM RUSTY

2uarterback Roger Staubach had just finished a five-year stint as a naval officer when he reported to the Dallas Cowboys in 1969 as a 27-year-old rookie.

The 1963 Heisman Trophy winner from Navy wondered if the layoff had eroded his passing skills. He got his answer quickly in the opening game of the 1969 season against the St. Louis Cardinals. Craig Morton, the Cowboys' number-one quarterback, was nursing injuries, so Dallas coach Tom Landry had no choice but to go with the rookie.

"I was very nervous," Staubach recalled. "It was not only my first game but I thought, if things didn't go right, it could have been my last."

Staubach did more than survive—he fired one touchdown pass and ran for 140 yards as the Cowboys defeated St. Louis 24-3. His first scoring pass as a professional went to wide receiver Lance Rentzel.

"I remember I was on the run when I made that throw," Staubach said. "I was just trying to get rid of it. It wasn't a great pass, but Lance made a nice play on it and scored.

"Coach Landry wasn't happy with my scrambling, then or ever. It caused a running feud between us. But I put up with his play calling and he put up with my scrambling."

> **COWBOYS FACT:** Dallas Cowboys quarterback Roger Staubach threw one of the most famous "Hail Mary" passes of all time. It occurred in the 1975 NFC playoff game between Dallas and the Minnesota Vikings.
>
> Trailing the Vikes 14-10 with 32 seconds to play, Staubach dropped back from the 50-yard line and heaved a pass 60 yards in the air. Wide receiver Drew Pearson saw the pass was short and adjusted his route.
>
> He grabbed the pass at the goal line and rolled into the end zone for the winning score.

ROGER STAUBACH

After serving as Cowboys quarterback Craig Morton's backup for two seasons, Roger Staubach won the starting job in 1971. That season, he won the NFL passing title, the first of four he captured in his career.

Although Staubach was the Heisman Trophy winner as a junior at the United States Naval Academy in 1963, the five years of required service he owed the Navy scared off most professional teams. He wasn't drafted until the tenth round by the Cowboys. It proved to be one of the greatest tenth-round picks in history.

During his 11-year career, Staubach would toss 153 touchdown passes and play in four Super Bowls, leading the Cowboys to victories in Super Bowls VI and XII. He was named the Most Valuable Player in Super Bowl VI against Miami after passing for 119 yards and two touchdowns with no interceptions.

When Staubach retired after the 1979 season, he was the highest ranked quarterback of all time, surpassing Hall of Famers like Sammy Baugh, Johnny Unitas and Joe Namath. But more important than the statistics was Staubach's ability to perform under pressure. He brought the Cowboys from behind in the fourth quarter to win 23 times, and 17 of those times he did it in the final two minutes.

Staubach completed 1,685 passes for 22,700 yards and rushed for 2,264 yards and 20 touchdowns. He was inducted into the Pro Football Hall of Fame in 1985.

DALLAS

THE SUPER BOWL BREAKTHROUGH

*T*om Landry led the Dallas Cowboys to 270 victories over 29 seasons, but winning the Super Bowl for the first time was his sweetest moment as a head coach. Landry took the reins of the expansion Cowboys in 1960, then watched as the club floundered to an 0-11-1 record. After failing to coax a victory out of the Cowboys in that inaugural season, it took Landry just six years to build his club into a perennial playoff team. Dallas won its first Eastern Conference title in 1966, but their leap from conference champion to NFL title-holder and Super Bowl winner was akin to hopping the Grand Canyon. The Cowboys had trouble taking their game to the next level.

Vince Lombardi's Green Bay Packers were the thorn in Landry's side in 1966 and 1967. Both seasons the Cowboys faced Green Bay in the NFL Championship Game and each year Dallas was sent home a loser.

The most aggravating Dallas loss came in the Ice Bowl in 1967, so called because it was played in minus-15-degree weather at Lambeau Field. In the closing seconds of that game, Green Bay quarterback Bart Starr scored on a sneak to take the NFL title from the Cowboys.

"We had played in championship games before and lost," Landry said. "There was the Ice Bowl game when we were defeated in the final seconds. That was a tough, tough defeat. Then, in 1970, we got to our first Super Bowl and Baltimore beat us on the last play of the game."

Jim O'Brien's 32-yard field goal gave the Colts a 16-13 win over Dallas in Super Bowl V. That was the last straw. After the Cowboys' heartbreaking Super Bowl loss to Baltimore, Landry was more determined than ever to bring a championship to Dallas. He got his chance the following season in 1971, when Dallas confronted Miami in Super Bowl VI.

"I'd have to say the most memorable moment in my football career came in Super Bowl VI against the Miami Dolphins," Landry said. "To finally win a Super Bowl for the first time was very special to me. We basically went into that Super Bowl against Miami with the same team that lost to Baltimore a year earlier. I was awful sure we would beat Miami. We were very well prepared. I don't think I was ever as confident of winning a game as I was before that Super Bowl."

Using a ball-control offense, the Cowboys amassed 252 yards rushing while quarterback Roger Staubach fired a pair of touchdown passes. Meanwhile, the Cowboys defense shut down Miami's attack in a 24-3 Super Bowl victory.

"One of the plays I'll always remember in that game involved Bob Lilly, our defensive tackle, chasing Bob Griese around the field," Landry said. "Griese had dropped back to pass and Lilly was on him quick. Griese seemed to get away, but Bob chased Griese around like a cutting horse. They went to the right, then to the left, then the right, and by the time Lilly caught him they were both ready to drop. But Bob stayed with it. Griese ended up losing 29 yards on the play."

Just as Lilly refused to give up, neither would the Cowboys quit in their quest for a Super Bowl win. And in 1971, they finally made their breakthrough.

COWBOYS

TOM LANDRY

*B*efore starting his coaching career, Landry played with the New York Yankees of the All-American Football Conference and New York Giants of the NFL, where he was a feared defensive back and skilled punter. He intercepted 32 passes during his seven-year playing career and averaged 41 yards per punt.

After serving as an assistant coach with the New York Giants, the Cowboys offered Landry his first head coaching job. He built them into a perennial playoff contender and for 20 consecutive seasons, between 1966 and 1986,

Dallas finished with a winning record. During that span, the Cowboys won two Super Bowls, five NFC titles and 14 division championships.

During his 29 years at the helm of the Cowboys, Landry's overall record, including postseason games, was 270-178-6. Only George Halas and Don Shula have won more games in the professional ranks.

COACHING HISTORY:
Dallas Cowboys 1960-1988

BOB LILLY

*D*efensive tackle Bob Lilly was one of pro football's true ironmen. After graduating from Texas Christian he was the Dallas Cowboys' first-ever pick in 1961. He went on to play in 292 games for the Cowboys, missing just one contest in his 14-year career. Lilly was selected for 11 Pro Bowls and was the anchor of Dallas' "Doomsday Defense" of the 1960s and 1970s. In 1980, he became the first player to spend his entire career with Dallas and be elected to the Hall of Fame. He played from 1961 to 1974.

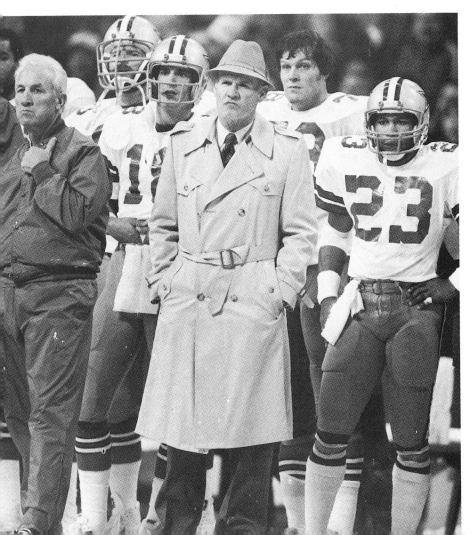

Maximum Overdrive

It is under extreme stress that a man's true colors are exposed.

During the 1986 AFC Championship Game, fourth-year quarterback John Elway faced a fierce winter gale, a strong Cleveland Browns defense, the taunts of 80,000 rabid fans at Cleveland's Municipal Stadium and a sprained ankle when his team took the field with the game on the line. The Broncos trailed the Browns 20-13 with 5:32 remaining and the ball just past their own one-yard line.

"I knew we had to put it in the other end zone," Elway said. "We were backed up. We just had to dig down and find out what we were made of."

As Elway conferred with Bronco coach Dan Reeves on the sideline, the rest of his offensive unit huddled in its own end zone, waiting to see if coach and quarterback could concoct a play to get them out of the hole and start a come-from-behind miracle.

"John was tremendous," wide receiver Steve Watson said. "He came into the huddle and told us to do our best, to work hard, and we'd be able to do it."

And they did. Elway patiently moved the Broncos downfield. He faced a critical third-and-18 situation at the Cleveland 48, but found wideout Mark Jackson with a 20-yard toss to keep the drive alive.

During the drive, Elway calmly passed for 73 yards and ran for 20 more to set up the game's most dramatic play, a five-yard touchdown pass to Jackson, which pulled the Broncos within an extra point of tying the game. Rich Karlis made good on the extra point, sending the game into overtime.

"That drive is something I might not be able to do again," Elway said. "The day before the big game, you dream of doing things like that. But you never expect them to happen. That was the best drive I've ever been involved in."

In all, Elway led the Broncos 98 yards in 15 plays to tie the score.

But just tying the game was not enough. In overtime, Elway finished up one of his best days as a professional with a nine-play, 60-yard march which ended on a 33-yard Karlis field goal. It gave Denver the AFC Title and a date in Super Bowl XXI against the New York Giants.

Quarterback John Elway was named NFL Player of the Year in 1987 when he led the Denver Broncos to the AFC Championship and a spot in the Super Bowl against the Washington Redskins.

break virtually all of Denver's team passing records. More importantly, Elway proved he had what it takes to be a consistent winner. He led the Broncos to AFC Western Division titles in 1984, 1986, 1987, 1989 and 1991. In 1987, Elway was selected NFL Player of the Year.

Under Elway's command, the Broncos appeared in three Super Bowls in four years between the 1986 and 1989 seasons. Unfortunately, Denver was unable to convert one of those appearances into a championship victory.

"Elway might be the best quarterback in the game," said offensive coordinator and former Denver Broncos assistant coach Mike Shanahan. "He can carry a team on his own athletic ability. He was the key to the Broncos' Super Bowl appearances."

Elway has appeared in four Pro Bowls. He is ranked among the top-ten quarterbacks of all time for pass attempts, completions and yards. Elway has been playing for the Denver Broncos since 1983.

JOHN ELWAY

Elway followed a roundabout road to the Broncos. He joined the team after being selected by the Baltimore Colts with the first pick in the 1983 draft. Elway, who also starred in baseball at Stanford University, threatened to sign with the New York Yankees rather than play with the Colts. Baltimore obliged by trading Elway to Denver. He immediately was billed as the Broncos' savior and signed a $5 million contract with the club in 1983.

Once in a Bronco uniform, it took just four years for him to

Flash of Green

Denver Broncos head coach Dan Reeves grabbed a piece of rookie Paul Green's jersey. The wide-eyed tight end bent down and the bespectacled coach whispered the play into his ear.

Green's whole life had narrowed to this one moment. Seventy thousand fans were wedged into the Louisiana Superdome. Two thousand journalists sat poised for the next play. Billions watched on satellite from around the world. It was Super Bowl XXIV, the Broncos against the San Francisco 49ers.

"White six, 324 Zebra, X go," Reeves said.

Green had dreamed of this moment since he was a kid growing up in the lush farmland of central California. He had poured his heart into football while at Clovis High School. He gave even more as a two-year starter at the University of Southern California. It all built up to the most difficult year of his life, his rookie season with the Denver Broncos. As a fourth-round draft choice, there was no guarantee he would survive in the NFL. So he worked extra hard, studied plays until his eyes burned, perfected blocking techniques until his body screamed, ran extra pass patterns until he was on the brink of exhaustion.

"White six, 324 Zebra, X go." The play plowed through his head like a locomotive. "I can't believe this!" Green thought. "This is my play."

He raced across the Astroturf to the crown of midfield. For the first time in his life, he would stick his head into an NFL game-day huddle.

Green was one of the nameless members of the developmental squad. He took his lumps and worked his tail off during the week in practice, but according to NFL rules, on game day he couldn't suit up. He was just another face on the sideline. Miraculously, because of another player's injury, Green was lifted from the developmental squad and placed on the active roster for the last game of the year, which just happened to be the Super Bowl.

Not only was Green in an NFL game for the first time, playing before millions of television viewers around the world, but "White six, 324 Zebra, X go" meant that Green was the primary receiver on a pass to the end zone. Adrenaline surged through every part of his body. His heart was beating uncontrollably.

In the huddle, Green spit the play in the direction of quarterback John Elway.

"Say whaaat!?" a voice shrieked. It was Clarence Kay, Denver's starting tight end, and the man Green was replacing.

"No damn way, rookie. This is my play," Kay screamed.

"But I'm supposed to..."

"You want me to kick your butt in front of the whole damn world? Get out of the huddle!" Kay shouted.

Green reluctantly obeyed the veteran tight end and returned to the Broncos' sideline, realizing that his possible moment of glory had slipped away. Then he watched as the play developed.

Kay slithered off the line and brushed past 49ers linebacker Bill Romanowski. He raced up the sideline with Romanowski tailing close behind. Elway spied Kay and lofted a well-placed

pass to the back of the end zone. Kay leaped and got one hand on the ball, but Romanowski recovered in time to tip it from Kay's grasp. A flag was dropped on the play and Romanowski was whistled for pass interference. The penalty set up Denver's only touchdown as the 49ers obliterated the Broncos 55-10 in the most lopsided loss in Super Bowl history.

But on the sideline Green couldn't help thinking he might have shaken Romanowski to make the catch. He was younger, lighter and faster than Kay. He didn't reflect upon the final result so much as on his missed opportunity at fame.

PAUL GREEN

Green's Broncos career was short and unspectacular. His luck wasn't much better when he was signed by the Seattle Seahawks in 1992. He started the first four games of the season and caught nine passes before suffering a broken shoulder and spending the rest of the year on injured reserve.

PLAYING HISTORY:
Denver Broncos 1989-1990
Seattle Seahawks 1992-1994

Program from Super Bowl XXIV on January 28, 1990 in New Orleans. The Broncos fell to the San Francisco 49ers, 55-10.

Now He Gets Respect

*N*o one noticed young Karl Mecklenburg's athletic ability. In virtually every game he tried, he was the last guy chosen.

Certainly he wasn't appreciated in high school, where he was unceremoniously cut from the basketball, baseball and hockey teams. As a last resort, he decided to give football a shot. He's been trying to prove himself ever since.

Mecklenburg became a prep football star by the time he was a senior, but still he got no respect. Not a single college called to offer a scholarship. His only choice was to enroll at the University of Minnesota and try his luck as a walk-on player. He eventually became a starter for the Gophers.

Then, when the NFL draft rolled around, scouts said he had no chance to make it as a professional. It was the same story he'd heard in high school and college. But the Denver Broncos threw caution to the wind and drafted Mecklenburg with a throwaway pick on the 12th and final round of the 1983 draft.

Mecklenburg's prayers had been answered. All he needed was a fair shot. He made the Broncos as a reserve defensive end. He felt he had something to prove.

The chance Mecklenburg was looking for came early in his career, in a game against the Los Angeles Raiders. It was Raiders running back Marcus Allen who became the scapegoat for the years of disrespect Mecklenburg endured.

The Raiders were leading Denver 7-6 in the second quarter during an early fall game in 1985 at Mile High Stadium. Raiders quarterback Jim Plunkett drifted back on second down and looked to throw the ball long.

Allen decoyed a block in the backfield, then flared into the left flat. Plunkett could find no one open deep, so he dumped off a pass to Allen. The throw was a bit high and Allen leaped to make the catch.

The football had barely reached the Raiders running back when Mecklenburg exploded through him. He hit Allen shoulder high with all of his considerable force. Allen's head snapped back and he landed with a crunch as the pass fell incomplete.

"I knew I hit him pretty good because his eyes rolled back and he was just staring at the sky," Mecklenburg said. "It felt great. I was kind of lucky because I got him in the most vulnerable position you can get a back in. In a way, I was kind of glad to see him get up because he could've been badly hurt. But in another way, I wasn't because he was such a big part of that team."

When Broncos defensive coordinator Joe Collier saw the damage Mecklenburg created, he developed more defensive schemes especially suited for his new linebacker. He began using his versatile star at every position he could. Against the Pittsburgh Steelers in 1985, Mecklenburg seemingly was everywhere at once. He played all four linebacker spots and all three positions as a down lineman.

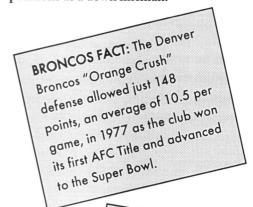

BRONCOS FACT: The Denver Broncos "Orange Crush" defense allowed just 148 points, an average of 10.5 per game, in 1977 as the club won its first AFC Title and advanced to the Super Bowl.

BRONCOS FACT: Rick Upchurch scored eight touchdowns on punt returns, an NFL record, during his career with Denver from 1975 to 1983.

KARL MECKLENBURG

Denver's Karl Mecklenburg (77) puts a knock on Kansas City Chiefs quarterback Bill Kenney (9). Mecklenburg recorded a team-high 13 sacks in 1985.

Mecklenburg has established himself firmly as one of the Broncos' most versatile defensive ends. In the 1985 season, Mecklenburg recorded a team-record 13 quarterback sacks. Mecklenburg started playing for the Denver Broncos in 1983.

BRONCOS FACT: The first draft pick in Denver history was Trinity College center Roger LeClerc in 1960. He signed instead with the Chicago Bears, but came back to play for Denver in 1967 for one final season.

91

Hit the Ground Running

The Denver Broncos faced a prodigious task late in the 1974 season. They were taking on the playoff-bound Oakland Raiders in front of a packed house at the Oakland Coliseum.

Oakland had mounted a nine-game winning streak in 1974, and at 9-1 was clearly the class of the AFC. Denver struggled along at 4-5-1, trying to save face. In 29 previous regular season meetings between the two clubs, Denver had won just six times. It was like sending an unarmed David to meet Goliath.

"We went into Oakland as big underdogs," said John Ralston, the Broncos head coach that season. "We were hoping to mix it up against that great team and keep them off balance. But to tell you the truth we were not really sure what would work."

The Raiders defensive line, one of the league's most dominant, included Bubba Smith, Art Thoms and Otis Sistrunk. Phil Villapiano and veteran Dan Conners anchored the linebacking corps. On paper they appeared to overmatch Denver's offensive line, which included Claudie Minor, Bobby Maples and rugged tight end Riley Odoms. But games aren't played on paper and the Broncos were not intimidated. In fact, they manhandled the Raiders in the trenches.

"Our offensive line did an outstanding job that day," said Ralston, who was in his third year as the Broncos head coach. "The guys up front blocked extremely well. Our running game started to click right off the bat so we stayed with it. We didn't do anything fancy. We went right up the middle, just man against man. Once you get the running game going, a lot of other options open up."

With rookie fullback Jon Keyworth and tailback Otis Armstrong in the backfield, the Broncos rushed for nearly 300 yards. Keyworth accounted for 146 yards, while Armstrong picked up 144 yards on the ground. It was the start of something special. Armstrong, the club's first-round draft pick in 1973, finished the year with a franchise record 1,407 rushing yards and averaged over 100 yards per game on the ground.

Behind Denver's quality line play and outstanding running attack, the Broncos defeated Oakland, 20-17.

"I really enjoyed that game. It was probably the most memorable of my pro career, because we took on a great team and went right at them," Ralston said. "It was probably the only time since I have been a coach where I was able to run at will on an opponent. And we are not talking about a bad team. The Raiders were a fantastic defensive team. It was just one of those days when everything seemed to go right for us."

The game also seemed to get the Broncos on track. They established themselves as one of the best running teams in the league and won their next three games. Denver finished the season in second place behind the Raiders in the AFC West with a 7-6-1 record.

JOHN RALSTON

*F*or Ralston, Denver was just another stop in a long and storied coaching career. He joined the Broncos as head coach and general manager at the end of the 1971 season after successful stints at Utah State and Stanford University. He took a Bronco team that was in turmoil and quickly taught the club how to win.

"John Ralston really changed the (team's) attitude when he came in as coach," said the Broncos quarterback at the time, Charley Johnson. "He always had a positive attitude. He never dwelled on the negatives and that positive attitude wore off on a lot of other people."

After leading the Broncos to a 9-5 record in 1976, Ralston resigned and returned to the collegiate ranks as a head coach, most recently at San Jose State. He compiled a 34-33-3 record during his five-year tenure with the Denver Broncos, from 1972 to 1976.

Promotional poster for the 1977 Denver Broncos.

Roadhouse Blues

In his heyday, the cocky, whiskey-voiced Bobby Layne was as fine a field general as pro football has produced. Few of his breed have commanded the respect and allegiance of the supporting troops as did Layne, both on and off the field. Simply put, he ran the team his way. Perhaps no one put the redhead in better focus than old friend Doak Walker, a marvelously gifted running back with the Detroit Lions of the 1950s.

"Everybody walked softly around Bobby," Walker said. "Even the assistant coaches were afraid of him. They knew the kind of power he had with the club."

As a self-imposed dictator of sorts, Layne was not loath to make use of his authority. He regularly employed rookies to perform such menial tasks as running errands, doing his laundry and serving as chauffeurs. One of his more memorable men-in-waiting was Alex Karras, who would go on to become an All-Pro defensive tackle.

Karras joined the Detroit club in 1958. Almost immediately Layne appropriated his off-duty services.

"He always called me Tippy," Karras said. "I can't tell you why. But it was 'Tippy this' and 'Tippy that.' And it got to me after a while."

Principal among Karras' chores was to drive

Layne to his favorite after-hours watering hole in neighboring Pontiac, Michigan.

"I'd take him up there practically every night," Karras said. "The place was a little roadhouse. It provided drinking, a band and gambling. Bobby loved to sing. He didn't have much of a voice. Sounded like gravel rattling in a tin can. But he was loud. And that's all he seemed to care about."

Usually, Karras would nap in the driver's seat until the roadhouse closed, then drive Layne home while the quarterback lay in the backseat, bellowing boisterous ballads.

"One night, I had to go to the can something fierce," Karras said. "So I went inside the roadhouse. On the way out, I grabbed a beer, then struck up a conversation with this gal. One thing led to another and the place closed. I hurry to the car and Bobby's already behind the wheel. Uh-uh, he insists he's not gonna move. So he drives back to town singing at the top of his lungs with one foot propped up on the dashboard. We had to be doing 90 or better. I'm on the floor of the backseat praying like an altar boy."

The incident taught Karras a valuable lesson. His life was more important than his bladder.

"After that I stayed in the car, loaded kidneys or not."

BOBBY LAYNE

*L*ayne broke into professional football in 1948 with the Chicago Bears after earning All-America honors at the University of Texas. But it was with the Detroit Lions from 1950 to 1958 that his career blossomed. Although he was never outstanding statistically, he possessed all the intangible elements that make up a successful quarterback. He was a strong-willed leader with determination, competitive fire and coolness under pressure.

The 6-foot-2, 190-pounder guided the Lions to NFL championships in 1952 and 1953, as well as to the Western Conference title in 1954.

The 1953 NFL Championship Game may have been Layne's consummate moment as a professional. In a rematch of the 1952 title contest, the Lions trailed coach Paul Brown's Cleveland Browns 16-10 late in the fourth quarter. Layne had been largely ineffective to that point, completing just 37 percent of his passes. But with the league championship on the line, he suddenly came to life. He completed three of his next five passes to put the Lions within scoring distance. Then, with less than two minutes to go, Layne threw a 33-yard scoring pass to Jim Doran. Doak Walker kicked the

Quarterback Bobby Layne guided the Detroit Lions to NFL titles in 1952 and 1953, and a Western Conference crown in 1954. Although he never produced outstanding statistics, he was known for his fiery leadership and calm under pressure.

extra point to give Detroit its second straight league crown.

During his career, Layne completed 1,814 of his 3,700 passes for 26,768 yards and 196 touchdowns. He also rushed 611 times for 2,451 yards and scored 372 points.

In 1967, Layne was inducted into the Pro Football Hall of Fame.

PLAYING HISTORY:
Chicago Bears 1948
New York Bulldogs 1949
Detroit Lions 1950-1958
Pittsburgh Steelers 1958-1962

All in the Family

Alex Karras was the black knight of NFL defensive linemen.

He excelled before the era of 300-pound elephants who brutalize blockers with their might and bulk. Karras was small by those standards, about 250 pounds at his beefiest, perhaps 6-foot-2 on his tiptoes.

But he was very quick, very nasty and very strong.

Even siblings were a target for Karras wrath.

Alex's brother Ted Karras labored as an offensive guard and tackle with the Chicago Bears in the 1960s. One Sunday, Bears coach George Halas made a series of changes on the offensive line.

The new right guard was unable to handle Alex Karras and resorted to holding as a means of controlling him on the line. Karras responded with a punch to the midsection. On the next play, Karras was held again. This time he responded with a shot to the face.

On the third play, Karras got fed up after being held once more. He clenched his fists and was ready to pulverize the offender. But Karras was unable to see more than a blur without his eye glasses and knew his opponent only by the color of his jersey. As he went after the offending guard, he heard a voice.

"Dammit, Alex, knock it off. This is your brother Ted."

Plum Out of Luck

Alex Karras spoke openly of his hatred for quarterbacks.

"They're all blond-haired milk-drinkers," he said during his days as king of the Lions' court in the 1960s.

It was during this period that the Lions and Packers were angry rivals. Green Bay had built a dynasty under coach Vince Lombardi and quarterback Bart Starr. It began with an NFL championship in 1961 and extended through Super Bowl II in 1968. The Lions were perennial runners up.

But in 1962, the Lions believed they had a club that was at least the equal of Lombardi's reigning NFL champions. And on October 7, 1962, they had a chance to prove it.

Both teams were 3-0 going into the contest at Green Bay and were playing for control of the Western Conference. Detroit had the football and a 7-6 lead in the final minutes of the game. Quarterback Milt Plum faced a crucial third-down situation. If he picked up a first down, the Lions would retain possession and be able to run out the clock.

But as Plum set up and released his pass, receiver Terry Barr had his feet slide out from under him. Green Bay defensive back Herb Adderley had an easy interception. He returned it along the sideline before being wrestled down from behind. Then Paul Hornung entered the game and kicked his third field goal of the day to give Green Bay a 9-7 win.

That was when Karras started hating all quarterbacks, even his own. In the locker room, he seethed momentarily, then removed his helmet and fired it across the room at Plum's head. The projectile was only slightly off target.

"Yeah, I threw my helmet at Plum and I just missed," Karras recalled. "And I'm still sorry I missed."

Alex Karras was a four-time All-Pro defensive tackle with the Detroit Lions. Karras and Green Bay's Paul Hornung were suspended by NFL commissioner Pete Rozelle for the entire 1963 season after allegedly betting on football games.

LIONS FACT: Future U.S. Supreme Court Justice Byron "Whizzer" White returned from Oxford in 1940, where he studied with a Rhodes Scholarship, to join the Detroit Lions. The tailback led the NFL in rushing in 1940 with 514 yards and five touchdowns. After the 1941 season, White entered military service as World War II began to heat up, and later attended Yale Law School. He became one of the most respected justices in U.S. history.

ALEX KARRAS

Karras was drafted by the Detroit Lions in 1958 after winning the Outland Trophy at the University of Iowa as the nation's best lineman. He also placed second in the Heisman Trophy balloting that year.

With the Lions, Karras was a four-time All-Pro. Karras played with the Detroit Lions from 1958 to 1971.

BOOK MARK

Alex Karras and the Detroit Lions' rivalry with the Green Bay Packers extended through the 1960s and finally, in 1968, the Lions turned it around.

On this day, the Lions' pass rush overwhelmed the Packers' famed offensive line, made notorious by guard Jerry Kramer's best-selling book *Instant Replay*.

Karras was sickened by the idea of an offensive lineman like Kramer bathing in the spotlight as a respected author.

On the fifth sack of quarterback Bart Starr, Karras strode through Kramer's attempt at a block and smothered both blocker and quarterback. Karras arose and stood over the fallen duo.

"Put that in your (expletive) book," Karras said.

Parting Shot

The Detroit Lions were laden with talent both on the field and off in 1957, with legendary quarterback Bobby Layne as the ring leader. Layne held more clout with the club than coach Buddy Parker. Parker knew it and hated it.

Two days before the Lions' first exhibition game, the city of Detroit held its annual "Meet the Lions" dinner to wish the team well in the upcoming season.

While most of the team was busy eating dinner and waiting for the usual speeches by the mayor and head coach, others were having a rousing time at the bar in the back of the room. And, of course, Bobby Layne was the bar's toastmaster.

As the night wore on, Layne and his cronies got louder and more rambunctious. Finally, head coach Buddy Parker, the night's keynote speaker, was announced. A hush came over the crowd as he took the stage. He generally gave a stirring speech to the Lions players and fans, inspiring his team to new heights in the coming season. This year was different.

Parker walked slowly to the podium, stepped to the microphone and said, "This team of ours has been the worst I've ever seen in training. I can't control this group and don't want to get involved in another losing season. I quit and I'm leaving tonight."

With that, Parker left the room as the crowd watched in stunned silence.

The Lions didn't seem to notice, however. Under new head coach George Wilson, they posted an 8-4 record, then blasted the Cleveland Browns 59-14 to win the NFL Championship.

BUDDY PARKER

Raymond K. "Buddy" Parker began his coaching career in 1949 with the Chicago Cardinals and ended it in 1965 with his resignation from the Pittsburgh Steelers. He had his greatest success as coach of the Detroit Lions, where his club won three straight Western Conference titles from 1952 to 1954. He posted a 107-76-9 coaching record. Parker was a running back in the NFL for nine seasons before he became a coach. He rushed 180 times for 489 yards and four touchdowns during his career.

PLAYING HISTORY:
Detroit Lions 1935-1936
Chicago Cardinals 1937-1943

COACHING HISTORY:
Chicago Cardinals 1949
Detroit Lions 1951-1956
Pittsburgh Steelers 1957-1964

Hold the Stuffing

Thanksgiving would be incomplete without a Detroit Lions football game. The Lions have been part of the turkey day tradition since 1934, participating in nearly 60 Thanksgiving Day contests. During his 15-year tenure with the Lions from 1958 to 1972, linebacker Wayne Walker became an indispensable part of the act.

Walker made a career of terrorizing quarterbacks from his linebacker position with the Lions. But he also hoodwinked his share of Detroit players.

It all began when Walker decided to post a flyer in the Lions locker room saying that a certain market in downtown Detroit was giving away free Thanksgiving turkeys to the club's players and coaches. Walker watched in amusement as the players, not wanting to miss a freebie, quickly vacated the locker room after practice in order to find the store. They soon discovered the address was really an abandoned lot under a freeway.

Happy with his new prank, Walker decided to refine and retry the turkey giveaway trick each year. And every season he got a few new takers.

Before long, Walker began to work in cahoots with actual supermarkets. Players would be given directions to the store where one of the market's managers would meet the players with a large package wrapped in butcher paper. When the players returned home and unwrapped the package they found a 20-pound block of ice rather than a turkey.

Late in his career, the only players who fell for Walker's prank were unsuspecting rookies. One year, Walker instructed several first-year players that they were required to wear Indian war paint and headdresses to the store in order to receive their free turkeys. At least two players showed up at the market in Indian garb. The manager then snapped their photos as they happily received their complimentary "turkey."

And at practice the following Monday, the pictures were prominently displayed on the locker room wall to the amusement of all but the humiliated rookies.

LIONS FACT: Karl Sweetan won the starting quarterback job in 1966 after spending the previous year with the Pontiac Arrows, a semi-pro team. He connected with Pat Studstill on a 99-yard touchdown that season, tying an NFL record.

LIONS FACT: Earl "Dutch" Clark, a Hall of Fame quarterback, tailback and kicker, who also coached the Detroit Lions in the 1930s, was the last man in NFL history to regularly use the dropkick to boot field goals and extra points.

WAYNE WALKER

Wayne Walker was a fourth-round draft pick of the Detroit Lions in 1958 after starring at center for the University of Idaho. The Lions promptly switched Walker to outside linebacker. He was selected to the Pro Bowl three times and in 1968 was named the Lions' Most Valuable Defensive Player. Walker appeared in 200 games for the Lions, a team record.

Walker played for the Detroit Lions from 1958 to 1972.

MAN OF STEEL

*T*hroughout the Green Bay Packers' championship years of the 1960s, middle linebacker Ray Nitschke was coach Vince Lombardi's hammer man. He was a ferocious and hard-hitting linebacker who rarely missed a defensive down. He seemed indestructible.

"Vince Lombardi knew a lot about his people," said Nitschke, who played for the famed taskmaster in all nine of Lombardi's seasons in Green Bay.

In 1960, during Nitschke's third season in the NFL's smallest city and Lombardi's second as the Packers head coach, he got a first-hand look at Lombardi's insight. It was in July during two-a-days and the weather had turned for the worse.

"It was very muggy," Nitschke said, "and it was one of the few times Lombardi showed any compassion for his players in training camp. He told us we could take off our shoulder pads and our helmets. Then we continued with practice."

The Pro Football Hall of Famer placed his pads and helmet near the photographers' tower, a tall metal scaffolding from which a member of the Packers' staff usually filmed practice and Lombardi often watched it. After shedding his gear, Nitschke sprinted back to the huddle.

The air began to mist as the dark clouds of a summer storm rolled in. The weather grew more intense and soon Nitschke realized his equipment

The Fabulous GREEN BAY PACKERS

50¢

A PUBLICATION OF THE MILWAUKEE JOURNAL

could be ruined by the moisture.

"I didn't want my pads and helmet to get wet and mildewed," he said.

Nitschke ran to the tower and put his equipment back on.

"Right then, when I was standing under the tower, it came crashing down," Nitschke said. "The wind knocked the scaffolding down with me underneath it."

Players, coaches and front-office personnel sprinted in unison toward the collapsed tower. From a distance, Lombardi yelled, "Who's that guy on the ground?"

"It's Nitschke," one of the Packers replied.

Lombardi looked relieved.

"Nitschke? He's all right," the coach said. "Everybody get back to practice."

"Apparently the coach felt it would take more than half a ton of steel to dent my head," Nitschke said. "It was the first time I'd ever been tackled by a tower, but he was right. I wasn't hurt much. The scaffolding bounced off my pads, knocking me down, and a big bolt went right through my headgear, stopping just short of my skull. There was about an inch of space between my helmet and my head and most of the space was taken up by a sponge liner.

"The hole in my helmet was about four inches above my left temple. The helmet saved my life. If I hadn't put my helmet on, I might have spent the rest of the season in the cemetery."

PACKERS FACT: Hall of Fame linebacker Ray Nitschke was an all-state quarterback in high school.

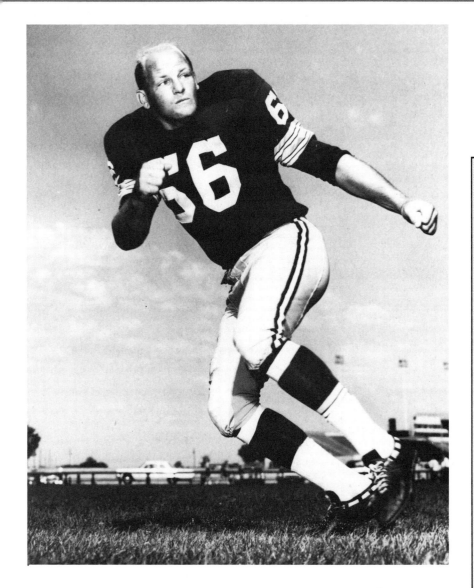

Photo from Richard Wolffers Auctions, Inc., San Francisco

RAY NITSCHKE

During his 15 NFL seasons, the University of Illinois graduate, a third-round draft choice, was a hard-nosed but clean-playing middle linebacker. Nitschke anchored the Packers' defense during their dynasty years in the 1970s. Besides being a rugged run stopper, he was a top-notch pass defender and intercepted 25 passes in his career. Two of the thefts he returned for touchdowns.

Nitschke was selected All-Pro three times and was named the Most Valuable Player of the 1962 NFL Championship Game, which the Packers won 16-7 over the New York Giants.

For its 50th anniversary in 1969, the National Football League selected Nitschke to its 50-year All-Pro Team.

In 1978, Nitschke was inducted into the Pro Football Hall of Fame. He played his entire career with the Green Bay Packers, from 1958 to 1972.

PACKERS FACT: Johnny "Blood" McNally earned his colorful nickname as a student at St. John's College of Minnesota.

An excellent running back, McNally wanted to try pro football without giving up his college eligibility. He adopted the name "Johnny Blood" for his pro debut after walking past a movie theater and noticing a sign advertising the movie *Blood and Sand*.

During his 15-year NFL career, McNally had a tendency to ignore team rules and curfews. He once missed the team train but caught up with it by driving his car along the railroad tracks. As he approached the train, a passenger in the car took the steering wheel while McNally jumped out and on to the speeding train.

PACKERS FACT: In Super Bowl II against the Oakland Raiders, Green Bay defensive back Herb Adderley became the first player to return an intercepted pass for a touchdown in a Super Bowl game.

Shrewd Negotiator

Green Bay Packer lore has it that early in 1964, popular starting center Jim Ringo became the first player to bring an agent to his salary negotiation with the club's dictatorial coach and general manager Vince Lombardi.

The Packers had finished 11-2-1 in 1963, half a game behind the first-place Chicago Bears. It ended three consecutive championship game appearances by Green Bay. Lombardi was dissatisfied with his club's finish.

But Ringo had enjoyed an excellent season. He made All-Pro for the fifth year in a row. When he met with Lombardi to discuss his upcoming contract, he brought along an agent.

Lombardi had made it clear that he was not about to begin negotiating with unruly lawyers or players' representatives. The story goes that Lombardi met Ringo's agent, excused himself from the room, then returned five minutes later.

"I am afraid you have come to the wrong city to discuss Mr. James Ringo's contract," Lombardi is said to have told the agent. "Mr. James Ringo is now the property of the Philadelphia Eagles."

Just like that, Jim Ringo, seven times an All-Pro as a member of the Green Bay Packers and a man who would later be inducted into the Pro Football Hall of Fame, was gone from the Packer family.

But separating fact from fiction is often the most important part of football lore.

It is true Ringo's agent did talk to Lombardi. And it is true Lombardi did resent agents until 1966, when he accepted the inevitable. But in reality, the trade had been arranged even before the agent and Lombardi met. And it had been arranged at the request of Ringo, who wanted to be closer to his Pennsylvania home, for reasons known to this day only by Lombardi and Ringo.

"Vince and I were the only ones who knew why I was traded," Ringo said. "It was more personal than anything. I still had a wonderful rapport with Vince afterward."

For years after Ringo's trade, Lombardi perpetuated the myth that players with greedy agents might be ushered out of the coach's office quickly. He found it to be a useful story in managing his players and his budget. The players reasoned that if an All-Pro center like Ringo was dispensable, then just about anyone could be sent packing. And very few people wanted to be traded away from Lombardi's perennial NFL-champion Green Bay Packers.

JIM RINGO
PLAYING HISTORY:
Green Bay Packers 1953-1963
Philadelphia Eagles 1964-1967
COACHING HISTORY:
Buffalo Bills 1976-1977

Vince Lombardi (right) chats with Green Bay co-captains Jim Ringo (left) and Bill Forester (center) as they prepare for the 1960 NFL Championship Game against the Philadelphia Eagles. Philadelphia won it, 17-13.

JIM RINGO

After Ringo's decade-long run as a seven-time All-Pro center for the Packers, he finished his career with four stellar seasons in Philadelphia, where he started 56 consecutive league games and played in two more Pro Bowls.

In 1976, Ringo was named head coach of the Buffalo Bills. Although he had a distinguished on-field career, Ringo's coaching stint with the Bills was not as celebrated. He soon discovered that the job Lombardi performed as a head coach was a difficult one.

Ringo took over as the Buffalo Bills' skipper five games into the 1976 season, after Lou Saban was fired. Despite the presence of O.J. Simpson in his backfield, Ringo was unable to coax a win out of his team. They lost nine straight games to close out the 1976 season. The losses continued to mount in 1977 as the Bills dropped their first four games before finally beating Atlanta, 3-0.

Ringo ended the 1977 season with a 3-11 record. He retired after the 1977 season and compiled a 3-20 lifetime coaching record.

In 1981, Ringo was inducted into the Pro Football Hall of Fame.

If You Can't Beat 'Em, Join 'Em

Philadelphia Eagles defensive tackle Reggie White became a free agent at the end of the 1992 season and put on an elaborate show while searching for a new football home.

He was offered diamonds, rubies and pearls in virtually every NFL city he visited. But in his heart, he knew all along where he really wanted to play. It had nothing to do with money, jewels or even a sign from God.

He found out on November 15, 1992, at Milwaukee County Stadium. The Philadelphia Eagles with Reggie White, Randall Cunningham and the rest of the boys had come to town to take on the Green Bay Packers.

Brett Favre was still learning the ropes as the Packers starting quarterback. In fact, he was starting just the seventh game of his career. On Green Bay's second possession of the game, the Packers had the ball at the 32-yard line with 2:20 left to play.

On the first play of the drive, Favre launched an 11-yard completion. As he unloaded the ball, 6-foot-5, 295-pound Reggie White barreled into Favre. Their combined total weight of 508 pounds landed together on the quarterback's left (non-throwing) shoulder. Needless to say, the shoulder was separated.

Although visibly in pain, Favre stayed in the game without missing a single snap. Four plays later, he dropped back and threw a five-yard scoring pass to wide out Sterling Sharpe.

Shot up with a painkiller at halftime, Favre could not lift his left arm as high as his shoulder and discovered he could not hand off to the left side. But he continued to play in the second half. The Eagles saw Favre's difficulty and tried to work on it by pressuring the right side.

White was held sackless that day and Green Bay upset the playoff-bound Eagles, 27-24. It was only Green Bay's fourth win in its initial 10 games under first-year head coach Mike Holmgren. But it commenced six straight wins in the season's final seven weeks and the Packers missed the playoffs by only one game.

After the Eagles contest, Favre claimed he had never been hit so hard in his entire life, which included his collegiate years at Southern Mississippi University. His shoulder was such that he couldn't tie his shoes, put on a coat or even drive a car.

Although Favre's shoulder bothered him for the remainder of the season, he missed nary a play.

The following winter, Green Bay was making its proposal for White in the first-ever bidding war for unrestricted free agents. When he came to town on his recruiting visit, the league's most sought-after free agent had lunch with Favre.

White told Favre how impressed he was that the second-year quarterback had stayed in the game after the hit he took against the Eagles. White said he thought for sure he had put Favre out of the game. The quarterback admitted he thought he was done, too.

When White signed with the Packers, he said Favre's toughness and his potential for success were major factors in his decision to sign with Green Bay.

As the 1993 training camp opened, White pledged his loyalty to Favre.

"I told Brett if a guy tries to hit that shoulder again, I'll be the first one out on the field for him this year," White said.

Favre had a simple reply, "Thank God he's on our side."

Teaming White and Favre made a difference. In 1993, the Packers made their first playoff appearance since 1982.

REGGIE WHITE

*T*he Philadelphia Eagles used their first pick in the 1984 supplemental draft to select White, a standout defensive end at the University of Tennessee. He played in seven straight Pro Bowls with Philadelphia from 1987 to 1993, earning Most Valuable Player honors in 1987 after making four sacks in the game. That same year, White set an NFC record with 21 sacks and was named NFL Defensive Player of the Year. He signed with the Packers as a free agent prior to the 1993 campaign.

PLAYING HISTORY:
Philadelphia Stars (USFL) 1984-85
Philadelphia Eagles 1985-1992
Green Bay Packers 1993-

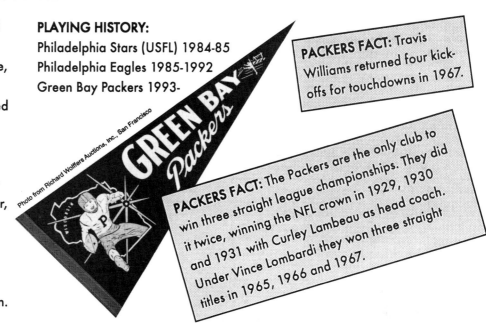

Photo from Richard Wolffers Auctions, Inc., San Francisco

GREEN BAY *Packers*

PACKERS FACT: Travis Williams returned four kick-offs for touchdowns in 1967.

PACKERS FACT: The Packers are the only club to win three straight league championships. They did it twice, winning the NFL crown in 1929, 1930 and 1931 with Curley Lambeau as head coach. Under Vince Lombardi they won three straight titles in 1965, 1966 and 1967.

BELOW: Reggie White (92) reaches down to recover a fumble after the Green Bay Packers bury Chicago Bears quarterback Jim Harbaugh (4). White is assisted by Tony Bennett (90), LeRoy Butler (36) and Johnny Holland (50).

And It Wasn't Even the Fourth of July

The Houston Oilers' Gregg Bingham was a typical inside linebacker—he loved chaos and mayhem.

Bingham created turmoil for Houston's opponents from 1973 to 1984 and off the field he enjoyed an occasional fracas. But not even Bingham was prepared for the greeting he got from fullback Tim Wilson at an Oilers training camp during the early 1980s.

Wilson was a closet pyromaniac who loved to see things blown to bits. To fulfill his fantasies, Wilson always kept an arsenal of fireworks and used them liberally.

After a rough day at Houston's summer training camp, Bingham and All-Pro running back Earl Campbell strolled back to the team dormitory. They pressed the elevator button and waited, exhausted.

Suddenly, the elevator doors swung open and Bingham and Campbell ducked for cover.

They were greeted by what looked like World War III. Stuffed inside the elevator were Roman candles and a variety of other pyrotechnic devices exploding in rapid-fire succession.

Unable to fend off the fireworks, Bingham and Campbell scrambled down the hall, squeezed into a tiny broom closet and quickly slammed the door.

But a Roman candle had also scurried down the hallway and managed to land in the closet, right behind them. Unable to find the door handle in the dark and confusion, the two Pro Bowl players yelled, screamed and held on to one another until the sparkler finally burned itself out.

Can You Describe the Missing Dog?

Thomas "Hollywood" Henderson was a talented but flaky linebacker who starred with the Dallas Cowboys in the late 1970s. He was traded to the San Francisco 49ers in 1980, but was soon waived by the club, citing Henderson's "erratic behavior." Henderson's crazy antics continued during his one season with the Oilers.

On several occasions during games, Henderson instructed Oilers' staff members to leave the sideline, purchase two hot dogs and have them waiting for him in his locker at halftime.

During one game, the club's equipment manager was in the locker room prior to the half. He spotted the hot dogs and unwittingly ate them. When

Henderson got to his locker and discovered the frankfurters were missing, he was furious. He demanded that stadium security be called in so he could file a missing hot dogs report.

Early in the second half, a time-out was called and the equipment manager went into the Oilers huddle with water. As he handed Henderson a bottle, Henderson noticed a spot of mustard on the equipment manager's face. Suddenly it clicked and Henderson went ballistic. He chased the equipment man out of the huddle, then called a time-out to scream and chase him some more.

OILERS FACT: Houston won the first two AFL championships in 1960 and 1961, defeating the Los Angeles Chargers both times. For winning the first AFL title in 1960, the Oilers received $1,025.73 each.

Clutch Performance

Gregg Bingham took offense to Hollywood Henderson's behavior and decided to get even.

After years of flying to and from games, Bingham had discovered a few quirks in the interiors of airplanes.

On the ride home, Henderson inevitably made a trip to the restroom. From his seat, Bingham pressed his feet against the restroom's adjoining wall, knowing full well that the pressure would cause the door to jam and become inoperable.

Henderson was trapped inside the restroom for over an hour, screaming, begging and pounding on the door before Bingham finally obeyed the stewardess and allowed the wacky linebacker to escape from his latrine prison.

Bingham figured it was just another clutch performance by an NFL veteran.

Photo from Richard Wolffers Auctions, Inc., San Francisco

GREGG BINGHAM

Bingham was a fourth-round draft pick of the Oilers in 1973 out of Purdue. He was named to the All-Rookie Team that year. An excellent pass defender and run stopper at linebacker, he made 21 interceptions during his 12-year career. He was also the club's leading tackler every season from 1974 to 1983. Bingham played for the Oilers from 1973 to 1984.

OILERS FACT: Warren Moon completed 404 passes in 1991, a single-season record.

THOMAS HENDERSON

Thomas "Hollywood" Henderson joined the Dallas Cowboys in 1975 out of Oklahoma's tiny Langston College. He was an important cog at outside linebacker in the Cowboys' famed "Doomsday Defense" of the late 1970s and earned two Pro Bowl berths. Henderson's flamboyance led to the nickname Hollywood, but also helped him land in coach Tom Landry's dog house. He was cut by Landry late in the 1979 season.

PLAYING HISTORY:
Dallas Cowboys 1975-1979
San Francisco 49ers 1980
Houston Oilers 1980

BELOW: Oilers linebacker Gregg Bingham (54) races toward the end zone with a loose football in a 1979 playoff game against the Denver Broncos. Bingham anchored the Houston defense from 1973 to 1984.

A Snapper Comeback?

One day in the late 1970s, Pro Bowl tight end Mike Barber was rambling down a Louisiana byway, heading for the Houston Oilers training facility, when he spied a dark blob near the side of the road.

He pulled over to get a closer look and discovered a dead alligator. Barber hoisted the man-sized reptile into his vehicle, slammed the door and continued on down the road.

At the Oiler camp, Barber snuck into a small room where defensive backs gathered to watch films and discuss strategy. He planted the dead gator in a stack of towels and waited outside.

Eventually, the defensive backs pranced off the practice field, drenched in sweat after a rugged workout. They began peeling towels off the stack to dry themselves before reviewing their weekly game plan. It was not long before the alligator was unveiled.

From outside the room, Barber heard the screams of grown men and the clatter of desks being overturned as the defensive backs scurried into the hallway.

Barber waltzed into the frightened crowd and said, "What's wrong?"

The secondary men were too scared to even speak. Barber recognized the fear in their eyes and tried to calm them.

"It was just a joke," Barber said as he strolled into the room and put his hand on the reptile. "This gator's dead."

But some of the players weren't convinced and they refused to reenter the room.

An Oilers security man was summoned to the scene. He took the alligator away and tossed it in a nearby bayou. Barber thought the incident was over.

But city officials discovered a live alligator in the area a few days later. Newspaper headlines warned families to keep children away from the bayou.

And Barber wondered just how "dead" his alligator really had been.

OILERS FACT: Biology teacher Charley Hennigan wrote a letter to the Oilers in 1958 asking the newly formed AFL team for a tryout. He not only made the team; in 1961, he caught 61 passes for 1,746 yards, pro football's single-season yardage record. Then in 1964, he caught 101 passes, a single-season mark that stood until 1984.

OILERS FACT: With George Blanda at quarterback in 1961, the Oilers became the first pro football team to score 500 points in a single season.

MIKE BARBER

Besides being an excellent tight end, Barber was a team leader and offensive tough guy. During his 10-year career, Barber caught 222 passes for 2,788 yards and 17 touchdowns.

PLAYING HISTORY:
Houston Oilers 1976-1981
Los Angeles Rams 1982-1985
Denver Broncos 1985

Houston Oilers tight end Mike Barber (86) shakes loose from Seattle Seahawk Keith Simpson to pick up a first down. He caught 222 passes during his 10-year career.

NYLON STALKING

On cold days, Mike Barber and linebacker Gregg Bingham took it upon themselves to convince the rest of the team that frigid weather would not be a factor in the upcoming game.

In 1980, they had one of their sternest tests. That's when the Oilers met the Cleveland Browns in three-degree temperature, with a 20-mile-an-hour wind whipping off the chilled waters of Lake Erie.

Several players had brought along nylons to wear under their uniform to fight off the cold. Before going out for the pregame warmup at Cleveland Stadium, Bingham and Barber accosted teammates they spotted slipping on nylons and insulted their manhood, calling them pansies and other derogatory names.

The Oilers then returned to the heated locker room for last minute instructions and a team prayer. Bingham was still dishing dirt at his teammates, when, out of the corner of his eye, he saw Barber sneak into the bathroom. He followed Barber, slipped into the adjoining stall and quietly climbed onto the commode. He peered over the partition just in time to see Barber plunging one leg into a pair of nylons.

"I couldn't believe it," Bingham recalled. "I called him everything in the book."

Barber was shamed momentarily, but not enough to keep from wearing the nylons.

Tastes Great, Less Filling

The Houston Oilers were on the brink of going to the Super Bowl in the late 1970s and were desperately looking for that special player who would push them over the top.

That's when they sent a couple of draft choices to the Oakland Raiders to acquire four-time Pro Bowl tight end Dave Casper in 1980.

Casper was greeted with awe by many of his new Oiler teammates. After all, he came from the Raiders, the winningest team in pro sports, as well as one of the wildest. He also had a Super Bowl ring, something the Oilers were still striving for.

On his first day at the Oiler compound, the towering tight end appeared deadly serious as he was fitted with pads and practice equipment by scurrying attendants. Casper donned his Oilers helmet and promptly plowed headfirst into the wall.

"Are you alright?" asked a bewildered equipment man.

"I'm fine," Casper said. "But there's something wrong with this helmet."

"What's wrong with it?"

"It doesn't hurt when I hit something," Casper said. Then, suddenly, Casper took a running head-long dive out the equipment room's half-door, landing with a thud in the middle of the locker room. His new teammates looked on in amazement.

Casper was soon informed by the Houston coaches that he was obligated to take special care of his helmet and was to wear it on the field at all times. This was something new for Casper. In Oakland, the players routinely slipped off their helmets and used them as seats on the sideline.

Casper was faced with one other problem. During the offseason, he had gained several unwanted pounds and was still trying to shed weight. After listening to several dieting theories, he devised one of his own in Houston.

One night, in an effort to impress the coaches with his newfound respect for Oiler head gear, Casper showed up at a team dinner wearing his helmet. He made his way through the food line and piled his tray high with steak, mashed potatoes, vegetables and several pies. While the Oiler players watched in hushed fascination, Casper found a seat to his liking, then proceeded to chew the victuals with gusto. But instead of swallowing his meal, he spit it through his facemask bit by bit. Soon he was surrounded by scraps of food and portions of the evening fare dangled repulsively from the bars of his facemask.

But that was all part of the Casper diet. He figured that chewing the food without swallowing it would give him the necessary nutrients without the fat.

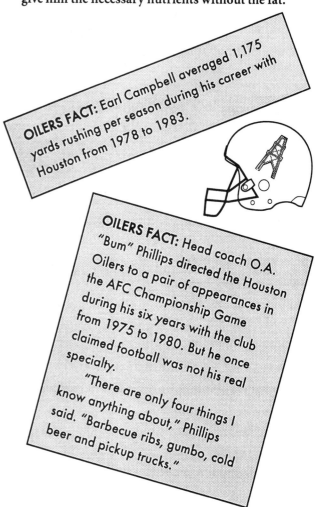

OILERS FACT: Earl Campbell averaged 1,175 yards rushing per season during his career with Houston from 1978 to 1983.

OILERS FACT: Head coach O.A. "Bum" Phillips directed the Houston Oilers to a pair of appearances in the AFC Championship Game during his six years with the club from 1975 to 1980. But he once claimed football was not his real specialty.

"There are only four things I know anything about," Phillips said. "Barbecue ribs, gumbo, cold beer and pickup trucks."

DAVE CASPER

Dave Casper was one of the top pass-catching tight ends of his era. He caught 378 passes for 5,216 yards and 52 touchdowns during his 11-year career. He had his best seasons with the Oakland Raiders, where he acquired the nickname "Ghost," and was a four-time Pro Bowl selection. In his first season with Houston, he nabbed 56 passes for a team-high 796 yards and four touchdowns. He was the Oilers' leading receiver in 1982 with 36 catches for six scores.

PLAYING HISTORY:
Oakland Raiders 1974-1980
Houston Oilers 1980-1982
Minnesota Vikings 1983
Los Angeles Raiders 1984

Dave Casper (87) in a pushing match with the Pittsburgh Steelers' Jack Lambert (58) in a 1980 game at Houston.

The Weighting Game

At 6-foot-3 and 280 pounds, Art Donovan could cover a lot of ground at defensive tackle. But Baltimore Colts head coach Weeb Ewbank thought his performance would be enhanced if he lost a little weight.

"I tried explaining to Weeb that I was already a light eater," he said. "What I didn't tell him is what I meant. I never start eating until it gets light. Then I eat everything."

Donovan's condition dates back to when he was a rotund youth pigging out on the culinary delights of New York's Coney Island.

"I could do 25 hot dogs just standing there," he recalled. "The vendor's eyes would be bugging out. I'd say, 'I can eat 50 if you put 'em on the cuff.' And the guy would end up getting beat on the deal. But if they were kosher style I'd cut back to 35. Easy enough going down—only tough to keep there, you know?"

In the 1954 season, the Colts coach was insistent. Along with dieting, Ewbank wanted Donovan to embark on a systemized training program complete with weightlifting.

"I think I did 13 pushups in 13 years," Donovan said. "I asked him, 'Do you want a gymnast or a football player?' He let me off the hook, but he put a clause in my contract calling for a $1,000 fine if I weighed more than 270 pounds before a game."

After that, to the amazement of his teammates, Donovan did show up for his pregame weigh-ins at the desired weight.

"The whole team gathered around to watch the weigh-in," former linebacker Dick Szymanski said. "Artie would make a real show of it. First, he'd get on the scale wearing his socks, shorts and undershirt. Before anybody could get a reading, he'd jump off the scale and remove his socks. Then he'd get back on the scale. Same thing. He'd jump off right away and drop his shorts. Then his undershirt went and finally his false teeth. And the bar would settle right at 270 where the club wanted him."

Unwilling to part with that much money on a weekly basis, Donovan devised his own regimen for beating the scale.

The secret to Donovan's regimen? "I'd eat dinner on Monday and then I wouldn't eat again until after I weighed in on Friday," he said. "But after that I'd make up for lost time. Come the game, I'd be back to 280."

———— ⬮ ————

When not eating, Donovan encouraged others to eat—for profit.

"There was this rookie who could really go at it," Donovan said. "I asked him, 'What's your long suit?' He says, 'Chicken.' So we agreed to set up something with a local guy who fancied himself a real trencher. The night of the contest I show up at the restaurant and the rookie's already there downing pork chops and beer. I say, 'Hey, are you nuts or something?' He says, 'Don't worry, I'm just warming up.' Sure enough, the kid eats the local under the table and we collect. The only trouble is he couldn't play for squat and they cut him. Sad, because you don't come across his kind of talent often."

ART DONOVAN

Donovan reported to the original Baltimore Colts as a 25-year-old rookie in 1950 after being named second team All-New England as a two-way lineman at Boston College. The former U.S. Marine and World War II veteran then played for three teams in three years (Colts, Yankees, Texans), all of which folded. In 1953, the Colts were granted a new franchise and Donovan signed with Baltimore once again. An excellent pass rusher, he was named All-Pro four times as a defensive lineman with the Colts.

On the field, Donovan was a key element in the Baltimore Colts' championship seasons of 1958 and 1959. When his 12-year NFL career ended in 1961, he became the first Colt elected to the Pro Football Hall of Fame.

PLAYING HISTORY:
Baltimore Colts 1950
New York Yankees 1951
Dallas Texans 1952
Baltimore Colts 1953-1961

COLTS FACT: Defensive linemen are often noted for their hard-headedness, but few were as stubborn as former Baltimore Colts star Art Donovan.

"We're playing the Los Angeles Rams," recalled Dick Szymanski, a center and linebacker with the Colts from 1955 to 1968, "and their quarterback, Norm Van Brocklin, calls an audible. Art Donovan and I are supposed to shift, but he just stays put. I yell at him, 'Move over, Fatso.'

"He does. Then he says, 'Naw, you're supposed to move, not me.' And back he comes.

"'No, you fat (bleep),' I yell, 'you move.' But he won't. Now he's cussing me pretty good.

"Van Brocklin can't believe it. Finally he signals for a time-out and says, 'When you clowns get it settled, let me know.' And he walks off the field."

113

OR PERHAPS YOU MEANT THE *OTHER* MARCHETTI

Had it not been for an unexpected knock on the door, answered by Gino Marchetti, the world of professional football would have one less Hall of Famer. Running backs would have enjoyed more peaceful afternoons. And quarterbacks would have reason to offer thanks that Marchetti wasn't around to punish them.

World War II had just ended. Marchetti, like the rest of the returning servicemen, was elated to be back on American soil. For him, it meant Antioch, California.

The war had been difficult. His parents, Italian immigrants, lacked naturalization papers and were placed in an internment camp. Meanwhile, Gino, only 18 years old, was engaged in one of the most violent encounters of the war, the Battle of the Bulge.

Back home in Antioch, Sunday afternoons were especially enjoyable for Marchetti. He had no urgent plans. He played football for a semi-pro team and when the games were over, he enjoyed drinking a beer or two with the boys.

When the knock sounded on Marchetti's door, he walked across the living room, opened it and listened to the following questions.

"Is your name Marchetti?" a man wanted to know. "Do you play football?"

The 6-foot-4, 245-pound Marchetti answered affirmatively to both questions. The caller then

introduced himself as the football coach at Modesto Junior College. He wanted to know if Marchetti was interested in playing there.

Since Marchetti had no definite plans, not even tentative ones, the idea had appeal.

Yes, he'd give it a whirl, he said. Modesto was nearby and he'd surely know some of his classmates and teammates. And Modesto turned out to be more enjoyable than he thought. It introduced him to college life and to formal football training.

But a funny thing happened once football practice began. The coach realized there had been a case of mistaken identity. He had come to the right address and was looking for Marchetti— there was no mistake about that. But he spoke with the wrong Marchetti. It was Gino's younger brother, Ernie, he was hoping to recruit for Modesto. Ernie had already gone off to St. Mary's College.

Nevertheless, the mistake worked out for both parties. Gino Marchetti's play was impressive enough to have the University of San Francisco solicit his services. Then, after an undefeated season at USF, Marchetti was the second-round draft choice of the NFL's Dallas Texans, beginning a distinguished 12-year pro football career that carried him to the Hall of Fame. Meanwhile, his brother Ernie Marchetti enjoyed a fine collegiate football career at St. Mary's, but never played in the professional ranks.

GINO MARCHETTI

After drafting Gino Marchetti to play for them in 1952, the Dallas Texans collapsed in bankruptcy midway through the season. The franchise then moved to Baltimore and was rechristened the Colts. For the next 10 years, Marchetti was the best defensive end of the era and one of the most superb of all time.

In his 11 years with Baltimore, he played in the Pro Bowl 10 times.

"No defensive end was ever better," said Don Shula, Marchetti's teammate in Baltimore and later the winningest coach in NFL history. "He had speed, power and love of the game. He could do it all, play the run, pressure the passer and never let up. Football players don't come any better than Gino Marchetti."

Marchetti was elected to the Pro Football Hall of Fame in 1972, his first year of eligibility.

PLAYING HISTORY:
Dallas Texans 1952
Baltimore Colts 1953-1964

COLTS FACT: Halfback Tom Matte became an instant hero in Baltimore as the 1965 season was winding down.

In the 12th week of the season, quarterback Johnny Unitas tore up a knee. His replacement Gary Cuozzo dislocated a shoulder the following week. In the final game of the season, the Colts needed a win over the powerful Los Angeles Rams to earn a playoff spot. But Baltimore was without a quarterback.

Coach Don Shula gave Matte a quick cram course on the intricacies of the quarterback position and equipped him with a wrist band that had the team's basic plays written on it. Matte led the Colts to a 20-17 win over Los Angeles.

The next week Baltimore played Green Bay in a playoff. The Packers needed overtime to beat Baltimore, 13-10.

KIDS SAY THE DARNDEST THINGS

It was the Sunday after Christmas, 1959, and the Baltimore Colts were playing the New York Giants at Baltimore's Memorial Stadium for the NFL Championship.

The Giants were heavily favored and Frank Gifford, New York's star halfback, was one of the reasons.

Gifford was the key to the Giants' offense. He was the club's leading rusher that season with 540 yards and averaged over five yards per carry. He'd also developed into an effective flanker and was the Giants' top receiver with 42 catches.

But Gifford was considered a "pretty boy" by the Colts. They knew that Gifford was training to become a broadcaster after his career ended and saw him as an athlete who really wanted to be a movie star. The Baltimore defense thought they might be able to rough him up and stifle the Giants' offense.

Baltimore defensive back Johnny Sample, in only his second year in the league, had been assigned to cover Gifford in the title clash. Anytime Gifford released from the backfield, it was Sample's job to get in his face.

"Stopping him became a personal crusade for me," Sample said. "If I reduced his effectiveness in the game, it would certainly improve the Colts' chances for a win."

Gifford and Sample were not strangers. In a contest between the Giants and the Colts a year earlier, the two had a verbal confrontation after Sample leveled New York receiver Kyle Rote and put him out of the game.

Sample told Gifford he was the next target.

"Gifford said to me, 'Kid, you talk too much,'" Sample recalled.

But a year later, as the two clubs prepared to take the field for the NFL Championship Game, Sample wasn't the only vocal player on the Baltimore sideline.

Several of the Colts made comments about their intent to ruin Gifford's Hollywood profile. Sample was one of the primary instigators.

"We yelled things at him. Every time I got close to him, I told him, 'I'm going to mess up your face,'" Sample said.

Soon enough, Gifford registered a complaint with the officials about the harassment.

"He was just yapping," Gifford said. "He yapped all through the game. Kids will do that."

But it looked like the Giants would have the last laugh. After three quarters of play, New York held a 9-7 lead.

Then, suddenly, Colts quarterback Johnny Unitas began firing on all cylinders. Early in the fourth quarter, he ran four yards to give the Colts a 14-9 advantage. On the Colts' next possession, he directed the offense 70 yards and finished the drive with a 12-yard scoring pass to Jerry Richardson.

But it was Sample who iced the game. After the Giants took the ensuing kickoff, he intercepted a Charley Conerly pass and returned it 42 yards for a touchdown, giving the Colts a 28-9 lead.

Less than three minutes later, Sample did it again. He intercepted another Conerly pass and returned it 34 yards to set up a Steve Myhra field goal.

The Colts went on to win their second straight NFL title over New York, 31-16, and Sample was a primary reason. He intercepted two passes, returning them 76 yards and accounting for 10 points, and knocked down four passes.

Although Gifford's face was unblemished after the game, Sample proved to be a one-man wrecking crew.

time. Everything involved with the game, I think, served to catch the fancy of the viewing public. The strategies employed by both teams, the timing and coordination of the event itself, and the trading back and forth in the scoring, all worked perfectly to make it a great sales promotion for the NFL."

"Some sportswriters called it the greatest game ever played," said former Giants linebacker Sam Huff, who was on the losing sideline that day. "I don't know if it was that or not. But it was probably the most exciting. It had everything. Only problem was the wrong team won."

JOHNNY UNITAS

*U*nitas was a ninth-round draft choice of the Pittsburgh Steelers in 1955, but he was cut early in training camp. The Baltimore Colts signed him as a free agent the following year.

Unitas developed into one of the game's greatest quarterbacks. He was the NFL Player of the Year three times and played in 10 Pro Bowls. Unitas ended his 18-year career with 2,830 completions in 5,186 attempts for 40,239 yards and 290 touchdowns. He set an NFL record by throwing for at least one touchdown in 47 straight games.

In 1979, he was elected to the Pro Football Hall of Fame in his first year of eligibility.

PLAYING HISTORY:
Baltimore Colts 1956-1972
San Diego Chargers 1973

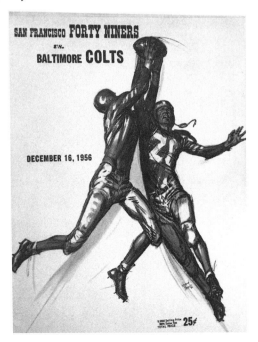

Photo from Richard Wolffers Auctions, Inc., San Francisco

ABOVE: Coach Weeb Ewbank's World Champion Colts' jacket and signed football from 1958.
BELOW: San Francisco 49ers versus Baltimore Colts game program from 1956.

BELOW: Johnny Unitas (19) became a household name after he quarterbacked the Baltimore Colts to the 1958 NFL Championship over the New York Giants in overtime. It has been called the greatest game ever played.

SAN FRANCISCO **FORTY NINERS**
vs.
BALTIMORE COLTS

DECEMBER 16, 1956

25¢

Punt or They'll Riot

The quickest way to make enemies in the NFL is to run up the score in a game.

Former Kansas City Chiefs coach Hank Stram was well aware of that fact when his club had a two touchdown lead on the Denver Broncos at Mile High Stadium.

With time winding down in the fourth quarter, Denver's hometown fans were becoming more and more vocal. They were upset at the play of the Broncos, and the players on the field could feel the crowd's unruliness turning to ugliness.

But the brunt of the fans' anger and frustration was directed at the Kansas City Chiefs. Chiefs coach Hank Stram thought it was best to finish up the fourth quarter as quickly as possible. He wanted to get his team off the field and into the safety of the locker room.

"Hank Stram told Lennie (Dawson) he didn't want any sustained drive," former Chiefs defensive end Jerry Mays recalled. "He said, 'Just throw three long passes, then punt it and let's get the heck out of here.' He didn't want us down near the goal line because he was afraid someone would get hurt."

Dawson understood Stram's concern, but his competitive nature wouldn't allow him to deliberately throw an incomplete pass.

"So Lennie goes back and throws a long pass for a touchdown," said Mays, who spent 10 years with the Chiefs. "Now the Denver fans are going wild. We're ahead by three touchdowns, so Hank says we're not even going to kick it down near the goal line. Just squib kick it so the Broncos will recover at about the 30-yard line."

Chiefs kicker Jan Stenerud understood the instructions and performed his duty flawlessly. But Denver's kick return team wouldn't cooperate.

"Well, Stenerud kicks it and the ball bounces off a Denver guy's knee and we recover," Mays said. "The fans now think we've deliberately kicked an onside kick and they're ready to riot.

"After the game, we walked off the field with our helmets on because they were throwing beer cans and everything at us. Doak Walker, who was a scout for the Broncos, walked over to me and said, 'Jerry, I'll give you $300 for the use of your helmet for 10 minutes.'"

———————— ————————

JERRY MAYS began his career with the Dallas Texans in 1961 after an impressive collegiate career at Southern Methodist University. He was selected in the fifth round by the Texans, then moved to Kansas City with the franchise when they relocated after the 1962 season. He started at defensive end for the Chiefs in Super Bowls I and IV and retired after the 1970 season.

In Super Bowl IV, it was the relentless pressure of Mays and the rest of the Chiefs' front four that distracted Minnesota Vikings quarterback Joe Kapp and led to Kansas City's only Super Bowl championship, a 23-7 victory over the Minnesota Vikings.

Mays played in six AFL All-Star games. He was selected to the Kansas City Chiefs' 25th anniversary all-time team in 1987, where he joined Art Still as the club's all-time defensive ends. He was also selected to the Chiefs Hall of Fame in 1971.

PLAYING HISTORY:
Dallas Texans 1961-1962
Kansas City Chiefs 1963-1970

No-Fall Policy

Bobby Bell knew what was coming. With the Denver Broncos trailing the Kansas City Chiefs, 24-17, late in the game, Denver was forced to go for the onside kick.

Bell was a member of the Kansas City Chiefs' "hands team," the special teams' unit organized to defend against opponents' onside kicks. He was well aware the Broncos probably would be dribbling one in his direction.

"We were playing in the old Municipal Stadium," Bell said as he recalled the 1969 encounter between the two clubs. "The Broncos were behind and needed the ball."

Despite his reputation as a fierce defensive end and line-backer, the 6-foot-4, 230-pound Bell was an excellent ball handler with good speed. He proved it by intercepting 25 passes during his career for 479 yards and six touchdowns.

Denver kicker Bobby Howfield bounded the ball right at Bell and a swarm of Broncos surged in his direction.

"The ball took a good bounce right into my hands," he said.

And Bell, a former all-state prep quarterback from North Carolina who was familiar with the end zone, knew what to do with the football.

"I said, 'Uh-uh, I'm not falling down with the ball. Why should I fall down with the ball?' I just picked it up and started running as fast as I could," Bell said. "The guys who kicked off looked at me and were waiting for me to fall on the ball. The next thing they knew, I had run right past them."

The Broncos' kickoff team watched in shocked amazement as Bell bounced off one tackler, then scampered 55 yards to the end zone. The touchdown sealed a Kansas City victory.

"I remember at the All-Star Game later that year," Bell said, "the Denver coaches told me they saw me pick up the ball and they were yelling, 'Dammit, Bell, fall on the ball...fall on the ball.' They could see I was gone. It was about 55 yards."

CHIEFS FACT: Defensive tackle Joe Phillips, who joined the Chiefs in 1992, will have no problem finding work after hanging up his football shoes. After earning a law degree at the University of San Diego, he passed the California and Missouri state bars. He also has a stockbroker's license and appeared on the HBO series "First and Ten."

BOBBY BELL

*A*warded the Outland Trophy in 1962 as the country's top interior lineman while playing for the University of Minnesota, Bell was not drafted until the seventh round by the Kansas City Chiefs in the 1963 draft. Many scouts thought he was too small to be an interior lineman in the professional ranks. Chiefs coach Hank Stram believed otherwise. He decided to use him initially as a defensive end.

Later, Bell was converted to the outside linebacker position where he was able to take advantage of his athletic skill as both a pass defender and run stopper. For 12 seasons, from 1963 to 1974, he was the cornerstone of the Kansas City defense. Twice he helped the Chiefs advance to the Super Bowl.

Bell played in six AFL All-Star games, prior to the NFL-AFL merger, and in four Pro Bowls. In 1969, he was picked to the AFL's all-time team.

In 1983, Bell was the first Chiefs player to be elected to the Pro Football Hall of Fame. He played with the Chiefs from 1963 to 1974.

CHIEFS FACT: The Kansas City Chiefs began as the Dallas Texans in 1960 and relocated to Kansas City in 1963. During the 10-year existence of the AFL, the Dallas Texans/Kansas City Chiefs posted the league's best record at 87-48-5. They won three AFL championships.

CHIEFS FACT: Nigerian-born running back Christian Okoye had never participated in football until his sophomore season at Azusa Pacific. During his first season, Azusa Pacific coaches placed arrows on the field to show him the direction to run. In 1987, the Chiefs used their second-round daft pick to select Okoye.

THE KING OF COOL

During his 14-year career with the Kansas City Chiefs, quarterback Len Dawson was known as "Lennie the Cool" for his calm demeanor under pressure. Never was the tag more appropriate than at Super Bowl IV.

Runner-up in the AFL West in 1969, the Chiefs upset the defending Super Bowl-champion Jets, 13-6, in the first round of the playoffs. Kansas City then avenged two regular season losses to Oakland with a 17-7 win over the Raiders in the AFL Championship Game. The victory propelled Kansas City into Super Bowl IV against the Minnesota Vikings.

Five days before Super Bowl IV, Dawson's name was one of several that surfaced in a gambling probe in Detroit. A man named Donald Dawson (no relation) who was a "casual acquaintance," had been arrested in a Justice Department investigation into nationwide sports gambling.

"I knew the guy," said Dawson. "I didn't know him well, hadn't seen him in years. But I was the quarterback in the Super Bowl. I was just one of a lot of guys who were mentioned.

"Looking back, it was completely irresponsible. But you could see what was happening. Some politician in Detroit was trying to make a name for himself."

Dawson was notified that he "might" be subpoenaed. The revelation was enough to create five days of turmoil for Dawson. In the days prior to the

Super Bowl, he found his hotel room under siege.

"It was different then," said Dawson. "Now they have security people at the hotels. But I had people knocking on my doors or calling me at all hours. I finally changed rooms.

"The allegation didn't affect just me. It affected the team, my family. My kids couldn't go to school and didn't want to go to the game."

Worrying about the gambling probe and the Super Bowl wreaked havoc with Dawson's health. He got sick the night before the game, slept very little and consumed only milk, crackers and a candy bar on Super Bowl morning.

But you'd never know it once the ball was put in play. Although Kansas City was a 12-point underdog to Minnesota, Dawson performed flawlessly. He completed 12 of 17 passes for 142 yards, including a 46-yard game-clinching touchdown pass, and earned Most Valuable Player honors as the Chiefs thumped the Vikings, 23-7.

"Once I hit the field, I was able to put all that other stuff out of my mind," said Dawson. "Also, I was fortunate that I started well. My first completion went for a first down. Had it been the other way around, it might have been different."

The gambling allegations were dismissed soon after the game, but they affected Dawson's ability to enjoy his Super Bowl victory.

"It wasn't so much joy I felt," Dawson said. "Just relief."

Kansas City quarterback Len Dawson looks over the game plan with coach Hank Stram. They combined their talents to lead the Chiefs to an upset victory over the Minnesota Vikings in Super Bowl IV.

LEN DAWSON

*T*he Super Bowl MVP award culminated Dawson's long road to stardom. It began in 1957 when he was the first-round pick of the Pittsburgh Steelers. But after throwing just 45 passes in his first five seasons of pro football with Pittsburgh and then Cleveland, Dawson joined the AFL's Dallas Texans. He led the Texans to their first AFL title and won Player of the Year honors in 1962. The following season the Texans moved to Kansas City and became the Chiefs.

Dawson stayed with the Chiefs for the remainder of his career, retiring in 1975 after winning four AFL passing titles and leading his team to three championships. In 19 pro seasons, he completed 2,136 of 3,731 passes for 28,711 yards and 239 touchdowns. Seven times he was selected to postseason All-Star teams.

Dawson was named to the Pro Football Hall of Fame in 1987.

PLAYING HISTORY:
Pittsburgh Steelers 1957-1959
Cleveland Browns 1960-1961
Dallas Texans 1962
Kansas City Chiefs 1963-1975

Proving Ground

Playing for the Kansas City Chiefs in the fledgling days of the American Football League was not always determined by athletic ability. In many cases, it was purely a test of survival.

"The Chiefs' first training camp was held at New Mexico Military Institute in Roswell and was run worse than a military camp," said Smokey Stover, a seven-year linebacker with the Dallas Texans and later the Chiefs. "But even before I got there, I had to go through a tryout camp in Dallas where we had 129 guys try out."

It was designed to weed out the unfit rather than determine who had football playing ability.

"That first day all we did was calisthenics," Stover said. "They'd have one coach lead us until he couldn't do anymore, then another would jump in and lead. And we had five coaches!"

Some 30 players quit that first day. Eventually 17 were chosen to proceed to the Roswell camp where they joined more than 100 other football prospects. Stover was among the invitees.

"You didn't dare get hurt or you were gone," said Walt Corey, a former linebacker with the Chiefs. "I remember the first day, they lined us up in two rows and we went head-to-head. If you whipped the guy across from you, you got to come back the next day."

The worst part about Roswell was not the sadistic nature of the coaches, but the heat and mosquitoes.

"It was about 110 in the daytime and 85 at night with no such thing as air conditioning," remembers former wide receiver Chris Burford. "The mosquitoes were so big that six or seven could come down and take off with one of our guys. It was too hot to sleep with a sheet, but you had to have one just to keep the mosquitoes off."

If the mosquitoes didn't cause discomfort, then the unbearable heat and the ensuing unquenchable thirst were sure to aggravate the most determined athlete.

"There were irrigation ditches near the field and after practice we'd be so hot we'd just run and fall into the ditches to get cool," Stover said. "They worked us so hard, and it was so hot, that when I weighed in, I had to put two 10-pound weights under my arms. I was down to 188 pounds, but I wanted it to show 208."

CHIEFS FACT: Kicker Nick Lowrey went undrafted after graduating from Dartmouth in 1978 and was cut 11 times by eight different teams before catching on with the Kansas City Chiefs in 1980. He went on to become the most accurate field goal kicker in NFL history and is ranked among the top five scorers of all time.

SMOKEY STOVER

In 1960, Stover signed as a free agent with the Dallas Texans, one of the American Football League's original clubs, after distinguishing himself at Northeast Louisiana University. During his seven-year professional career, Stover intercepted six passes from his linebacker position. With the Chiefs, Stover played a pivotal role in the club's drive to an AFL title in 1966 and then to Super Bowl I.

PLAYING HISTORY:
Dallas Texans 1960-1962
Kansas City Chiefs 1963-1966

CHIEFS FACT: The Kansas City Chiefs played the Green Bay Packers in the first AFL-NFL Championship Game. It was later renamed the Super Bowl. Green Bay beat the Chiefs 35-10.

LIGHTEN UP

The first Chiefs team almost never got off the ground—literally. When training camp broke, about 60 players, along with coaches, trainers and equipment, were jammed into a four-engine DC-6 for the ride to Kansas City, where the team had set up its permanent headquarters.

"The plane was so loaded that they took a couple people, set them on the commodes and strapped them in," Smokey Stover recalled.

But the plane was too heavy for takeoff. The pilot decided to dump fuel to make the aircraft lighter in order to get off the ground. It still wasn't enough.

"Finally the plane's captain came back and told our general manager we couldn't take off," Stover said. "We were overloaded. The general manager's comment was, 'I'll take responsibility.'

"So we took off, and for the longest time, we were just off the ground before we finally got up in the air. Later, the captain came out of the cabin and you could see he was just wringing with sweat. He said he'd never do that again."

The Last Laugh

Despite being underdogs in the 1969 Super Bowl match-up against two-touchdown favorites the Minnesota Vikings, the Kansas City Chiefs were proud of their roots in the AFL. Before the game, they were given jerseys with the AFL's 10-year anniversary patch on the sleeve. It was a simple emblem defining the end of the league before its assimilation into the NFL in 1970. But its symbolism was not lost on the players.

"They were like a bunch of kids eating ice cream cones," Stram said. "Most of them had played in the days the NFL looked down its nose at the AFL."

To the Chiefs, the patch was something special. They were finally accepted on equal footing. But as the game progressed, the Chiefs felt they didn't get the respect they deserved from Minnesota. At one point, the Vikings even found Coach Stram's strategy to be humorous.

"One of the biggest factors in that game, something that people usually take for granted, was Jan Stenerud's three field goals," Stram said. "Both teams were on the same side of the field that day, and when I sent Jan in to kick his 48-yarder, the Vikings actually laughed. They thought I was crazy kicking from the 48."

But it was Stram who got the final chuckle.

"When (Stenerud) kicked it, it looked like it would never come down. The Vikings were stunned."

The mirth on the Minnesota bench subsided as Stenerud's field goal gave the Chiefs a 3-0 lead. By halftime, the snickering had turned to sighs as the Chiefs built a 20-0 lead on three Stenerud field goals and a five-yard run by Mike Garrett.

Kansas City eventually coasted to a 23-7 victory, making history as the second AFL team to win a Super Bowl. It was the first of Minnesota's four Super Bowl losses.

Chiefs coach Hank Stram with the club's first-round draft choice in 1968, Texas A&M guard Maurice "Mo" Moorman.

CHIEFS FACT: The first two Super Bowls were actually called the AFL-NFL World Championship Game. It was Kansas City Chiefs owner Lamar Hunt who initiated the term "Super Bowl" for pro football's biggest event.

Lamar Hunt's seven-year-old daughter Sharron had a toy called a super ball. It gave Hunt an idea.

"In the AFL-NFL meetings, we had been referring to the 'championship game,' Hunt said. "Subconsciously I may have been thinking about Sharron's toy. But one day, I happened to come out and call the game the 'Super Bowl.' Somehow the name stuck."

HANK STRAM

Stram began his pro coaching career with the AFL's Dallas Texans in 1960, the league's first year of existence. In 1963, the Texans became the Kansas City Chiefs. Under Stram's direction, the Chiefs/Texans had the winningest record in AFL history, with a 129-78-10 record, and won the AFL title three times. In 15 seasons with the club, he had just three losing campaigns.

Stram's Chiefs appeared in the first Super Bowl in 1966, although Kansas City lost to Green Bay 35-10. It wasn't until 1969 that Stram could claim the honor of having won a Super Bowl.

Stram also spent two seasons as head coach of the New Orleans Saints. He compiled a 136-100-10 record during his 17-year pro coaching career.

COACHING HISTORY:
Dallas Texans 1960-1962
Kansas City Chiefs 1963-1974
New Orleans Saints 1976-1977

Kansas City coach Hank Stram discusses strategy with injured quarterback Len Dawson (center) and back signal-caller Mike Livingston (10). Livingston returned to the field and threw a touchdown pass on the very next play.

JACK RUDNAY

On the field, Chiefs center Jack Rudnay was all business, earning Pro Bowl honors four times. For 13 years, from 1970 to 1982, he anchored the Chiefs offensive line.

Rudnay was selected out of Northwestern University in the fourth round in 1969. He was awarded the Mack Lee Hill Award, given annually to the Kansas City rookie who best exemplifies the spirit of the Chiefs late running back, "the man with the giant heart and quiet way." Hill was an outstanding running back with the Chiefs in 1964 and 1965. He gained over 1,203 yards in two seasons and averaged over five yards per carry.

In 1987, Rudnay was voted to the Chiefs 25th anniversary all-time team as a center. Rudnay played with the Chiefs from 1970 to 1982.

A Fine-Feathered Prank

When it came to playing practical jokes, no one did it better than Kansas City Chiefs center Jack Rudnay.

"He was in a class by himself," said Chiefs Hall of Fame quarterback Len Dawson. "He had a very active mind. There are just certain people who work in that direction."

One of Rudnay's best remembered pranks was performed on the Chiefs former equipment man, Bobby Yarborough.

"Bobby apparently got on the wrong side of some people," said former Chiefs running back and Rudnay roommate Ed Podolak. Rudnay was the man who engineered the payback.

After Yarborough left for breakfast one morning, several chickens that had dined on alfalfa pellets and water throughout the previous day found their way into Yarborough's room. By the time the equipment man returned late in the afternoon, the room was covered with feathers and chicken droppings.

Head coach Paul Wiggin was summoned to the scene to assess the damage. Wiggins tried to maintain his poise, and to calm the upset equipment man, but unfortunately for Yarborough, the coach was in on the joke.

CHIEFS FACT: Since 1988, the Kansas City Chiefs have drafted three winners of college football's Butkus Award, given each year to the nation's top linebacker. They are Derrick Thomas of Alabama, Percy Snow of Michigan State and Erick Anderson of Michigan.

Dallas Cowboys running back Emmitt Smith (22) gains yardage against the Buffalo Bills' Darryl Talley during Super Bowl XXVII. Smith gained 108 yards on 22 carries in the game.

Dallas Cowboys head coach Jimmy Johnson gets the traditional victory drenching during the closing moments of Dallas' 52-17 win over the Buffalo Bills in Super Bowl XXVII. Miraculously, Johnson's hair was not affected.

A commemorative patch from Super Bowl XXVII, when the Dallas Cowboys beat the Buffalo Bills 52 to 17.

Dallas Cowboys quarterback Roger Staubach's autographed helmet.

As repeat winners in Super Bowls XXVII and XXVIII, the Dallas Cowboys are entitled to their own Super Bowl caps.

DELL PRO FOOTBALL ANNUAL

No. 1 — 35c

STANLEY WOODWARD picks the winner of every game

33 pages on the All-Pro Squads— offense and defense

BOBBY LAYNE (above)
TOBIN ROTE (left)

LEFT: Quarterback Bobby Layne guided the Detroit Lions to NFL Championships in 1952 and 1953.

DENVER BRONCOS

BOTTOM: Cleveland's Jim Brown, considered by many to be the greatest running back of all time, won the rushing title eight out of his nine playing years.

Les Bingaman

Leon Hart

WHEN an opposing backfield man is hit by the above 300 pounds of muscle and bone, he usually remembers it. He does, that is, once the shock has worn off.

The 6'3" Bingaman has earned the reputation of being one of the finest middle guards in the pro game. Despite his size, Les moves with deceptive speed. This faculty of getting there fastest with the very mostest has gained big Bingaman the All-Pro defensive award for the last three years.

EVERY time Leon got his hands last season, he went for an average 20 yards. A former All-American, Notre Dame, he has proved to be best ends in the business since coming to test in '50.

A specialist in snaring the short then rolling over the opposition 265-pound bulk, Leon played a major Detroit's 11 wins, including the '53

SAN FRANCISCO FORTY NINERS

CLEVELAND BROWNS

OCTOBER 2, 1955

Bobby Layne

point your finger at one man who for the Lions' title last season, to single out Bobby Layne. gained a total of 4,121 yards rushing in '53, and Bobby, alone, ac- the yardage. The 26- is a perfect example of what can accomplish "Mr. Quarter-Layne is known as in the league, 80-pounder really justifies that title.

Doak Walker

No one has ever seen Doak eat a football, but that's about the only thing he can't do with it. The great 26-year-old halfback from Southern Methodist has been thrilling the grid world since 1947 with feats of passing, punting, running.

WHEN the Detroit fans start chanting "Hold that line", Lou is the key player sent in to make the goal line stand more effective and less penetrable.

One of the truly great offensive linemen, whether used at tackle or guard, the 27-year-old is also that solid block of granite on emergency defensive assignments. The 6'4", 250-pound graduate of William and Mary is one of the few men in the game who have seen action in Professional Bowl classics four years in succession.

Lou Creekmur

Rip-Roaring Lio

Detroit is stalking its third straight champio
ll-time record for the National Football Le
are five big reasons why they hope to ma

DENVER BRONC

AFC CHAMPI

Photo from Richard Wolffers Auctions, Inc., San #

The AFL-NFL World Championship Game held on January 15, 1967 was actually the first Super Bowl, although the term Super Bowl was not used until two years later. In the first title contest between the two leagues, only 61,946 people paid to see Green Bay defeat the Kansas City Chiefs 35-10. Since then, the Super Bowl has developed into the biggest event in pro sports.

The Fabulous GREEN BAY PACKERS

50¢

A PUBLICATION OF THE MILWAUKEE JOURNAL

The Green Bay Packers were hailed as the team of the 1960s after winning six NFL championships between 1960 and 1967 and Super Bowls I and II.

Quarterback Bart Starr was selected by the Packers in the 17th round in 1956, but rarely played during his first three years with the club. In 1960, he was handed the starting job and, over the next seven seasons, led the Packers to five NFL crowns and two Super Bowl wins.

THE COACH, THE MAN, THE LEGEND
LOMBARDI

75¢

HOW HE BECAME SPORT'S GREATEST LEADER
"I Loved That Man": The Players Talk About Him
His Words, His Deeds, His Inspiring Life Story

GREEN BAY Packers

Green Bay Packers coach Vince Lombardi accumulated a 105-35-6 record during his short reign as the NFL's premier coach in the 1960s. Felled by cancer in 1970 at the height of his career, he was selected to the Pro Football Hall of Fame a year later.

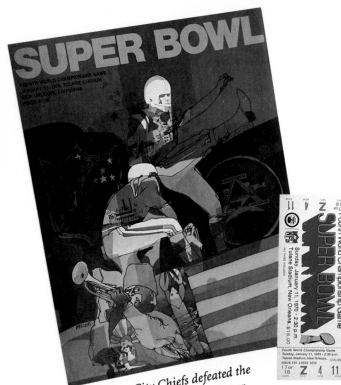

This pennant is a remnant of the Kansas City Chiefs' early years. The Chiefs began in 1960 as the Dallas Texans and were moved to Kansas City in 1963 by team owner and AFL pioneer Lamar Hunt.

The Kansas City Chiefs defeated the Minnesota Vikings, 23-7, in Super Bowl IV.

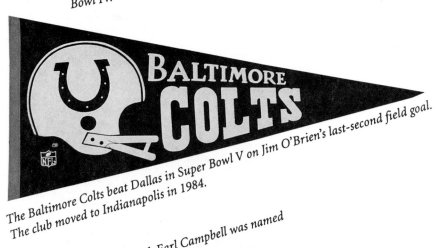

The Baltimore Colts beat Dallas in Super Bowl V on Jim O'Brien's last-second field goal. The club moved to Indianapolis in 1984.

Houston Oilers running back Earl Campbell was named the NFL's Most Valuable Player in 1979.

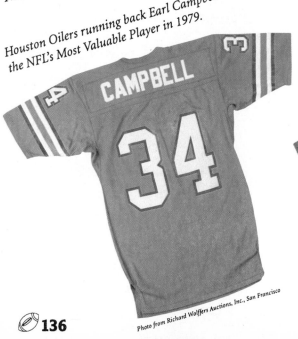

The Houston Oilers won the first two AFL crowns in 1960 and 1961, led by the quarterbacking of George Blanda.

Photo from Richard Wolffers Auctions, Inc., San Francisco

Jim Brown (32) hurdles over a pair of Pittsburgh Steelers to score a touchdown. Brown retired from football at the age of 30 in 1965. He ever missed a game during his nine seasons with Cleveland.

Miami Dolphins head coach Don Shula has guided six teams to the Super Bowl and has a 2-4 record in the game.

LIFE magazine cover featuring the Minnesota Vikings in November, 1961

Hank Stram spent 12 years as a college football coach before getting his first pro football job with the AFL's Dallas Texans in 1960, later to become the Kansas City Chiefs.

137

Nick of Time

The Miami Dolphins had the Oakland Raiders on the ropes in the 1974 AFC playoffs. Miami held a 26-21 lead with 31 seconds to play, but Raiders quarterback Kenny Stabler still had an ace in his pocket.

Stabler took the snap from center Jim Otto at the Dolphins eight-yard line. He rolled right and looked for wide receiver Fred Biletnikoff in the end zone. Biletnikoff was well covered.

Stabler felt pressure from behind and changed directions rolling to his left. He looked for his secondary receiver, then spotted Clarence Davis who had swung out of the backfield and into the end zone.

"I was at the back of the end zone and could see Kenny might be in trouble," Davis said. "When he rolled back to the left, he came in my direction. We were always taught that when the quarterback was in trouble to come back to the ball. We used to practice that. So I started to move up a little toward the line of scrimmage.

"The Miami linebackers, Nick Buoniconti was one, were right in front of me, and they began to move up just in case Stabler ran the ball. So I wasn't really open. The defenders were right there."

Miami's All-Pro defensive end Vern Den Herder was hot on the heels of Stabler. He grabbed the Raiders quarterback by the jersey and was in the act of tossing him to the Oakland Coliseum turf when Stabler heaved a desperation pass toward the end zone in the general vicinity of Davis.

"Kenny threw the ball in my direction," Davis said. "It looked like he tried to loft it over the linebackers' heads, but I could see it was going to be short, that it might be intercepted."

The 5-foot-10, 190-pound Davis was jostled mercilessly by three Miami defenders but struggled through them. Davis then made a leaping, twisting grab for the football.

"I was surrounded and just tried to get to the ball any way I could," Davis said. He did just that, making the catch while tumbling to the end zone turf. Davis found himself clutching the football amid a jumble of hands and legs clad in Miami uniforms. He sat momentarily stunned as the Oakland Coliseum exploded with joy. Pandemonium erupted as fans raced out of the stands. The Oakland players were swarmed and security guards had to be summoned to clear the field so the game's final seconds could be played out.

"I can't explain that feeling," Davis said. "It was just great. It was one of those moments you dream about as a kid, like hitting the winning homer in the World Series. You never forget a moment like that. That's a play that will always stay with me."

Davis' catch gave the Raiders a 28-26 win and sent them on to the AFC Championship Game where they were defeated by the Pittsburgh Steelers. But for Davis it was a moment that could never be tarnished.

LEFT: Raider Clarence Davis (28) scoots around end as Mo Bradshaw (81) prepares to block San Diego's Woodrow Lowe (51).

Photo from Richard Wolffers Auctions, Inc., San Francisco

CLARENCE DAVIS

*C*larence Davis joined the Raiders in 1971 as a highly touted rookie running back out of the University of Southern California. In his initial season with the Raiders, he didn't disappoint. He carried just 54 times, but averaged nearly six yards per carry.

Davis also proved to be a dependable receiver out of the backfield and was named All-Conference as a return specialist after averaging over 27 yards on kickoff returns.

Davis had one of his best seasons in 1976 as the Raiders went to Super Bowl XI. In the biggest game of his career, Davis rushed 16 times for 137 yards, an 8.6-yard average. Oakland went on to defeat Minnesota in the Super Bowl, 32-14.

In 1978, Davis retired. During his eight NFL seasons, he carried 804 times for 3,640 yards and averaged 4.5 yards per carry. He also scored 26 touchdowns on the ground.

An effective receiver out of the backfield, Davis nabbed 99 passes for 865 yards.

PLAYING HISTORY:
Oakland Raiders 1971-1978

Shoulder to Shoulder

Early in 1975, seven years of pounding began to catch up to Oakland Raiders powerhouse fullback Marv Hubbard. In a game against Atlanta, he took a shot from a Falcons linebacker and felt his left shoulder give way. It turned out the shoulder socket had been completely torn off.

Nearly two months later, Hubbard was back in the lineup against the Washington Redskins on Monday Night Football.

"We were on a roll that season and I had a feeling we were going to the Super Bowl," Hubbard said. "I wasn't going to miss it. I wanted to get ready to play."

But, early in the game, Hubbard dislocated his left shoulder again. He was out of commission for another four weeks.

"I was ready to play the last game of the season against Kansas City," Hubbard said. "We had the title locked up. (Coach) John Madden just wanted me to get some plays in during the first half to get my timing down, then I was going to sit out the second half. With two minutes to go, (Chiefs defensive end) Buck Buchanan grabs me by the arm and flings me to the ground. Then all 280 pounds of him fell on my right shoulder. We go in at halftime and take X-rays. Now I have a fracture in my right shoulder."

Three shoulder injuries in one season would have been enough for most players. But Hubbard still saw the Super Bowl up ahead.

"I asked the doctor if he could get it fixed for the playoffs," Hubbard said. "He said, 'Yeah, if you can stand the pain.'"

A week later, Hubbard was in uniform as the Raiders took on the Cincinnati Bengals in the first round of the playoffs. He had a fractured right shoulder and was still recovering from the dislocated left shoulder.

"They put doughnuts and ace bandages under my pads for protection," Hubbard said. "And they gave me xylocaine shots in both shoulders. It made them tingle a little bit."

Although he was barely able to move his arms, Hubbard carried 12 times in the game for 39 yards and Oakland defeated the Bengals 31-28.

And although the Raiders' run to the Super Bowl ended the following week at Pittsburgh as the Steelers downed Oakland 16-10 on an ice-covered field, Hubbard's persistence in the face of incredible physical adversity stood as a true testament to his incredible need to win.

MARV HUBBARD personified the Raiders' running attack of the 1970s. It was a straight-ahead game, man-on-man, running between the tackles. Between 1971 and 1975, Hubbard was the club's leading rusher. He averaged nearly five yards per carry and rarely rambled more than 15 yards a crack. In 1972, he gained 1,100 yards and was the AFC's third leading rusher behind O.J. Simpson and Larry Csonka. All of it came running north and south.

During his eight NFL seasons, Hubbard gained 4,544 yards and averaged 4.8 yards per carry. Only eight players in pro football history have a higher per-carry average. He played for the Raiders from 1969 to 1976.

The Longest Game

The Oakland Raiders of the 1970s were known around the NFL as a wild group of mavericks and outcasts. But every group of misfits needs a capable leader to rally around. For the Raiders, quarterback Ken "Snake" Stabler was that man. He was the last of a breed in the NFL: the swashbuckling field general who called his own plays.

Stabler wasn't blessed with great physical gifts. His arm strength was suspect and he often hobbled onto the field with bad knees. But Stabler's ticket to success in the NFL transcended athletic ability. It was his leadership that mattered. Above all, Stabler was a winner. His teammates believed in him.

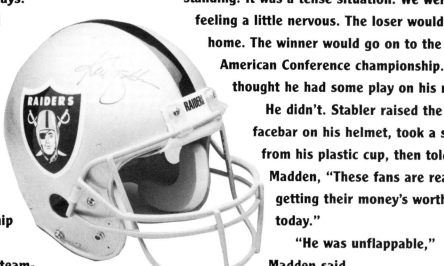

Photo from Richard Wolffers Auctions, Inc., San Francisco

"When Snake called a play," former All-Pro tackle and current Raider coach Art Shell said, "we knew it was the right play. He wouldn't have called it otherwise."

During his years as the Raiders starting quarterback, Ken Stabler guided the club to five division titles and a victory in Super Bowl XI over the Minnesota Vikings. But the consummate Stabler moment came a year later in the 1977 playoffs.

Oakland lost just three games in 1977, but finished in second place in the AFC West behind the Denver Broncos. The Raiders had to settle for a wildcard playoff berth against the Balti-more Colts. It turned into one of the longest games in NFL history, a grueling double overtime contest that was tied 31-31 after 75 minutes of play.

"As the sixth period was getting ready to start," said John Madden, the Raiders coach at the time, "Snake came over to where I was standing. It was a tense situation. We were all feeling a little nervous. The loser would go home. The winner would go on to the American Conference championship. I thought he had some play on his mind."

He didn't. Stabler raised the facebar on his helmet, took a sip from his plastic cup, then told Madden, "These fans are really getting their money's worth today."

"He was unflappable," Madden said.

But when the Raiders took the field in the second overtime period, Stabler knew exactly what to do.

"Snake came into the huddle with ice water in his veins," former All-Pro guard Gene Upshaw said. "That was why we were able to come from behind so often. Nothing ever bothered him."

Stabler seemed to think it was time to put the game to rest. He guided Oakland the length of the field, then hit tight end Dave Casper with a 10-yard touchdown pass to win the game. After nearly 80 minutes of play, Stabler had completed 21 of 40 passes for 345 yards and three touchdowns. And he'd given the fans more than their money's worth.

KEN STABLER

Stabler's road to stardom was a long and hard one. He was selected by the Raiders in the second round of the 1968 draft, but reported to camp nursing a knee injury suffered in the Sugar Bowl while playing for Alabama. He found himself third on the Raiders' depth chart behind Daryle Lamonica, the AFL Player of the Year in 1967, and wily old veteran George Blanda.

Stabler spent 1968 rehabilitating his knee, then walked out of camp in 1969 when he felt he wasn't getting the attention he deserved. He returned to the Raiders in 1970, but it wasn't until early in the 1973 season that he took the starting job away from Lamonica.

"Snake came in and said he didn't want to be the mop-up guy anymore," Madden said. "Basically I told him that was his job."

That week Stabler ran the opposing team's offense, while the Raiders first defensive unit worked on its coverages. He completed nearly every pass he threw. Madden decided it was time to make a move. He named Stabler the starting quarterback.

"Not because he came in and bitched about not playing," Madden said. "But because he didn't give up and pout. He went back out on the field and backed his claim for the position."

Stabler led the Raiders to the 1973 AFC Championship Game, where they were defeated by the Miami Dolphins, and remained the club's field general for seven seasons.

In 1984, Stabler retired after spending time with the Houston Oilers and New Orleans Saints. During his 15-year career, Stabler completed 2,270 passes for 27,938 yards and 194 touchdowns. He was the AFC Player of the Year in 1974 and 1976, and played in three Pro Bowls.

PLAYING HISTORY:
Oakland Raiders 1970-1979
Houston Oilers 1980-1981
New Orleans Saints 1982-1984

A Knight to Remember

Ted Hendricks was called "The Mad Stork." It was a fitting moniker for a tall, skinny outside linebacker known as much for his zany antics off the field as his ferocious play on it.

In a 15-year career that took him from Baltimore to Green Bay to the Raiders, and ultimately to the Pro Football Hall of Fame, Ted Hendricks is best known for his days with the freewheeling Oakland Raiders. Hendricks joined the club in 1975 and wasted no time endearing himself to his new teammates.

In those days, the Raiders held training camp in Santa Rosa, California. The playing field was adjacent to a large pasture where cows and horses grazed in the stifling summer heat. In one of his first practices with the club, Hendricks left the locker room and spied a white horse in the nearby pasture. The 6-foot-7 linebacker approached it cautiously, then quickly mounted it and steered the nag onto the practice field.

A group of startled Raiders, stretching their limbs nearby, watched in amazement as Hendricks swooped onto the field astride the horse, picked up an orange traffic cone used in practice drills, then raced around the gridiron pointing the cone as if it were a lance.

Then, just as suddenly, Hendricks rode back into the pasture, dismounted the horse, put on his helmet and reported to practice.

"It was just another day of training for us," said John Madden, who had seen his share of outlandish behavior during his 10 years as the club's head coach.

TED HENDRICKS

A punishing tackler who freely roamed from sideline to sideline, Hendricks could dismantle an offensive backfield almost single-handedly. But more than anything, Hendricks had an uncanny knack for making the big plays that changed the course of football games. He blocked 25 field goals or extra points during his 15-year career, recovered 16 fumbles, intercepted 26 passes and recorded four safeties, an NFL record. Three times he scored touchdowns on turnovers. And he holds the NFL record for fumble recoveries during postseason play. In other words, he made a habit of being in the right place at the right time.

During 15 NFL seasons, he never missed a game. He played in 215 straight contests until his retirement in 1983, the most by any linebacker in NFL history. Even in his final season, when he had abdominal muscle pulls so severe that he had to roll out of bed sideways and lay on the floor while he dressed, he refused to skip a game.

"Ted was a great natural athlete and an intense competitor," said former coach John Madden. "He got the reputation of being kind of an eccentric, but once a game started he went like gangbusters. Great players make great plays and I can't think of any defensive player who made more big plays for us than Ted Hendricks."

Hendricks collected four Super Bowl rings during his 15-year career and appeared in eight Pro Bowls. He was selected to the Pro Football Hall of Fame in 1990. It was the crowning moment to an illustrious professional career.

PLAYING HISTORY:
Baltimore Colts 1969-1973
Green Bay Packers 1974
Oakland/Los Angeles Raiders 1975-1983

Ain't Gatorade, That's For Sure

Among the Raiders' all-night party crew of the 1970s and early 1980s, Ted Hendricks was a legend. Even among the Raider misfits, Hendricks was one-of-a-kind. Whenever Raider alumni groups gather, stories abound about Hendricks and his old roommate and sidekick, defensive lineman John Matuszak. Some of those stories concern the expeditions Hendricks and Matuszak led to their favorite wineries, back when the Raiders trained in Santa Rosa near the Sonoma Valley wine country. Hendricks and Matuszak were not averse to visiting the wineries on the break between grueling two-a-day practices.

"Ted would come into the huddle after his forays and he'd be smiling with purple teeth and a purple tongue from the red wine," remembers former linebacker Phil Villapiano.

RAIDERS FACT: Oakland Raiders Hall of Fame wide receiver Fred Biletnikoff was considered a cool customer on the field, but before a football game he was a bundle of nerves.

While most players got ready for a contest by staring blankly at the walls or tending to their equipment, Biletnikoff smoked cigarettes, drank coffee and paced the locker room like a caged tiger. The nervous tension also caused him to vomit routinely before taking the field.

"When we heard Freddy in the bathroom calling for Earl," former Raiders coach John Madden said, "we knew he was ready to play."

RAIDERS FACT: Richard Sligh, a seven-foot, 300-pound tackle from North Carolina College who played for Oakland in 1967, is believed to be the tallest player in NFL history.

RAIDERS FACT: Jack Tatum returned a Green Bay fumble 104 yards for a touchdown in 1972.

Ref, Dumb and Blind

The defending Super Bowl champion Oakland Raiders had their hands full in the 1977 AFC Championship Game against the Denver Broncos.

Midway through the third quarter, the Broncos had a 7-3 lead and were driving for another score. The momentum was clearly with Denver and Oakland needed a big play to change it. With first-and-goal at the Raiders two-yard line, Denver running back Rob Lytle took a handoff from quarterback Craig Morton and vaulted over the left side of the line. Raiders safety Jack Tatum was there to meet him, putting a ferocious hit on Lytle that echoed throughout Mile High Stadium.

"Denver was on the goal line," Tatum said, "and I read the play. I saw Rob Lytle take the handoff from Morton and try to jump over the offensive line. I was right there. I came up and made a good hit on him and he fumbled. No question about it."

Tatum's thundering hit stopped Lytle in midair and jarred the ball loose. Raiders defensive tackle Mike McCoy recovered the fumble and began to rumble toward the Broncos goal line. Just then, a referee whistled the play dead and, after considerable discussion, the officials awarded the ball to Denver at the two-yard line.

"The refs ruled it wasn't a fumble," Tatum said, "but then came up with three different excuses as to why the Broncos should have the ball. One ref said there was an inadvertent whistle. Another said Lytle was already down. The inadvertent whistle was the call that stood. The bottom line was that Denver got the ball back."

But the damage was done. With another crack at the goal line, Broncos running back Jon Keyworth powered in for a touchdown, giving Denver a 14-3 lead.

"That was a 14-point swing," Tatum said. "It really put us in a hole."

Oakland rallied for two touchdowns in the fourth quarter as quarterback Ken Stabler hooked up with tight end Dave Casper on a pair of scoring passes. But Denver held on to win the AFC Championship Game 20-17.

"In the locker room, everyone was upset about that fumble call," Tatum said. "Mr. (Al) Davis had a few choice things to say about the refs which I probably shouldn't repeat. The guy who was really mad was (head coach) John Madden. Until this day, if you mention that game to him, he gets mad.

"Later, the officials apologized and said they blew the call. But that game probably makes me more mad then the Immaculate Reception game."

JACK TATUM

During his 10-year NFL career, Jack Tatum was known as "The Assassin." He was the hardest-hitting man in the football business. He played within the rules, but was so overly aggressive that opponents often labeled him "dirty."

Former Pittsburgh Steelers coach Chuck Noll, upset over the constant injuries his wide receivers suffered against Oakland, said in 1976 that Tatum and George Atkinson were part of the NFL's "criminal element."

Tatum's former coaches vehemently dispute that comment.

"I guarantee you one thing," John Madden said. "Jack Tatum never hit anybody from behind."

The torn and tattered bodies Tatum left strewn around the NFL attest to his ferocity. One incident in particular exhibited Tatum's savage play on the field.

During a 1978 preseason game between the Raiders and the New England Patriots, wide receiver Darryl Stingley ran a crossing route, venturing into Tatum's territory. As Stingley reached out for a pass, Tatum caught him in full stride with a clean hit just under the chin. Stingley crumpled lifelessly to the ground. He suffered a broken neck that left him paralyzed.

It was not the most savage hit of Tatum's career, but it was the most unfortunate. Raider-haters around the country blamed Stingley's life-threatening injury on the club's brutality.

In truth, it was a result of Tatum's dedication to aggressiveness. It was a legal tackle from a man with more interest in protecting his territory than making interceptions.

PLAYING HISTORY:
Oakland Raiders 1971-1979
Houston Oilers 1980

RAIDERS FACT: George Blanda was the oldest man ever to play pro football. He retired in 1975 at age 48 after playing with the Chicago Bears, Baltimore Colts, Houston Oilers and Oakland Raiders during his 26 seasons between 1949 and 1975. Blanda is also pro football's all-time leading scorer with 2,002 points.

Photo from Richard Wolffers Auctions, Inc., San Francisco

147

The Roast Beef Defense

In 1966, George Allen took over the head coaching job of the Los Angeles Rams and immediately found a fan in quarterback Roman Gabriel.

"One of the most memorable characters I ever met in football was George Allen," Gabriel said. "His whole life was devoted to winning football games. He never had a driver's license or car because he claimed he couldn't think about football when he was driving. He always used a driver, a former policeman named Bob Reese, who picked him up and drove him to practice or to do errands. George needed to think about football at all times."

Allen also served as the Ram's general manager and met personally with players to negotiate contracts. Inevitably, the discussions would turn away from money and focus on football philosophy.

"Once, during contract negotiations, George and I met at a local golf course for lunch," said Gabriel, who quarterbacked the Rams for 11 seasons and was named the league's MVP in 1969. "George wasn't as good a negotiator as he was a coach. He always seemed to get side-tracked away from the negotiation.

"I remember we both ordered roast beef, mashed potatoes and peas during this negotiation. As we were eating, he was talking about certain defenses he wanted to use during the upcoming season and he would get more and more excited. Pretty soon he had cut up his roast beef into small pieces and was using the beef and the peas to diagram plays on his plate. Of course, he was a defensive-oriented coach and he used the roast beef as his defensive players. The peas were soft and mushy so they were the offensive players. The contract was never discussed."

"George was completely focused on football, even after a game," Gabriel said. "Once we were leaving Los Angeles Memorial Coliseum after a game, it must have been 1966, and George was signing autographs for people. His wife, Etty, came along and said something to him. George glanced at her, but apparently it didn't register as to who she was. He said, 'Please get to the end of the line, Miss, if you'd like an autograph.' He thought it was just a woman cutting into the autograph line."

Although **GEORGE ALLEN** never played major college football, and had coached only bush-league college teams, Rams owner Dan Reeves took a chance on the charismatic leader. Between 1966 and 1970, Allen led the Rams to five straight winning seasons and two first-place finishes. In 1967, Allen was named NFL Coach of the Year, after leading the Rams to an 11-1-2 record. (For more about George Allen, see the Redskins chapter, pages 262-263.)

COACHING HISTORY:
Los Angeles Rams 1966-1970
Washington Redskins 1971-1977

RAMS

George Allen (left) is congratulated by coach Dick Vermeil of the Philadelphia Eagles after achieving his 100th victory as an NFL head coach. Allen reached his 100th win five years after leaving the Rams, while coaching the Washington Redskins in 1976.

Brains over Brawn

When Dick Bass reported to the Los Angeles Rams in 1960 as a first-round draft choice out of tiny College of Pacific in Stockton, California, he didn't expect to break into the starting lineup.

The Rams already had a stable of outstanding running backs that included Ollie Matson, Jon Arnett and Joe Marconi. Bass figured he'd have to make a name for himself as a blocking back or kick returner.

"When I first got to camp, hazing was still in effect," Bass said. "The rookies weren't supposed to start and the veterans let you know it."

But Bass was not intimidated by his older teammates, nor the opposition he faced in the league.

"When I came out of college, I had a good grasp of the game as far as fundamentals were concerned, but I think my attitude is what really mattered," he said. "I had a good mental approach to football. I never made a mental mistake."

It was Bass' quick wits and mental toughness that helped him survive his early days as a blocking back. On more than one occasion, he found himself matched up with a defensive lineman 100 pounds heavier than himself. Detroit Lions defensive tackle Roger Brown was one of them.

Brown, a perennial All-Pro, weighed in at 300 pounds and was stronger than a lowland gorilla. Bass knew he could never match muscles with the hard-charging Detroit Lion.

"I would talk to Roger while we were playing," Bass said. "And I guess he wasn't used to that. On this one play, rather than block him, I just fell down in front of him, right at his ankles. I guess that really mixed him up, because he stopped and just looked down at me."

While Bass played possum at Brown's feet, and the oversized defensive tackle paused to stare at Bass, the Rams made a sizable gain on a running play that went right past the mesmerized defensive tackle.

"I guess that was one of those situations where quick thinking outdid size and muscle," Bass said.

How to Level the Opposition

Running back Dick Bass often tangled with Baltimore Colts defensive end Eugene "Big Daddy" Lipscomb. Lipscomb was one of the terrors of the league early in Bass' career. At 6-foot-6 and 310 pounds, he physically dominated the smaller players of the day. But Lipscomb also had a gentle side. He would often help the quarterback to his feet after a sack and carefully brush the dirt off the player's uniform.

Lipscomb once was asked about the technique he used to rush the quarterback. He said, "I pick 'em up one by one, then I throw 'em away until I come to the one with the ball. Him I keep."

Bass was not intimidated by the menacing Lipscomb, but he was never overjoyed to see him either. He learned that one of the best ways to neutralize Big Daddy was to make him angry.

"For his size, Big Daddy was exceptionally quick," Bass said. "He had great lateral movement and could cover the field sideline to sideline.

"One time I was carrying the ball and there he was right in front of me. I just lowered a shoulder. I caught him on his heels, a little off balance and knocked him straight on his butt. Then I kept right on going. I ran right up his chest with my cleats.

"That really made him mad. Coming back to the huddle, I told him we were going to come right at him again. I could see him getting madder and madder. And you could tell when he was getting mad because he would get himself so worked up, sometimes he would cry. It probably wasn't smart to get the opponent worked up like that, but that's the way we played back then."

RAMS FACT: Tom Fears had 18 pass receptions against the Packers in 1950, a single-game record.

RAMS FACT: The close proximity to Hollywood allowed several Rams to begin a career in television and movies. Fred Dryer acted in television's Hunter and Merlin Olsen appeared in both Father Murphy and Aaron's Way.

DICK BASS

During his 10-year NFL career, Bass scored 41 touchdowns. In two different seasons, he rushed for over 1,000 yards. From 1960 to 1969, he was the Rams' top ground gainer. When he retired after 10 seasons, he was the club's all-time leading rusher with 5,417 yards and a 5.4-yard average. Lawrence McCutcheon and Eric Dickerson later broke his record.

Dick Bass played with the Los Angeles Rams from 1960 to 1969.

151

Hitting the Big Time

Some players remember the Super Bowl wins. Others recall dramatic catches or exciting runs. For Elroy "Crazy Legs" Hirsch, who made his share of great catches and dazzling runs during a 12-year career that landed him in the Pro Football Hall of Fame, his favorite memory is of the simple moment when he realized he'd made it to the big time.

"I'll never forget playing in the 1946 College All-Star Game," said Hirsch, who earned the nickname "Crazy Legs" because his limbs seemed to churn in six directions at once as he left tacklers stranded behind him. "Before the game, they darkened the stadium and announced everyone's name, one at a time. When the public address announcer called out your name, you ran on the field and they put a big spotlight on you. They played your college theme song as you ran out. It doesn't sound like much, but I thought it was one of my greatest experiences as a player."

For the country boy from Wausau, Wisconsin, playing under the lights at Chicago's Soldier Field, in the annual game which pitted the college all-star team against the reigning NFL

champion, was a dream come true. It was his final game as a collegian before joining the professional ranks. Shortly after the All-Star Game, Hirsch signed with the Chicago Rockets of the All-American Football Conference for $7,000.

Hirsch didn't disappoint the 97,000 fans in attendance at Soldier Field. This was his coming-out party.

Early in the game against the reigning NFL champion Los Angeles Rams, Hirsch took a pitchout from quarterback Otto Graham and raced 68 yards to score. Then, in the third quarter, he caught a 35-yard touchdown pass from Graham. The all-stars walked off the field with a 16-0 triumph. For scoring the game's only touchdowns, Hirsch was named Most Outstanding Player.

"That was a big day for me," Hirsch said. "We were playing in front of that huge crowd and against the Rams, who were the best team in the league at that time, so it meant a lot."

And the Rams were equally impressed. Three years later, they signed Hirsch to a contract. It was with the Rams that Hirsch eventually found his way into the record books as one of the greatest flankers in the game.

RIGHT: Elroy Hirsch of the Los Angeles Rams is dragged down from behind by New York Yankees defensive back Pete Layden during a 1950 game.

RAMS FACT: UCLA All-Americans Kenny Washington and wide receiver Woody Strode were signed by the Rams in 1946. They became the first African-Americans to play pro football in the modern era, along with Cleveland Brown stars Marion Motley and Bill Willis.

RAMS FACT: The Rams were the first team to have a helmet logo. In 1947, halfback Fred Gehrke painted a pair of Rams' horns on a Los Angeles helmet. The team management liked the new look and had Gehrke paint horns on every helmet. Gehrke started a trend. Not long afterward, almost every team in the NFL had a team logo painted on their helmets.

RAMS FACT: Norm Van Brocklin threw for 554 yards, a single-game record, against the New York Yanks in 1951, completing 27 of 41 passes.

ELROY HIRSCH PLAYING HISTORY:
Chicago Rockets 1946-1948
Los Angeles Rams 1949-1957

ELROY "CRAZY LEGS" HIRSCH

Under Rams coach Joe Stydahar, Hirsch became the first halfback to be split wide as a flanker. The Rams emphasis on passing proved to be a bonanza for Hirsch. In 1951, he had one of the greatest seasons ever for a pass receiver, catching 66 passes for 1,495 yards, an NFL yardage record. He averaged over 22 yards a catch, scored 17 touchdowns and was the league's leading scorer. Six of his scores were on receptions of over 70 yards. Hirsch's record-breaking statistics helped the Rams win their first world championship.

Hirsch hauled in 387 passes and averaged over 18 yards per reception during his professional career. But it was Hirsch's ability to run with the football after a catch that attracted attention. With the ball clutched under his arm, he ran with the speed and evasiveness of a running back.

In 1969, Hirsch was inducted into the Pro Football Hall of Fame.

A Voodoo Solution

Eugene "Mercury" Morris, the prized halfback of the Miami Dolphins, struggled through the 1974 season. He was hampered with a knee injury and gained just over 200 yards the entire year. As the club prepared for the playoffs and the defense of their 1973 Super Bowl crown, they hoped Morris would be ready to contribute.

One day, Dolphins head coach Don Shula approached Morris after the star running back was examined by the team doctor.

"Doc says you can play," Shula reported. "We're going to have you return kickoffs."

Morris looked down at his knee, which was shrivelled to two-thirds the size of his healthy one. Morris knew returning kickoffs with a knee injury was like being a slow-moving target in a shooting gallery.

"Return kickoffs?" Morris said to himself. "He's trying to kill me."

A sense of desperation told Morris he had to see the Rootman. Morris trudged down to 54th and 12th streets in downtown Miami and visited a Haitian witch doctor, the Rootman.

"There was burning incense in the lobby, but you should have seen the guys in there," Morris said. "Lawyers with briefcases, businessmen. They all wanted to know the outcome of their cases or their transactions."

Morris told the Rootman he didn't want to hurt Shula. He just wanted Shula to change his mind about the kickoff duty.

The night before the Dolphins were to leave for their Oakland playoff game, Morris did as the Rootman told him. He chewed roots and put a Don Shula doll in a box. Then he buried the box in his back yard at exactly 2:00 in the morning and bellowed some chants into the chilly night air.

That Sunday, as the Dolphins prepared to take on the Raiders at the Oakland Coliseum, Morris gnawed on more roots prior to the game. He also took out a piece of paper with a spiderweb drawn on it and the word "confused" scrawled in the middle of the web. He placed the paper in his shoe.

Early in the game, cornerback Lloyd Mumphord missed a tackle and was benched by an angry Shula. Then in the second half, cornerback Tim Foley was injured and Shula replaced him with Henry Stuckey, rather than putting Mumphord back in the game. It was a mistake and everybody seemed to know it but the head coach.

"Stuckey had trouble playing somebody on his nose," Morris said of the cornerback's coverage skills. The Raiders spotted a mismatch and immediately hit receiver Cliff Branch on a 72-yard touchdown pass.

"Then defensive coordinator Vince Costello started yelling, 'Why is Stuckey in there?'" Morris recalled. "Someone on the bench said, 'He must be confused.'"

The Raiders won the game in the waning seconds when quarterback Ken Stabler blindly tossed a wobbly pass to the end zone as he was being tackled. The ball floated past three Miami defenders into the waiting arms of Clarence Davis for the winning score.

But the Rootman must have given Morris the correct formula. Chewing roots, baying at the moon and placing scraps of paper in a shoe worked on that December day. Morris never did return kicks and somebody on the Dolphins squad was definitely confused.

Tackle Wayne Moore knew what Morris had done.

"Couldn't you have waited one more week?" Moore complained in the postgame locker room. "We could have gotten one more check."

MERCURY MORRIS

During Morris' eight-year playing career, he carried 804 times for 4,133 yards and 31 touchdowns. He averaged over five yards per carry. In the early 1970s, Morris teamed with Larry Csonka and Jim Kiick to give the Dolphins one of the most devastating and explosive backfields in NFL history. Csonka and Morris became the first backfield mates ever to gain over 1,000 yards each in 1972. That same year the Dolphins posted a perfect 17-0 record on their way to a Super Bowl victory.

PLAYING HISTORY:
Miami Dolphins 1969-1975
San Diego Chargers 1976

DON WHO?

One reason for Don Shula's success as head coach of the Miami Dolphins is his complete dedication and immersion into the game of football. Like a chess master, he dreams about strategy. But sometimes he gets so wrapped up in the X's ands O's that popular culture simply passes him by.

A case in point involves a locker room incident with popular actor Don Johnson. Johnson starred in the hit television show "Miami Vice" during the 1980s. The show was often filmed in the city of Miami. After one game, Johnson was shuttled into the Dolphins' locker room to meet the players and hobnob with Shula.

Johnson was introduced to the coach as someone who plays a role with "Miami Vice." Shula was obviously pleased to meet Johnson and said, "You guys do a great job on Miami's streets. It's always nice to meet a police officer."

Shula had never heard of Johnson or the television show.

PRINCE WHO?

Although Don Shula is a modest man, on several occasions his vanity has gotten the best of him and forced him into humorous situations.

One time, he was flying to London on a well-earned vacation. As the plane touched down, Shula looked out the window and saw 200 reporters assembled on the tarmac. He bolted into the bathroom, quickly shaved and splashed on some aftershave lotion.

"How did they know I was here?" he asked a stewardess.

But as he left the plane he was mildly disappointed when the media flocked to a young man in a flowing purple cape who emerged from the first-class section. It was the rock star Prince who the British tabloids were interested in. Shula was ignored as he disembarked.

... AND WHO ARE YOU?

A similar thing happened when Shula was the young head coach of the Baltimore Colts in the late 1960s. About a week after his Colts lost to the Jets in Super Bowl III, Shula and his wife went to a Baltimore theater to catch one of the latest film releases. The Shulas entered the crowded theater and found the last two seats near the front.

Just then, everyone began cheering. Shula thought it was time for an impromptu speech. He told the crowd how much he appreciated their support, despite the disappointing Super Bowl loss, and described the team's fine season. Then he took his seat.

Pleased with himself, he watched the movie roll onto the screen. A man behind Shula leaned forward and said, "Look, buddy, I don't know who you think you are, but the reason we were clapping was because they wouldn't start the movie until everyone was in the theater. Since you were the last two, we cheered."

DOLPHINS

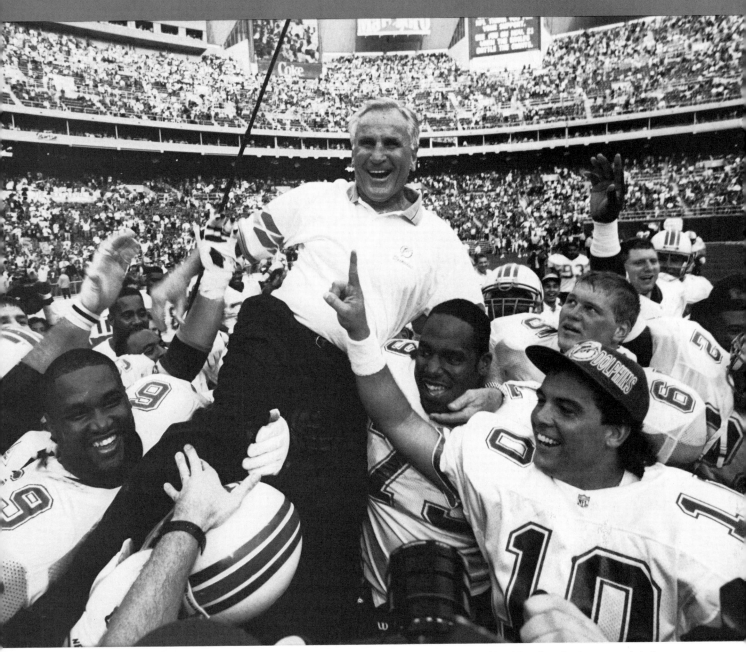

Don Shula gets a ride off the field from his Miami players after winning his 325th game, making him the winningest coach in league history.

DON SHULA

Shula began his head coaching career with the Baltimore Colts in 1963. In 1970, the Dolphins hired Shula away from the Colts. Miami gave up a first-round draft choice to secure his services. It was the best deal they ever made.

Shula promptly coached the Dolphins to four consecutive AFC Eastern Division titles. The 1972 Dolphins posted a 17-0 record, the only perfect season recorded in NFL history, and were victorious in Super Bowl VII. The following year, the Dolphins won Super Bowl VIII

over the Minnesota Vikings. In all, Shula has led his club to six Super Bowls.

In 1993, Shula became the winningest coach in league annals and was named *Sports Illustrated's* Sportsman of the Year.

And Then I Was Picked Up By That UFO, Which Is Where I Met Elvis...

Having spun an elaborate and somewhat ill-advised yarn, Alfred Oglesby hoped the truth would set him free.

Unfortunately for the Miami Dolphins' third-year nose tackle, the truth left him bound to a palm tree with several rolls of athletic tape. Not that the sight of a 6-foot-3, 278-pound man taped to a tree seemed particularly out of the ordinary during the first week of the Dolphins' 1992 training camp.

Especially when one considers the events which occurred four days earlier.

Shortly after lunch on July 23, Miami coach Don Shula told reporters that Oglesby failed to attend morning practice on the campus of St. Thomas University. Thirty minutes after Shula's announcement, Metro Dade police arrived with details of a green BMW which had been abandoned some five miles from training camp.

The car, which belonged to Miami left tackle Richmond Webb, was found parked in the middle of a road with doors locked and hazard lights flashing. Webb, who was sharing an apartment with Oglesby at the time, had lent him the car following the previous night's team meetings.

"He just said he was going to step out for a minute and we haven't heard from him since," Webb said. "It's not like him to disappear."

By 4 p.m., as they quietly marched out for afternoon practice, it was apparent Dolphin players feared the worst.

Those fears were laid to rest, however, when Oglesby called the team office at 5:30. A club official picked up the 25-year-old at a nearby housing complex called "Le Club" and brought him back to camp.

After a brief meeting with Shula, Oglesby greeted the media with an extraordinary tale.

"I was leaving the bar and two cars pulled up and the one guy pulled a gun on me," Oglesby said. "They jumped in the car and abducted me. They took me out and made me drive about eight or nine miles. Then they dropped me off and took off in Richmond's car.

"I was late because I had to walk about nine miles just to get near here. The last three or four miles I finally got a ride...The abductors wanted the car. They didn't want me."

"When something like this happens, you have the worst dreams of what it could be," Shula said. "It's a really scary story."

Perhaps the only thing more frightening than the story was that Oglesby actually thought people would believe it.

When reporters questioned the validity of a professional athlete needing 19 hours to walk nine miles and find a phone, the story began to unravel. In addition, it had been discovered that Oglesby and three other Dolphins were seen the previous night at an adult entertainment lounge called 'Bootlegger.'

Sensing that his story was beginning to unravel in every imaginable way, Oglesby paid a second visit to Shula's office. The coach, who earlier in the afternoon expressed genuine concern for the well-being of his young player, was livid. He left camp without issuing a statement.

Meanwhile, two hours after his first press conference, Oglesby once again stood in front of the media, this time with a more plausible, albeit embarrassing, version.

"I left Bootlegger and went over to a friend's apartment," Oglesby said. "We had some drinks and I fell asleep. When I woke up, my friend was gone and (Webb's) car was gone. Then I was stuck. So I sat there awhile to figure out what I was going to do. That's when I made up the first story.

"I panicked. I wouldn't have made it here on time and I didn't have any money on me. It was real immature. But I didn't want to lose my job."

Instead, he lost $4,000, the amount he was fined by Shula. The fun, however, was just beginning.

Because of Oglesby's antics, Shula revoked the veteran players' privilege of staying home during camp. Many of these players exacted their revenge the following Monday.

Around 10 p.m., Oglesby was using a pay phone to enjoy a conversation with his girlfriend. The talk was cut short when some 20 players ambushed Oglesby and dragged him, kicking and screaming, into a nearby courtyard. Fellow nose tackle Shawn Lee was kind enough to pick up the dangling phone and apologize to Oglesby's girlfriend.

"Sorry, Alfred can't come to the phone," Lee said. "He's tied up right now."

It took several rolls of adhesive tape to finish the job, but this time the Dolphins made certain Oglesby stuck to the facts. But he didn't stick with the club. Oglesby was released midway through the season.

ALFRED OGLESBY joined the Miami Dolphins as a rookie in 1990 after a standout collegiate career at University of Houston.

PLAYING HISTORY:
Miami Dolphins 1990-1992
Green Bay Packers 1992-1993
New York Jets 1994-

DAN MARINO

Dan Marino has been one of pro football's most dominating passers since being selected in the first round by the Miami Dolphins in 1983. The former University of Pittsburgh star set two nearly untouchable NFL single season records in 1984 as he threw for 5,084 yards and 48 touchdowns. He led the Dolphins to the Super Bowl that year. Marino is one of just four quarterbacks in pro football history to throw for over 40,000 yards in his career, and is second in career touchdown passes to Fran Tarkenton. He has played for the Miami Dolphins continously since 1983.

Photo from Richard Wolffers Auctions, Inc., San Francisco

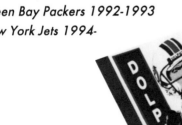

DOLPHINS FACT: Dan Marino is the only quarterback in pro football history to throw 40 or more touchdown passes in a season. He has done it twice, throwing 48 scoring passes in 1984 and 44 in 1986.

THE KICKER'S LAST PASS

*F*or 16 years, Garo Yepremian distinguished himself as a placekicker in the NFL. He had a lively leg despite his diminutive 5-foot-8, 170-pound build, and won many a game from double-digit range, particularly while in the employ of the Miami Dolphins.

Slightly balding and with boyish features, Yepremian, who sold neckties in the off-season, seemed almost out of place among his bulky teammates. During games, he sat quietly on the bench and viewed the on-field carnage with a somewhat anxious expression. He responded sheepishly to the violence.

"Bam, whup, crunch," he intoned, his hands gesticulating wildly. "No thank you very much."

The Dolphins' Armenian kicker also understood the animosity some players felt toward the noncombatants who won games with their toe. An especially vociferous critic of imported kicking specialists was the Detroit Lions standout defensive tackle Alex Karras.

"'I keeck a touchdown,'" Karras said mockingly. "'Hurrah for me.' Personally, I'd like to break off their leg and screw it in their ear. Anybody who doesn't pass, run, block or tackle shouldn't be allowed to decide the outcome of a game. Football is for football players."

Yepremian generally shrugged off the derision and scorn with a self-deprecating smile. Then one day, his worst fears were realized.

It happened in Super Bowl VII at the Los Angeles Memorial Coliseum with 90,182 spectators in the stands and millions more watching via network television. The Dolphins entered the game with a perfect 16-0 record as the AFC champion. Opposing them were the NFC champion Washington Redskins.

With two minutes left in the game and Miami leading 14-0, Yepremian and holder Earl Morrall trotted onto the field for a 42-yard field goal attempt. Yepremian recalls what happened next.

"The snap comes back and the ball is down," he said. "But I don't hit it so good. Whack! Now the ball comes bouncing back. I say to Earl, 'Pick it up.' And he say to me, 'You pick it up.' 'No,' I say, 'you pick it up.' He does not. So I grab the ball and run toward the sideline. Many big people are chasing me. I do not know what to do. Then I think, I will pass the ball. Surprise them, you know? Only the ball slips out of my hand. They (Redskins) pick it up and run for a touchdown. Very bad."

Redskins defensive back Mike Bass scooped up the football and dashed 49 yards to paydirt. Suddenly, the Redskins had new life.

Yepremian trotted to the bench with his head down and made himself as inconspicuous as possible.

"I try to get as far down the field as I can," Yepremian said. "I do not want Coach (Don) Shula to even see me. I feel it is not a good time for us to talk. But he sees me and he say, 'You should have eaten it.' I say nothing and he is busy, so we talk no more. And that is that."

On the Dolphins bench, a lynch mob was looking for the nearest tree.

"Oh, I wanted to strangle him," guard Larry Little said. "You work so hard to get that far, then he's throwing that stupid pass. If 45 guys could kill, Garo wouldn't have been making those stupid ties in the off-season."

Miami managed to prevail 14-7 to preserve its perfect 17-0 season and capture a Super Bowl crown. But Yepremian's embarrassing moment was never forgotten.

DOLPHINS

DOLPHINS FACT: In the Dolphins' very first game in 1966, Miami running back Joe Auer took the opening kickoff and raced 95 yards for a touchdown against the Oakland Raiders.

BELOW: Garo Yepremian's attempted field goal is blocked by the Washington Redskins, the ball bounces back into Yepremian's hands, and the kicker attempts to pass—much to the chagrin of Dolphin fans and teammates.

DOLPHINS FACT: Kicker Garo Yepremian ended the longest game in NFL history, a playoff game that went six quarters between the Dolphins and the Kansas City Chiefs, with a 37-yard field goal to beat the Chiefs 27-24.

GARO YEPREMIAN

Yepremian scored 1,074 points during his 14 NFL seasons and was accurate on 210 of his 313 field goal attempts. He had his best years with the Miami Dolphins during the 1970s. In 1971, he scored 117 points to lead the NFL. A year later, he was the league's most accurate kicker as he made 82 percent of his field goal attempts, converting 19 of 23.

PLAYING HISTORY:
Detroit Lions 1966-1967
Miami Dolphins 1970-1978
New Orleans Saints 1979
Tampa Bay Buccaneers 1980-1981

Later, Alligator

When Miami Dolphins fullback Larry Csonka wasn't rambling through opposing secondaries, quite often he was pulling pranks on coaches and teammates. Head coach Don Shula was one of Csonka's victims.

Csonka and defensive end Manny Fernandez snatched a baby alligator from a nearby swamp during training camp in south Florida one year. They snuck the alligator into Shula's shower and then calmly waited.

Finally, they heard Shula scream, then race out of the shower clad in a hastily wrapped towel.

"He laughed about it later," said Hall of Fame guard Larry Little, who paved the way for Csonka during the 1970s. "He has a good sense of humor."

But that was only half of the story, because the alligator mysteriously disappeared. According to Dolphins lore, it was tossed into a nearby pond and eventually grew into a full-sized reptile able to devour a man with one snap of the jaws.

The legend is revived each year at the Dolphins' Rookie Night. During dinner, first-year players are required to sing their alma mater's fight song. If the vocalization is not performed to the satisfaction of club veterans, the rookie is hauled out and tossed in the pond to see first-hand whether the alligator is still in residence.

DOLPHINS FACT: Earl Morrall may have been the best backup quarterback of all time. With the Baltimore Colts in 1968, he won the NFL passing title as a replacement for the injured Johnny Unitas and was named NFL Player of the Year. With Miami in 1972, he took over after quarterback Bob Griese was injured and won the AFC passing championship, guiding the Dolphins through most of their perfect season.

On Top of the World

Larry Csonka left the Miami Dolphins for the World Football League in 1975, but the big fullback returned to the Dolphins in 1979 for his final NFL season.

During Csonka's hiatus, the Pittsburgh Steelers had stolen the spotlight from the Dolphins, winning three Super Bowls. The turn of events irked head coach Don Shula, who couldn't stand to see Steelers coach Chuck Noll win a title at the expense of the Dolphins, despite being his good friend.

One day, Csonka caught Shula off by himself, daydreaming.

"What are you doing Don?" Csonka asked his startled head coach. Shula reacted with a snappy comeback.

"Oh, just thinking how lonely it is at the top," he replied.

"You must know how Chuck Noll feels then," Csonka said.

**LARRY CSONKA
PLAYING HISTORY:**
Miami Dolphins 1968-1974
Memphis Southmen (WFL) 1975
New York Giants 1976-1978
Miami Dolphins 1979

LARRY CSONKA

"Csonka," said former All-Pro defensive tackle Alex Karras as though savoring the word. "The guy's gotta be a football player with a name like that. Great football players have names like Butkus, Butz and Csonka. They sound like a guy getting hit in the gut. And that's what pro football is all about. Csonka. Yeah, it fits."

For reasons other than Karras' convoluted logic, Larry Csonka fit in the NFL. He could dispense punishment as well as take it. At 6-foot-3 and 235 pounds, he fit the mold for the prototype fullback. He moved the ball like something with treads, the type of vehicle that knew just one direction, straight ahead.

"Since I was a kid," Csonka said. "I've had a habit of leading with my face. And it shows."

By the time Csonka called it quits in 1979 after 12 professional seasons, his nose had undergone nearly a dozen realignments by force. His wife Pam has noted, "I kind of like the way the nose bends. I think he'd look strange if it were straightened."

Other entries from the Csonka medical file show several concussions, an arthritic elbow and knee, and a cracked eardrum. And Csonka can't begin to count the Monday mornings when just getting out of bed was a feat in itself.

In 1972, Miami head coach Don Shula lost starting quarterback Bob Griese midway through the season and decided to base his

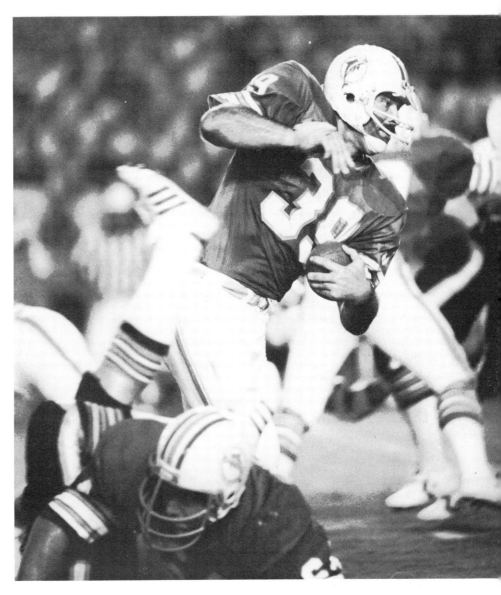

offensive attack around a strong running game. With veteran quarterback Earl Morrall at the controls, the Dolphins went to work using Csonka, Mercury Morris and Jim Kiick in the backfield. Shula's Dolphins ran through the regular season with a perfect 14-0 record. Csonka gained 1,117 yards while Morris ran for 1,000. Both men averaged over five yards per carry.

Csonka was at his best in the big games. He ran for a game-high 112 yards in Super Bowl VII and

took Most Valuable Player honors in Super Bowl VIII after rushing for 145 yards.

In 1979, Csonka retired from football with 8,081 yards on 1,891 carries, tenth best in NFL history. He scored 64 touchdowns on the ground and averaged 4.3 yards per carry during his career. He was also a sure-handed ball carrier who fumbled only 21 times in 12 seasons.

Csonka was elected to the Pro Football Hall of Fame in 1987.

TALKING IT OVER...AND OVER

*J*oe Kapp earned a reputation in the National Football League as much for his fiery temper and bravado as his quarterbacking skill.

He joined the Minnesota Vikings in 1967 and rescued the club from the NFL basement. Two years later, he had the Vikings in the Super Bowl.

But while Kapp impressed his coaches and teammates with his leadership and fire, he provoked and irritated opponents with his cockiness.

"The first time we ever saw him he gave us a little lip," said Deacon Jones, the former Los Angeles Rams defensive end, who is now a member of the Pro Football Hall of Fame. "He came up to the line of scrimmage and said, '(Expletive) you, Rams. I'm coming right at you.' I couldn't believe it. This was his first year in the NFL."

And that was before Kapp had an adequate supporting cast. The Rams stomped Minnesota that day 39-3. But Kapp never quit.

"He was still talking at the end of the game," Jones said. "You could see he was going to be trouble if he ever got some players around him, because of that intensity."

Vikings coach Bud Grant saw that Kapp got the help he needed. In 1969, Minnesota boasted the best offense in the NFL and posted a 12-2 regular season record. The Vikings exploded for wins of 52-14 over Baltimore, 51-3 against Cleveland, and 52-15 over the Steelers. Kapp ripped the Colts defense for seven touchdown passes, tying a league record.

He played against the Green Bay Packers with his fractured left wrist in a cast. He completed just four passes for 41 yards, but the Vikings beat Green Bay, 9-7. Near the end of the game, he taunted the Packers, saying, "You can't even beat me when I have one arm."

HAIL TO THE CHIEFS

*K*app guided the Vikings to Super Bowl IV, where they were upset by the Kansas City Chiefs, 23-7. Just a year earlier, the Jets had beaten the Colts to prove the AFL could play with the NFL. But Minnesota seemed unbeatable.

"Most of us thought the Jets beating Baltimore was a fluke," said Kapp. "All of us just assumed that the AFL was full of gimmicks and couldn't compete with the best of the NFL."

But Kansas City turned the tables on Minnesota in the first half of the Super Bowl. The Chiefs dominated line play and jumped out to a 20-0 halftime lead.

"The first series of the game I got hit about as hard as I ever had," Kapp said. "And they just kept coming at us all day long. We were supposed to be the team to beat, the team with the best offense. We gained a lot of respect for the AFL real quick."

The Chiefs defensive line of Aaron Brown, Jerry Mays, Curley Culp and Buck Buchanan harassed Kapp on passing plays, forcing him to hurry his throws. He completed 16 of 25 passes, but the relentless pressure led to two interceptions. He finally had to leave the game with a shoulder separation.

Kansas City cruised to a 23-7 victory. Kapp believes the AFL's two Super Bowl wins played a large role in the AFL-NFL merger of 1970.

"I don't think we would have the NFL as we know it now if not for those two games," Kapp said. "Before then, nobody thought any team from the AFL could compete with the NFL. If Baltimore and the Vikings had won, the AFL may have stayed a 'second' pro football league."

Steamrolling

At 6-foot-3 and 220 pounds and with bad knees, Kapp was a plodding runner. But he loved to take off downfield and delighted in confronting linebackers. He averaged five yards per rushing attempt in 1969.

Midway through the 1969 campaign, in a contest with Cleveland, Kapp ran a bootleg up the sideline and found 245-pound linebacker Jim Houston in his way.

"I never thought of going out of bounds," he said. "Who's Jim Houston? He's just one guy. I popped him one."

The collision was heard in the press box. Only one man got up. Houston was carried to the sideline for smelling salts and an early departure. Kapp went back to the huddle, then threw a 20-yard pass to fullback Bill Brown.

VIKINGS FACT: Former Minnesota Vikings quarterback Joe Kapp was known for his love of contact. Once, he was knocked out cold in a game against the Detroit Lions. On the sideline, Kapp was finally revived and watched as his replacement, Gary Cuozzo, suffered a broken collarbone. Kapp raced back onto the field and finished the game.

"Football is an animal game," Kapp said. "I'm an animal. Any guy good at it is an animal. Is it normal to wake up in the morning in a sweat because you can't wait to beat another human's guts out?"

JOE KAPP

Kapp played just four seasons in the NFL after spending several years in the Canadian Football League. He completed 49 percent of his 918 passes for 5,911 yards and 40 touchdowns.

PLAYING HISTORY:
Calgary Stampeders (CFL) 1959-1960
Vancouver Lions (CFL) 1961-1966
Minnesota Vikings 1967-1969
Boston Patriots 1970

Stat's All, Folks

Tucked away in the Super Bowl record book is a statistic that former Minnesota Viking defensive back Paul Krause remembers far too well.

Krause holds the single-game record for most tackles in a Super Bowl game with 14. But it's not a record he carries with pride.

"It was Super Bowl VIII against Miami," Krause said with a laugh, again visualizing that January day at Rice Stadium in Houston. "As a safety, I'm not expected to make a lot of tackles on running backs, but I had Csonka coming at me the whole game."

The Dolphins had one of the dominant running attack's in the league that season. Running backs Larry Csonka, Mercury Morris and Jim Kiick teamed up to gain over 2,500 yards on the ground and average nearly five yards per rushing attempt. Csonka carried the Dolphins' offensive load in the Super Bowl.

Krause, a 6-foot-3, 205-pound safety, was one of the game's great pass defenders and is the NFL's all-time pass interception leader. He was never known as a hard hitter. In fact, most of his tackles in Super Bowl VIII were of the self-defense variety. He wasn't foolish enough to believe he could deliver a punishing blow to Csonka, a 235-pound fullback.

"Csonka had a unique running style—none," Krause said. "He'd rather lower a shoulder on you than try to run around you. If he got by me, it was touchdown time. I was able to stop him, but he was putting the hurt on me, not the other way around."

Miami's offensive line consisted of Wayne Moore, Bob Kuchenberg, Jim Langer, Larry Little and Norm Evans. They consistently beat Minnesota's famed defensive front four, "the Purple People Eaters," off the ball.

As the Miami line ripped the Vikings defensive front to shreds, Csonka rambled for 145 yards on 33 carries, with two touchdowns. He was named the game's Most Valuable Player.

Miami's running game was so dominant that Dolphins quarterback Bob Griese bothered to pass just seven times, a Super Bowl low, and completed six. Miami beat the Vikings handily, 24-7.

Krause doesn't brag about his record-setting day in Super Bowl VIII.

"It's not the kind of record you want to have," Krause said. "By getting that many tackles, that meant they had players running with the ball in our secondary all day, which is pretty much what they had. I still see Number 39 in my dreams sometimes."

It's a dream that quickly turns into a nightmare.

VIKINGS FACT: The Minnesota Vikings were conceived after a bit of backroom intrigue.

Minneapolis originally was granted a charter franchise in the American Football League that began operation in 1960. Early in 1960, the NFL informed the Minneapolis business group organizing the club that they could have an NFL franchise beginning in 1961. They withdrew from the AFL and the Vikings were born in 1961.

The final AFL franchise was awarded to Oakland.

Photo from Richard Wolffers Auctions, Inc., San Francisco

VIKINGS FACT: Quarterback Fran Tarkenton threw 342 career touchdown passes, an NFL record.

VIKINGS FACT: In the Vikings' very first game in 1961, quarterback Fran Tarkenton came off the bench to throw four touchdown passes and run for a fifth as Minnesota upset the Chicago Bears, 37-13.

PAUL KRAUSE

Krause ended his 15-year career with an NFL-record 81 pass interceptions, which he returned for 1,185 yards and three touchdowns. He led the league in interceptions with 12 in 1964, his rookie season, and with 10 in 1975. He was selected to play in eight Pro Bowls.

PLAYING HISTORY:
Minnesota Vikings 1964-1979

Right Play...Wrong Way

Defensive end Jim Marshall recovered a record 29 fumbles during his 19-year career with the Minnesota Vikings. But he'll be best remembered for recovering a fumble against the San Francisco 49ers in 1964, then sprinting 66 yards the wrong way.

It was a sunny afternoon at Kezar Stadium when San Francisco quarterback Billy Kilmer dropped back to pass and was buried under a wall of charging Minnesota defensive linemen. The ball trickled loose from Kilmer. Marshall scooped it up and noticed there was nothing but daylight between him and the end zone. He lit out at top speed, sensing his moment of glory had finally arrived.

As he raced down the sideline he noticed his teammates waving frantically in his direction. Thinking they were cheering him on, Marshall sprinted faster and, as he reached the end zone, he jubilantly tossed the ball into the air.

And that's when Marshall sensed something was amiss. San Francisco center Bruce Bosley raced over to the ecstatic Marshall and shook his hand in congratulation. The Vikings defensive end turned around in confusion, searching for the referee, and noticed he was signaling for a safety, rather than a touchdown. Instead of scoring six points for the Vikings, Marshall had given two points to the 49ers.

"There were several of us chasing Marshall but nobody really tried to tackle him because we could see he was going to take it all the way in for a safety," Bosley recalled. "I remember going up to him and congratulating him and at first he was kind of bewildered. Then I guess it sunk in as to what had happened and he grabbed his helmet as if to say 'Oh, no.'"

Later during his playing days with Minnesota, Marshall picked up a fumble and ran it into the correct end zone to score the only touchdown of his career.

VIKINGS FACT: Coach Bud Grant was a forward with the NBA champion Minneapolis Lakers during the 1949-50 season.

RIGHT: Bud Grant served as head coach of the Minnesota Vikings from 1967 to 1985. He led the Vikings to four Super Bowls, although they were defeated in each one. Grant's 168 coaching wins place him in the top ten of professional football coaches.

JIM MARSHALL

Jim Marshall was a 6-foot-4, 240-pound All-America tackle from Ohio State when he made his 1959 pro football debut with Saskatchewan in the Canadian Football League. The following season, the Cleveland Browns selected him in the fourth round of the draft. In 1961, Marshall was dealt to the Minnesota Vikings where he anchored the defensive line for 19 seasons, from 1961 to 1979, the longest tenure with a single club by any player in pro football history. He played in 282 consecutive games with Minnesota, an all-time record, and recovered 29 fumbles.

PLAYING HISTORY:
Saskatchewan Roughriders (CFL) 1959
Cleveland Browns 1960
Minnesota Vikings 1961-1979

VIKINGS FACT: "The Purple People Eaters" was the name given the Minnesota Vikings defensive front four in the late 1960s and early 1970s. The group consisted of defensive ends Carl Eller and Jim Marshall, and defensive tackles Alan Page and Gary Larsen. In 42 games from 1969 to 1971, they allowed just 34 touchdowns from scrimmage.

RIGHT: The fateful run—Minnesota Vikings' Jim Marshall scoops up a San Francisco 49ers fumble and runs 60 yards into his own end zone. In the bottom right photo, he is congratulated by Bruce Bosley (77) of the 49ers.

The Mystery Man

One of the strangest incidents from the Boston Patriots' rag-tag early years involves the mysterious man in the raincoat.

It occurred at Boston University's Nickerson Field in 1961, when the American Football League was in its second year of operation. The Patriots would eventually settle into Foxboro in 1971, but on a rainy Sunday in November 1961, Nickerson Field was the cozy home of the Patriots as they took on the Dallas Texans.

It was the second meeting between the two clubs that season. The Texans, who would soon move north and become the Kansas City Chiefs, lost at the Cotton Bowl in the first game, 18-17.

For the rematch, 25,063 fans packed the stadium despite a constant drizzle. At least 10,000 more were outside, hoping to buy tickets. It was only the second sellout in the Patriots' young history. The crowd inside ringed the field in anticipation of a great battle.

Mike Holovak had recently taken the Patriots head coaching job vacated by Lou Saban. Holovak believed in alternating his two quarterbacks, Butch Songin and Babe Parilli, to shuttle in plays. Both men threw a scoring pass in the first half.

Songin got Boston on the scoreboard first as he hooked up with Jim Colclough for a touchdown. The Patriots upped their lead to 14-0 on a Parilli-to-Gino Cappelletti scoring toss.

But coach Hank Stram brought his Texans right back. They tied the score just before halftime, then late in the fourth quarter found themselves trailing the Patriots, 28-21. Going into the final minute of the game, Dallas had one last shot to win it.

By the fourth quarter, many of the stadium ticket takers had left for the day. Security was lax during the early days of the AFL, so the gates were left unattended. Many of the 10,000 fans who had remained outside after discovering the game was sold out began to make their way through the unguarded gates. Soon the end zones and sidelines were bloated with spectators.

Meanwhile, on the field, the Texans pulled out all the stops in the game's final minute. Quarterback Cotton Davidson called a flea-flicker pass, took the ball on a handoff from Abner Haynes and looked for Chris Burford, his top receiver. He found him at the five-yard line where Burford was brought down.

Dallas had no more timeouts and the team raced to the line of scrimmage as the clock ticked down to 25 seconds.

Davidson called Burford's number again. This time, he ran a crossing route in the end zone. Davidson stepped back and saw Burford all alone. He let fly with his pass.

Suddenly, from the crowd that was 10 spectators deep, a man wearing a raincoat came forward. Seeing the pass was about to be caught, the man leapt out and knocked the ball from Burford's hands.

There was wild confusion as time ran out and the fans surged onto the field. The mysterious man in the raincoat blended back into the thick crowd and disappeared as quickly and mysteriously as he appeared. The game was over. Final score: Boston Patriots 28, Dallas Texans 21.

WILLIAM SULLIVAN

And that was the end of it, until Texans coach Hank Stram saw the game film the next day back in Dallas. He suspected the man in the raincoat was Boston Patriots team owner William Sullivan.

Sullivan later denied to the media that he was the 12th defender on the field that day. But he did admit to having a raincoat similar to the mystery man's. And he claimed it was just a coincidence that he wore it to the game that afternoon.

*I*n 1959, William Sullivan, Jr., headed a group of New England businessmen who purchased a franchise in the fledgling American Football League. Sullivan was named the first president of the new Boston Patriots. He chose Lou Saban to be his first head coach. In 1971, Sullivan moved the club to Foxboro and renamed it the New England Patriots. Sullivan sold controlling interest in the club to Victor Kiam in 1988. Sullivan was the owner of the Patriots from 1959 to 1988.

LEFT: Official Super Bowl XX game program from Sunday, January 26, 1986 when the New England Patriots faced the Chicago Bears. The Patriots were routed 46-10. It was the Patriots' only Super Bowl appearance.

The Unforgivable Ref

New England Patriots fans—and Patriots tackle Ray Hamilton—will never forgive referee Ben Dreith. Since 1976, the year the Patriots staged one of the biggest one-year turnarounds in NFL history, Ben Dreith has been a marked man from Connecticut to Maine.

Under coach Chuck Fairbanks, New England rebounded from a 3-11 record to go 11-3 in 1976 and earn a wildcard spot in the playoffs. Fairbanks, in his fourth year as the club's skipper, was named NFL Coach of the Year. On the field, quarterback Steve Grogan led a varied attack that featured pounding running backs Sam Cunningham and Dan Calhoun.

The Patriots met the Oakland Raiders in the first round of the playoffs. Earlier in the season, New England destroyed the Raiders in Foxboro, 49-17. It was Oakland's only loss of the regular season. This time, the two clubs met at the Oakland Coliseum.

After trailing 10-7 at halftime, Grogan took control in the third quarter. He connected with All-Pro tight end Russ Francis on a 26-yard touchdown pass to put the Patriots in front, then New England added another touchdown just five minutes later on Jess Phillips' three-yard run. After dominating the game for three quarters, New England led the Raiders 21-10 with just 15 minutes remaining.

But odd and eerie things can happen in Oakland, as New England soon found out.

Raiders quarterback Ken Stabler chose the final period to stage one of his finest performances ever. He started the fourth quarter by completing four straight passes and driving the Raiders 70 yards. Running back Mark van Eeghen capped the drive with a one-yard touchdown run.

With less than four minutes to go, Stabler was at it again. Starting from his own 32-yard line, Stabler connected on three of four passes. He mixed in a pair of running plays and suddenly the Raiders were within striking distance.

At the Patriots' 27-yard line, Oakland faced a third-and-18 with 57 seconds remaining. Stabler dropped back and felt the pocket collapse around him. He spotted running back Carl Garrett over the middle and tried to force the ball to him. As he did, he was leveled by 6-foot-1, 250-pound nose tackle Ray Hamilton. The pass fell incomplete.

"I came in on Stabler, tipped the ball, then hit him," Hamilton said. "I looked downfield to see what happened. When I looked back, the referee was throwing the flag."

"It was a hell of a defensive play by Hamilton," Fairbanks said. "It was completely legal. There was no penalty there."

Hamilton was called for roughing the passer by referee Ben Dreith. The controversial penalty gave Oakland a first down at the New England 13-yard line.

Given a reprieve, Stabler made the most of it. On first down, Pete Banaszak gained eight yards. In addition, Patriots defensive back Prentice McCray, who was still upset about the roughing the passer call, was whistled for unsportsmanlike conduct. Now, Oakland was in business at the four-yard line.

With 10 seconds on the clock, Stabler called a run-pass option in the huddle. After taking the snap, he faked a handoff to Banaszak, then sprinted around left end behind All-Pro guard Gene Upshaw. Stabler dove into the end zone for the winning score.

When the final gun sounded, the Patriots were indignant. They insisted they were robbed. Dreith was late throwing the flag on Hamilton, according to Fairbanks.

After the game, Fairbanks claims he tried to discuss the penalty with Dreith, who said in unprintable terms that he had nothing to say. Patriot coaches banged on Dreith's locker room door for several minutes and ran after his car as he left the parking lot.

"One of the officials yelled at me from the car," Patriots assistant coach Charlie Sumner claimed. "He yelled, 'How do you like it now, Coach?' Personally, I think we were cheated."

"Now I know why the Raiders always win at home," said Hamilton, who is now, ironically, a Raiders assistant coach. Nevertheless, he still maintains the Patriots were cheated and should have advanced to the Super Bowl that season. Former Patriots quarterback Steve Grogan concurs.

"That was the Super Bowl we should have won," Grogan said.

Instead, Oakland advanced to Super Bowl XI where they destroyed the Minnesota Vikings 32-14.

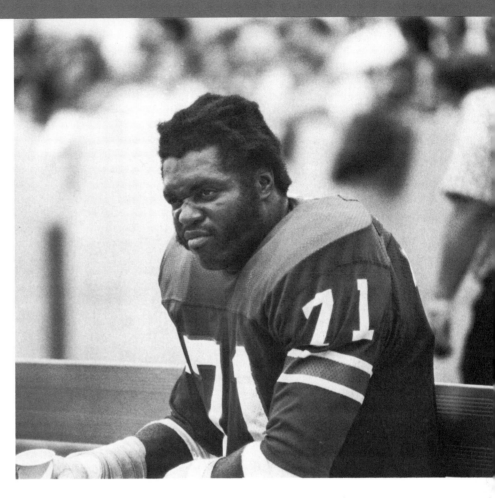

RAY HAMILTON

Hamilton was the New England Patriots' 14th-round draft pick in 1973 out of Oklahoma, where he was a two-time All-Big 8 selection. After spending nine seasons as a standout defensive tackle with the Patriots, Hamilton stayed with the club as a defensive line coach. In 1991, he joined the Tampa Bay Bucs as a defensive line coach and currently serves the Los Angeles Raiders as a defensive line coach.

Hamilton played with the New England Patriots from 1973 to 1981.

PATRIOTS FACT: At 5-foot-5, running back Mack Herron was one of the smallest men ever to play pro football. But in 1974, he led the Patriots in rushing, pass receptions, punt returns and kickoff returns. He gained a record 2,444 in combined yards.

All I Want For Xmas Is...My Coach

The New England Patriots have had some bizarre episodes in their past but none so strange as the scene that took place one December evening in Miami.

It began near the end of a triumphant 1978 season for coach Chuck Fairbanks and his Patriots. New England had put together one of the best running attacks in modern football history, rushing for nearly 200 yards per game, and had stormed through the regular season with an 11-4 record. The Patriots already had a playoff spot locked up. They had one final regular season game with the Miami Dolphins on Monday Night Football.

In the week leading up to the game, Fairbanks had been huddling with officials from the University of Colorado to finalize a contract. At the end of the 1978 campaign, he planned to leave the pro ranks and take the head coaching job at Colorado.

On the day of the Miami game, Fairbanks gathered his team together and made the announcement. It didn't come as much of a shock to the players, who expected Fairbanks to leave the Patriots at the end of the season. After all, they had already heard their head coach recruiting high school players for Colorado on the telephone.

Team owner Billy Sullivan was indignant at the news. He ordered Fairbanks to his office and was prepared to fire him. He then discovered the only move he could legally make was to suspend his head coach.

But Fairbanks wouldn't accept a suspension. He demanded that he be allowed to finish out the season with his club. After he was denied

access to the Patriots' charter flight to Miami, Fairbanks arranged his own transportation to the game.

The team arrived at the Orange Bowl unsure of who their coach would be that evening. Players asked reporters. Reporters questioned assistant coaches. Assistant coaches conferred amongst themselves. Finally, offensive coordinator Ron Erhardt and defensive coordinator Hank Bullough decided to work together as co-coaches.

"Does this mean there won't be a Christmas party at Fairbanks' house?" one player asked when informed of the suspension.

A few hours before the game, Fairbanks made his way to the Patriots locker room at the Orange Bowl. A flock of media representatives waited outside while Fairbanks had a chat with Sullivan. The Orange Bowl's security personnel patiently waited nearby.

Meanwhile, an unidentified friend of Fairbanks, who supplied the deposed head coach with a ride to the stadium, periodically stuck his head in the door and yelled, "Chuck, are you coming out?"

And he did, sooner than expected. Sullivan informed Fairbanks he was not allowed to coach the team that evening. In effect, Fairbanks was kicked out of the Patriots locker room.

The unsettled coaching situation had predictable results on the Patriots that night. Miami rolled over New England, 23-3.

But the problems had just begun. In the aftermath of the game, 11 team members banded together and asked that Fairbanks be reinstated for the playoffs. Sullivan finally rescinded his suspension and Fairbanks was temporarily rehired.

"The timing of the announcement was horrible," Fairbanks later admitted.

New England took on the Houston Oilers, the wildcard team, in the playoffs. Houston quarterback Dan Pastorini had a field day with the demoralized Patriots. He fired three touchdown passes in the first half and sent New England home for the holidays with a 31-14 drubbing to ponder. That was it for Fairbanks.

"People in the college game are always for you," Fairbanks said about his decision to leave the Patriots to coach the Colorado team. "The atmosphere is closer, friendlier."

But no more secure. Fairbanks was eventually fired from the University of Colorado as well.

CHUCK FAIRBANKS

The New England Patriots were a team in disarray when Chuck Fairbanks took over in 1973. The club had won just three games in 1972 and seemed headed into the AFC sewer.

Fairbanks revitalized the club. By 1976, the Patriots were a playoff team and Fairbanks was named Coach of the Year. He posted a 46-40 record during his six seasons as head coach at New England.

Chuck Fairbanks had his New England Patriots on the way to the playoffs in 1978 when he informed his team he would be stepping down as head coach at the end of the year to take a job at the University of Colorado. Indignant Patriots team owner William Sullivan suspended him. Here Fairbanks chats with Sam Adams (61) and Leon Gray (70).

Electrifying Introduction

The Clive Rush era in Boston lasted less than two years, but it began with one of the most bizarre incidents in Patriots history.

Before Super Bowl III between the New York Jets and the Baltimore Colts, Patriots owner William Sullivan had been in contact with New York offensive coordinator Clive Rush and the Colts' top assistant coach, Chuck Noll. He wanted one of the men to fill the Patriots head coaching job recently vacated by Mike Holovak. But Sullivan would wait until after the Super Bowl game to make his final decision.

The Jets, of course, pulled off one of the biggest upsets in pro football history in Super Bowl III. Despite being 18-point underdogs, they beat the Colts after quarterback Joe Namath guaranteed a victory. The Jets became the first AFL team ever to win a Super Bowl.

The Jets' stunning win persuaded Sullivan to hire Rush as his new head coach beginning with the 1969 season.

Years later, Sullivan admitted he was leaning toward hiring Noll, but when the Jets won the game he felt compelled to hire Rush because, "the Boston media would question why we hired the coach from the losing team and not the coach from the winning team."

Sullivan lamented that passing on Noll was one of his biggest mistakes as the team's owner. Noll was hired by Pittsburgh Steelers owner Art Rooney and went on to win four Super Bowl rings and a place in the Pro Football Hall of Fame.

Rush couldn't break away from his past with the Jets and, as soon as he took over the Patriots job, he started hiring numerous friends from the Jets franchise. One of them was former Jets receiver George Sauer, who became the Patriots general manager.

Rush called a press conference at the now-defunct Hotel Somerset to introduce Sauer to the media. He stepped up to the rostrum, put his right hand on the microphone to adjust it, then began to scream wildly.

The microphone was live with electricity and Rush was unable to pull himself away from the current that was surging through his body.

Dan Marr, then one of the minority owners of the club, jumped from his seat in the middle of the media gathering, knocked over television cameras that were filming the event and pulled the microphone cord from the wall socket, saving the life of his new head coach.

The 100 or more people in the room watched in stunned silence as Rush slumped in agony to the floor.

After a few minutes, Rush was back on his feet and feeling better. He bravely went to the rostrum again and got off what may have been his best line during a short and rocky coaching career.

"I heard the Boston press was tough, but I never expected this," Rush said.

CLIVE RUSH

If Rush thought the Boston media was brutal, it was nothing compared to coaching the Patriots.

Boston started the 1969 campaign by dropping seven consecutive games and sure enough, the media and fans made life miserable for Rush. Without an effective passing game, Rush was forced to rely on running backs Jim Nance and rookie Carl Garrett to carry the load. It wasn't enough. The Patriots finished the season with a 4-10 record.

Rush returned for the 1970 season and got off to a good start as the Patriots beat the Miami Dolphins in the league opener. But it was all downhill from there. Boston lost seven straight games and Rush was fired by owner William Sullivan with four games left in the season. Rush coached the Boston Patriots from 1969 to 1970.

PATRIOTS FACT: Kicker and wide receiver Gino Cappelletti scored 155 points for the Boston Patriots in 1964, the third highest single-season total in pro football history.

PATRIOTS FACT: Jim Nance rushed for an AFL-record 1,458 yards in 1965.

PATRIOTS FACT: In 1961, the Boston Patriots became the only team in football history to cancel a game because of a hurricane warning. The hurricane never materialized and the Patriots won the rescheduled game over the Buffalo Bills.

PATRIOTS FACT: During New England's run for the Super Bowl in 1985, linebacker Andre Tippett was the cornerstone behind the Patriots' opportunistic defense. Tippet was selected by the Patriots in the 1982 draft and the 240-pounder from the University of Iowa quickly developed into one of the league's best run stoppers. He played with the Patriots from 1982 to 1993.

What a Kick

It was fall, 1970. The New Orleans Saints were mired in yet another dismal season. It was so horrifying, in fact, that coach Tom Fears was fired after a 1-5-1 start and replaced by J.D. Roberts. As is often the case, the team rallied and played well under its new coach. At least for a while.

But on November 8, 1970, it appeared that the Saints had come up short to the Detroit Lions. With 11 seconds left, the Saints trailed 17-16 and were 72 yards from paydirt. The faithful were already filing out of old Tulane Stadium, a bit prematurely as it turned out.

From his own 28-yard line, New Orleans quarterback Billy Kilmer threw a 17-yard pass to Al Dodd, who stepped out of bounds at the Saints' 45 with two seconds left. There was time for only one play. Roberts' choice was to go with Tom Dempsey.

The rest was NFL history.

Dempsey was a remarkable athlete, all the more so because he overcame tremendous odds to compete in athletics. Born with a clubbed right foot and no right hand, there were many people who wouldn't give him the opportunity he wanted. But Dempsey saw no reason to let his handicap stop him. And it didn't.

In his second season with the Saints, Dempsey was making 65- and 70-yard field goals in practice routinely, but he had never had to recreate this feat on the field. Until now.

The snap from center Jackie Burkett was right on the money. Holder Joe Scarpati got the ball down 63 yards away from the uprights. Dempsey stepped forward and his custom-made right shoe made a sound like a cannon shot when it connected with the ball.

"I knew I had hit the ball extra hard and extra good," said Dempsey. "I was just wondering if it was going to stay straight or not."

Agonizing moments later, he had his answer. The ball just cleared the crossbar, touching off a celebration that is legendary to this day. Dempsey's field goal gave the Saints a 19-17 win over Detroit and sparked a mini-Mardi Gras on Bourbon Street.

"The party afterwards is what I remember most about the whole thing," said Dempsey, a Milwaukee native. "If you're going to set a record, this is the town to set it in. New Orleans people really know how to celebrate something."

And his accomplishment was worth all the celebration. Dempsey's 63-yard field goal record remains unbroken by any NFL player almost a quarter century later.

> SAINTS FACT: Saints kicker Morten Andersen, a native of Denmark, had never kicked a football until coming to the United States as part of a cultural exchange program in 1977. He is now the Saints all-time leading scorer and his 78-percent accuracy rate on field goals is third best of all time.

SAINTS

Tom Dempsey (19) steps up to the football to kick an NFL-record 63-yard field goal with two seconds to play, giving the New Orleans Saints a 19-17 win over the Detroit Lions. Joe Scarpati holds while Detroit's Alex Karras (71) provides the rush.

TOM DEMPSEY

Dempsey was good on 89 percent of his extra points tries and 62 percent of his field goal attempts. In 1973, playing with the Philadelphia Eagles, he scored 106 points, second best in the NFC. Dempsey ended his 11-year career with 729 points scored on 252 extra points and 159 field goals.

PLAYING HISTORY:
New Orleans Saints 1969-1970
Philadelphia Eagles 1971-1974
Los Angeles Rams 1975-1976
Houston Oilers 1977
Buffalo Bills 1978-1979

SAINTS FACT: In 1967, safety Dave Whitsell intercepted 10 passes to tie for the most in the NFL and was the first Saints player to appear in the Pro Bowl.

SAINTS FACT: Kicker Paige Cothren was the first player ever signed by the expansion New Orleans Saints in 1967.

179

The Prayer That God Didn't Hear

The dawning of a new era in New Orleans broke warm and sunny and without a hint that lightning was about to strike.

September 17, 1967 was a perfect day for football, a fact not lost on Saints rookie kick returner John Gilliam as he looked up into a cloudless, blue sky and awaited the kickoff that would signal the birth of a new franchise.

As he waited, Gilliam said a little prayer.

"I was praying, 'Please don't let the ball come to me,'" Gilliam said.

But when the Los Angeles Rams' Bruce Gossett booted the ball to start the game, sure enough, it drifted Gilliam's way. And once he caught the football, Gilliam figured he'd better do something with it. So he took off running at full tilt and when he finally came to a stop in the Los Angeles Rams end zone, he had himself a 94-yard touchdown and a place in New Orleans Saints' lore.

"The guys in the kickoff return wall did a great job," Gilliam said. "They blocked everybody. I saw a seam and just hit it. From there, it was history."

Gilliam's sparkling touchdown run electrified the overflow crowd of 80,000 at Tulane Stadium and sent such a charge through him that he heaved the ball into the stands instead of saving it as a keepsake.

And the return happened so fast—only seven seconds ticked off the stadium clock—that his wife missed it while in the restroom with their daughter.

John Gilliam

Gilliam, a 6-foot-1, 190-pounder, was originally drafted out of South Carolina State as a running back, but the New Orleans coaches noticed his speed and hands, which made him more of an asset as a pass catcher. Soon after, they decided to move their rookie to wide receiver.

In his first NFL season, he rushed just seven times for 41 yards. Instead he became an important part of the Saints' passing game and caught 22 passes for 264 yards and one touchdown.

Gilliam signed with the St. Louis Cardinals after two productive years with the Saints, then drifted around the NFL playing for five different teams. He returned to his original team, the New Orleans Saints, in 1977 for one final season.

He retired with 382 receptions for 7,056 yards and 48 touchdowns, and averaged nearly 19 yards per catch.

PLAYING HISTORY:
New Orleans Saints 1967-1968
St. Louis Cardinals 1969-1971
Minnesota Vikings 1972-1975
Atlanta Falcons 1976
Chicago Bears 1977
New Orleans Saints 1977

SAINTS FACT: Saints' defensive lineman Les Miller shares the NFL record for most fumbles returned for touchdowns with three.

SAINTS

Quarterback Archie Manning (8) unloads a pass against the Washington Redskins. Manning was named NFC Player of the Year in 1978, despite playing with a New Orleans team that finished with a 7-9 record.

SAINTS FACT: The Hilgenberg family has produced a long line of centers. Joel Hilgenberg has played both center and guard for the Saints. His brother Jay Hilgenberg is an All-Pro center with Cleveland. Their father, Jerry Hilgenberg, was an All-America center at University of Iowa in the 1950s. Uncle Wally Hilgenberg was the black sheep of the family, playing guard and linebacker with the Detroit Lions and Minnesota Vikings from 1964 to 1979.

SAINTS FACT: George Rogers set a franchise record in 1983 by rushing for 206 yards against the St. Louis Cardinals.

When You're Hot, You're Hot

It was without a doubt the hottest Archie Manning had ever been in his life.

Maybe it was the sheer anticipation of starting his first-ever NFL game. Maybe it was the prospect of facing the Los Angeles Rams' "Fearsome Foursome." Or maybe it was just the fact that mid-September in New Orleans is still downright hot.

Whatever the reason, Manning thought he was dying.

"They'd just installed turf in Tulane Stadium and it must have been about 130 degrees on the field," Manning said.

Always one to stretch hard, Manning also decided on some extra pregame sprints since the chances were good he was going to run for his life that day in 1971. And that's when it hit him.

"I went in the locker room after warmups and told Danny Abramowicz that I didn't think I could go," Manning said. "I had not one ounce of energy left. I felt like I was about to pass out. I was scared to death."

Abramowicz told Manning to change his clothes, drink some liquids and cool off.

"After that, the adrenaline got me pumped up again and I was all right," Manning said.

All right doesn't do the moment justice, however, because when Manning finished with the Rams that day, Saints fans everywhere were sure their prayers had been answered.

Admittedly, the Rams had an off day and the Saints had a good one. But the bottom line was that, with 70 seconds to play, the Saints trailed only 20-17 and had the ball on their own 30.

Mixing the run and the pass, Manning guided the Saints to the Rams' one-yard line and called time out with three seconds remaining.

The sideline scene that followed was right out of a Three Stooges movie.

"(Coach) J.D. Roberts just kept saying, 'We're gonna go for it,'" Manning said. "One of the assistants said we should do this and another said we should do that and the next thing I knew, the ref was tapping me on the shoulder and telling me time was up. And they hadn't even called a play.

"Danny (Abramowicz) met me about halfway to the huddle and asked what they called and I told him they hadn't called anything. So I called a little bootleg rollout and made it work."

Manning rolled right, turned it up and was hit near the goal line. But he stretched and stretched and finally brought the ball down—just barely—over the end line.

And so a New Orleans legend was born.

OPPOSITE: *Quarterback Archie Manning (8) was an All-America selection in high school and college, and played in two Pro Bowls with the Saints. A gifted quarterback, he was New Orleans' first-round pick in 1971. But Manning was forced to carry the offensive load for the hapless Saints and suffered numerous injuries during his career. Here, tackle Don Morrison (76) provides protection.*

SAINTS

ARCHIE MANNING

The former 6-foot-3, 210-pound University of Mississippi star with the rifle arm was chosen by the Saints with the second pick of the 1971 draft. Stanford quarterback Jim Plunkett, selected by New England in the draft, was the only man picked ahead of Manning.

Despite frequent injuries behind a patchwork New Orleans offensive line, Manning led the team in passing nine times. He played in two Pro Bowls and, in 1978, he was named NFC Player of the Year. That season, he guided the Saints to a 7-9 record, completing 291 of 471 passes for 3,416 yards and 17 touchdowns. It was the first of three consecutive seasons in which he threw for over 3,100 yards.

During his 14-year NFL career, Manning completed 2,011 of 3,642 passes for 23,911 yards and 125 touchdowns.

PLAYING HISTORY:
New Orleans Saints 1971-1982
Houston Oilers 1982-1983
Minnesota Vikings 1983-1984

Steel Nerves and Knocking Knees

Danny Abramowicz simply wouldn't take no for an answer.

A 17th-round draft choice of the New Orleans Saints in their expansion year of 1967, Abramowicz could figure the odds. He was a longshot to make the team.

As training camp moved into its third week, Abramowicz noticed the majority of the club's offensive work went to expansion draft veterans and early-round draft choices. He began feeling a sense of doom.

Before camp began, Abramowicz had even approached head coach Tom Fears and gotten assurances that he would receive a fair shake. He wanted Fears to know he could play despite his small-college background at Xavier (Ohio) University. But as the days passed and the offensive chances dwindled, Abramowicz could see the signs.

Finally, the dreaded nighttime knock came on Abramowicz's door. He was ordered to see Coach Fears with his playbook.

Abramowicz had other ideas, however.

"I hurried downstairs and walked into Coach Fears' office," Abramowicz said. "Before he could say anything, I said, 'Coach, you're not cutting me.' I said, 'You didn't give me a fair chance and I'm not leaving.'"

Fears had never met a rookie with such boldness. Taken aback, the Saints head coach sized up the brash rookie for a moment and made a quick decision.

"He said, 'Okay, go back upstairs. I'm going to give you another week,'" Abramowicz said.

It proved to be one of the best moves Fears ever made.

Given a reprieve, Abramowicz first played his way onto the team, then became a starter seven games into his rookie season. He made a stellar debut with New Orleans.

"I caught 12 passes for 156 yards my first game and remained there as a starter for the next six years," he said.

And he owes it all to the impetuousness of youth.

"One of the things I remember most about the whole thing is that I went outside the office after it was all over and my knees were shaking," Abramowicz said. "And I remember saying to myself, 'Whew. That worked.'"

DANNY ABRAMOWICZ

After his first game with the Saints, Abramowicz went on to catch a pass in a then-record 105 straight games and establish the standard by which Saints receivers since have been judged. At the end of his rookie season, he was the club's top receiver with 50 receptions good for 721 yards and six touchdowns.

Abramowicz led New Orleans in receiving in each of the franchise's first five seasons. In 1969, he earned All-Pro honors after leading the NFL with 73 catches for 1,051 yards and seven touchdowns.

Even now, Abramowicz stands a solid second on the Saints all-time receiving list with 309 catches for 4,875 yards and 37 touchdowns.

Abramowicz moved on to the San Francisco 49ers in 1973 in exchange for a pair of draft picks and finished out his on-field career two years later playing for the Buffalo Bills.

He caught 369 passes during his nine-year career for 5,686 yards and 39 touchdowns.

PLAYING HISTORY:
New Orleans Saints 1967-1973
San Francisco 49ers 1973-1974
Buffalo Bills 1975

Love-Hate Relationship

As the nose tackle who anchored the middle of the New York Giants three-man defensive front during their glory days in the 1980s, Jim Burt played out a curious love-hate scenario with Bill Parcells, who was at first a defensive coordinator and then head coach. From the very start, their relationship proved to be a prickly one.

"If I was injured, Parcells would be right in my ear," Burt said. "He'd say, 'When are you going to be back? When?' I'd say, 'Two or three days.' And he'd say, 'Which is it, two or three?' I'd say, 'I don't know for sure.' And he'd say, 'When are you going to know?' That's the way it went until I could hit again."

But, when fully mended, Burt often found it difficult to get back into the lineup. Once, Burt ran up behind Parcells, who was directing the defense from the sideline, and slammed a forearm into his back, knocking the coach onto the field.

"Get that guy the (expletive) out of here," Parcells screamed at no one in particular.

But two plays later he sent Burt in at nose tackle, confident his defensive anchor was healed and eager to play.

Publicly and otherwise, Burt referred to his mentor as the "Big Tuna" and the "Fat Man." None of these less-than-discreet characterizations escaped Parcells' notice. And though he never made mention of them to Burt, they undoubtedly acerbated the tension between them. Nevertheless, Parcells was always willing to help Burt improve on his technique.

"Parcells would get me down in my stance with a 20-pound dumbbell in each hand," Burt said. "Every 10 seconds, I had to snap up and pound the dumbbells against the weight room wall. This went on for 45 minutes until my arms were on fire. It was supposed to improve my technique. Parcells is an absolute psycho. You can expect almost anything from him."

One matter the two men agreed on was the care and feeding of opposing quarterbacks. Whenever Burt smashed to the turf a Joe Theismann, a Randall Cunningham or a Danny White, Parcells whooped it up along with the most ardent of the Giants faithful.

Gotcha!

Jim Burt scored a knockout shot at San Francisco's Joe Montana in a 1986 NFC divisional playoff game won by New York, 49-3.

"I got around (49ers center) Fred Quillan and there was Joe Montana right in my face," Burt recalled. "I flat ran through him. I came up under his shoulder pads and he left the ground. He went flying and I just jumped over him. By the sound of the crowd, I knew it was quite an impact."

Montana was rushed to the hospital with a severe concussion while several of the 49ers players cried, "Cheap shot." San Francisco guard Guy McIntyre told Burt, "We're going to get you for that."

The 49ers did. But not in the way McIntyre intended. In 1989, the 49ers signed Burt and he was in a San Francisco uniform for the 1990 NFC title game between the 49ers and Giants.

GIANTS

Nose tackle Jim Burt (64) and the New York Giants defense gang up on Washington fullback John Riggins (44).

JIM BURT

Jim Burt anchored the New York Giants defensive line for eight seasons after being drafted out of Miami in 1981 and was part of the Giants Super Bowl team in 1986. In 1989, he signed with the San Francisco 49ers as a free agent and helped guide them to a Super Bowl win.

PLAYING HISTORY:
New York Giants 1981-1988
San Francisco 49ers 1989-1991

187

BRING DAD AGAIN NEXT WEEK

Running backs often break off long touchdown plays by "running to daylight." When New York Giants defensive end George Martin made an epic 78-yard interception return for a touchdown in 1986, he described it as something entirely different.

"It was a sunny day when I caught the ball," Martin said, "and it was a cloudy day when I scored."

Martin's score against Denver couldn't have come at a better time. Denver led 6-3 in a defensive struggle and the Broncos were driving late in the first half behind quarterback John Elway.

On first-and-10 at the Giants 13-yard line, with less than a minute to play in the half, Elway tried to throw a pass to Gerald Willhite in the flat. Martin, lined up at left end, read the play immediately.

"The Broncos were setting up a screen play, and I saw the tackle set back," Martin said. "He tried to cut me, which happened all the time. When I saw John throw the ball, I think he was assuming I would be on the ground."

Instead, Martin batted the ball and made the interception.

"I just reached up instinctively and tipped the ball," he said. "It was all very spontaneous."

After tipping the ball with his right hand, Martin had to reach behind himself to gather it in for the interception. His skill as a backup tight end had never come in more handy.

During Martin's career with the Giants, he had been deployed often as a tight end on short-yardage and goal-line situations. He even caught a four-yard scoring pass from Phil Simms in 1980 against the Dallas Cowboys.

"Catching the ball was the easiest part of the play," Martin said of the interception. "I've always had very good hands. I consider catching the ball part of being a complete player."

If making the catch was the easy part, getting to the end zone was another matter for the then 33-year-old Giant. Martin took off to his left, hurdled Willhite and began an endless journey down the sideline to the end zone.

One of the biggest obstacles Martin faced before scoring was Elway. Near midfield, the Denver quarterback was poised to tackle Martin. For a brief moment, Martin showed him the football. Elway missed.

"I thought John would tackle me low, like most quarterbacks would," Martin said, "but he tried to tackle me high. That was a cardinal sin."

Later in the run, Martin faked a lateral to Giant linebacker Lawrence Taylor. Not wanting to risk a fumble, Martin decided to hold onto the ball.

"Lawrence was shouting, 'Give me the ball,'" Martin said. "And I was shouting, 'Give me a block.' My wife asked me later what it was Lawrence and I were yelling at each other."

Taylor ended up as one of several Giants who ran interference for Martin.

Near the end zone, Denver running back Sammy Winder had one last shot at making a tackle. But Giant rookie cornerback Mark Collins threw a block, one that came perilously close to being a clip, and Martin's 14-second, 78-yard trek came to an end.

After crossing the goal line, Martin was mobbed by his jubilant teammates, who suddenly found themselves ahead, 10-6, with 43 seconds left in the half.

The touchdown was important to Martin for personal reasons. His father, George Sr., had flown in from California's Napa Valley to attend his first-ever Giants game.

"After that, (Giant head coach) Bill Parcells, being the superstitious person he is, insisted my father had to be at every game," Martin said. "And he was."

GIANTS FACT: Emlen Tunnell broke his neck playing football at the University of Toledo and was told his playing days were over. Tunnell persisted, however, and became a star at the University of Iowa. The New York Giants signed him in 1948, making Tunnell the club's first African-American player. In 1967, he was selected to the Pro Football Hall of Fame.

GIANTS FACT: Hall of Fame tackle Steve Owens was the captain of the New York Giants in 1927 when the club allowed an all-time record low of just 20 points in 13 games. Owens was named coach of the Giants in 1931 and held the job for 23 years.

GIANTS FACT: Ali Haji-Shiekh kicked 35 field goals in 1983, the most ever by a kicker in one season.

BELOW: Giants defensive end George Martin intercepted a John Elway pass during a game in 1986 and returned it 78 yards for a touchdown. Martin's score, which came just before halftime, put the Giants in front of Denver 10-6.

GEORGE MARTIN

*I*n a 14-year career that ended after the 1988 season, Martin found the end zone seven times. He tallied five touchdowns on defense, one as a tight end and one on special teams. Martin also scored a safety in Super Bowl XXI.

But his 78-yard touchdown, which came in a 19-16 win over the Denver Broncos at Giants Stadium, ranks as one of his finest moments. Martin played for the New York Giants from 1975 to 1988.

Late Hitter

Sam Huff, a premier middle linebacker with the New York Giants in the late 1950s and early 1960s, had a reputation for playing the game a little on the shady side. More specifically, he was a notorious late hitter.

Former Giants safety and Hall of Fame defensive back Emlen Tunnell recalls an incident in which he made a tackle, then continued to lay prone on his victim. When the player protested, Tunnell explained, "I can't get off until Huff gets here."

Not surprisingly, Huff never denied the accusations.

"Yeah, I made some late hits," he said. "But it was nothing illegal. I always got there before the whistle."

An old Huff antagonist was the Green Bay Packers' battering-ram fullback Jim Taylor. Although not blessed with speed, size or moves, Taylor was a mean and dangerous runner who preferred to stomp over people than go around them. Opponents believed Taylor preferred dishing out punishment to picking up yards. When he was not carrying the football, he was also a rugged blocker.

Taylor and Huff clawed, punched, chewed and chopped one another at every opportunity. Both were rough customers not given to backing down.

"Sam was always giving you that little something extra in there," Taylor said. "The elbow, the forearm, the late hit. He kept trying to intimidate you all the time."

"Taylor deserved everything he got," Huff responded. "He would kick and scratch for extra yardage and if there was a slow whistle he would break out of your grasp and be gone."

When the Packers and Giants met for the 1962 NFL title on a raw, windy afternoon in Yankee Stadium, the two men butted heads all day long. Huff got the best of the Green Bay fullback for most of the afternoon. Taylor carried the ball 31 times for 85 yards, an average of just 2.7 yards per carry.

But it was Taylor who scored the Packers' only touchdown and then helped run out the clock in the fourth quarter to give Green Bay a 16-7 win and the NFL Championship. The victory was Taylor's revenge.

"After the gun, I jammed the ball in Sam's facemask," Taylor recalled. "I said, 'Well, that's the game, Mr. Huff, and you can stick this in your ear.' I smiled all the while."

Hearing Taylor's rendition of the incident, Huff countered, "Those weren't exactly his words as I remember. He suggested I stick the ball in a place other than my ear."

GIANTS FACT: The defensive maneuver known as a blitz is also termed a "red dog." The name stems from former Giants linebacker Don "Red" Ettinger, who was one of the first players to attempt the move. Ettinger, who played with New York from 1948 to 1950, had red hair and once said of the blitz, "I was just doggin' the quarterback." Hence, the name red dog.

SAM HUFF

*H*uff joined the Giants in 1956 after being named All-America at the University of West Virginia. During his eight seasons with New York, he played in four Pro Bowls and was named the NFL's top linebacker in 1959.

In 1964, Huff was traded to the Washington Redskins with whom he played until 1967. He retired for a year, then returned for one last season in 1969.

Although renowned as a run-stopper, Huff was an excellent pass defender as well. During his career, he intercepted 30 passes.

In 1982, Huff was elected to the Pro Football Hall of Fame.

PLAYING HISTORY:
New York Giants 1956-1963
Washington Redskins
1964-1967, 1969

GIANTS FACT: Quarterback Y.A. Tittle was considered washed up by the San Francisco 49ers when they traded him to New York in 1961 at the age of 34. Tittle led the Giants to the NFL Eastern Conference title in 1961, 1962 and 1963 and was named the league's MVP in 1961 and 1963.

NEW YORK

Monday Night Nightmare

Millions of viewers tuned into Monday Night Football on November 18, 1985 to watch the New York Giants take on the Washington Redskins. But they were largely unprepared for the mayhem they were about to witness.

Giants linebacker Lawrence Taylor and Redskins quarterback Joe Theismann were the principal players. It was a game neither of them would forget.

Washington had struggled early in the season, but at 5-5 the Redskins were still in the playoff picture. New York, with its dominating defense and ball-control offense, once again was on its way to the postseason tournament.

Nevertheless, from the opening kickoff it proved to be a typical Giants and Redskins game, characterized by pounding line play and top-notch defense. Redskins quarterback Joe Theismann, a longtime nemesis of the New York Giants, was unable to move his team with any consistency in the first quarter.

Then, midway through the second period, Theismann took the snap and rolled to his right. A dangerous quarterback when on the run, Theismann had his gaze fixed on a spread of receivers downfield. He sensed the New York defense closing and tried to sprint around the oncoming defensive line. Suddenly, the 6-foot-3, 240-pound Taylor was in his face.

"Theismann cut back and I got a handful of his jersey from behind," Taylor recalled. "Then (linebacker Harry) Carson hit him from the front. We had him sandwiched between us. But he was still trying to break away when (Gary) Reasons came over the top and landed on him."

Theismann crumpled under the weight of Reasons' descent and his pivot foot became jammed into the stadium turf. All the while he was locked in the combined embrace of Taylor and Carson. With the eyes of millions trained on him via the ABC cameras, Theismann went down, his immobilized leg bending at a terrible angle.

"I heard a pop," Taylor said, "and I thought it was the sound of helmets smacking together. But then I saw his (Theismann's) leg and the broken bones were sticking out. I almost lost it, man. I almost lost it right there. I started screaming at the Redskins' bench. I was halfway across the field, screaming for them to send help."

Remarkably, Theismann remained conscious throughout the ordeal, his competitive instinct still churning inside. As the Redskins team doctor and the training staff worked over him, Theismann wondered aloud about the extent of his injuries. Deep in his heart, he knew what they were. Meanwhile, ABC was running and rerunning the terrible incident in slow motion to the consternation of many viewers. Finally, Theismann was carried off the field.

"Joe (Theismann) yelled at us, 'You guys broke my leg. You broke my leg. But I'll be back,'" Taylor said. "I didn't say anything, but Carson said, 'Not soon, Joe.'"

Carson understood the severity of Theismann's injury. The Redskins quarterback never did make it back to the playing field. His career ended that night at RFK Stadium.

For Taylor, it was not just another night at the ballpark. Although he has been inflicting damage on NFL quarterbacks for years, Theismann's injury was something different.

"I love to hit and get hit," Taylor said. "There's nothing better than a good solid hit. I've put people out in my day, but I don't like to see people get seriously hurt. I don't want to see any broken bones."

Theismann's injury momentarily shook up the perennial All-Pro, but he quickly regained his composure. He still had a game to play. Indeed, Washington rallied around backup quarterback Jay Schroeder after the gruesome injury. He ignited a fire in the Redskins and led his club to a 23-21 victory.

LAWRENCE TAYLOR

*F*or Taylor, 1985 proved to be an All-Pro season. It was just one of a long list of awards the Giants linebacker received during his 13-year career. As a rookie in 1981, he had 10.5 sacks and forced six fumbles, prompting the NFL to name him the league's Most Valuable Defensive Player. Taylor played for the Giants from 1981 to 1993.

GIANTS FACT: Upon purchasing the New York Giants in 1925, new owner Tim Mara commented, "A franchise of any kind in New York should be worth $500."

RIGHT: New York Giants linebacker Lawrence Taylor (56) sacks and strips the football from Washington Redskins quarterback Mark Rypien (11) during a game in 1988.

GIANTS FACT: The New York Giants used sneakers to win the 1934 Championship Game at the Polo Fields. The Giants and Chicago Bears both slipped around on the icy field during the first half of the title clash. Then an ingenious Giants coach sent a clubhouse attendant to nearby Manhattan College to obtain as many pairs of basketball shoes as possible. At the intermission the Giants changed into the sneakers and the added traction allowed New York to score 27 points in the fourth quarter and beat the Bears, 30-13.

RIGHT: In 1986, Lawrence Taylor (56) was selected as the league's MVP. Here, he leaps to put pressure on Minnesota Vikings quarterback Jim McMahon (9).

On Second Thought, Reverse That Reverse

It was the final game of the 1963 season and the New York Jets were going nowhere.

Coach Weeb Ewbank's boys had struggled through a disastrous year, posting a 5-7-1 record. They were just minutes away from chalking up their eighth loss of the campaign at home against Kansas City. Late in the fourth quarter, they trailed the Chiefs, 48-0.

Most of the players on the New York side-lines were struggling to keep warm in the minus-20-degree weather. They'd lost interest in the contest long ago and were ready to pack up and go home for the winter.

Ewbank searched the sideline looking for able-bodied athletes. Like all teams in the early years of the AFL, the Jets carried only 34 players on the roster and Ewbank was quickly running out of men.

With the game out of reach, some of the players ending their careers that day were reluctant to enter the fray. They figured there was no sense in sustaining a debilitating injury in a vain quest for a victory that was out of reach. Ewbank understood, but was forced to play linebackers at defensive back and guards at linebacker.

With only minutes remaining in the game, the Jets had the ball one last time. But for Ewbank and most of the Jets veterans, the only logical strategy left was "to run the clock out and get the hell out of Dodge," said former Jets defensive back Bill Baird. Ewbank sent in taxi squad quarterback Eddie Chlebek to carry out his strategy.

But the 22-year-old Chlebek, in his first and only pro season, was eager to make something happen. He wanted to make an impression. He entered the game and promptly decided to do things his way. Chlebek called a flanker reverse with Don Maynard carrying the football.

In the huddle, Chlebek's call was greeted with blank stares. "You've got to be crazy!" Maynard said. But the quarterback stuck with the call and the Jets broke the huddle.

The ball was snapped and Chlebek made a superb fake to the fullback, crashing straight through the line. Chlebek took two more steps into the backfield and was ready to hand the ball off to Maynard, who was supposed to be circling back to the quarterback and then around the opposite end on the reverse.

But Maynard was still in his stance. He refused to move and Chlebek was stuck with the football. While Chlebek momentarily panicked, the gun sounded, ending the game. Just then, several Kansas City linemen broke through and smothered the rookie quarterback.

But the Jets horrid 1963 season was finally over.

As Don Maynard figured it, the game may have been a disaster, but at least he wouldn't be spending the offseason rehabilitating an injury caused by a taxi squad quarterback's ridiculous flanker reverse call.

Chlebek's career ended that day. In his sole season of pro football, he completed two of four passes for five yards.

DON MAYNARD

Maynard's 15-year career began in 1957 when he was drafted in the ninth round by the New York Giants. After being used mostly as a kick return specialist by the Giants, Maynard took his skills to the Canadian Football League for a year, then returned and was signed by the New York Titans, later the Jets, in the new American Football League.

Maynard's career reached its peak in the late 1960s when quarterback Joe Namath joined the Jets. In 1967, Maynard had his best season, hauling in 71 passes for 1,434 yards and 10 touchdowns. The following season, he played a vital role in the Jets' run to Super Bowl III. He played in three AFL All-Star games.

Maynard nabbed 633 passes for 11,834 yards in his career. When he retired in 1973, he was the leading receiver in NFL history, although the record has since been broken. Maynard also set the NFL mark for most 100-yard receiving games with 50.

In 1987, he was selected to the Pro Football Hall of Fame.

PLAYING HISTORY:
New York Giants 1958
Hamilton Tiger-Cats (CFL) 1959
New York Jets 1960-1972
St. Louis Cardinals 1973

JETS FACT: Wide receiver Don Maynard was the first player ever signed by the New York Titans. Maynard was playing in the Canadian Football League at the time.

Don Maynard was quarterback Joe Namath's favorite receiver with the New York Jets.

Faking It

Jim Turner played in a pair of Super Bowls, including Super Bowl III where his three field goals helped the New York Jets defeat the Baltimore Colts in one of pro football's biggest upsets. But the most exciting moment of his 16-year NFL career came when he unexpectedly scored a touchdown.

It happened during the 1977 season when Turner was wearing a Denver Broncos uniform. The Broncos were on their way to Super Bowl XII that year, but to get there they had to go through their hated division rivals, the Oakland Raiders.

Turner had learned the kicking trade as a boy growing up in Crockett, California, about 25 miles from Oakland. So this mid-season game at the Oakland Coliseum was a homecoming for him.

With quarterback Craig Morton at the controls, the Broncos took an early 14-7 lead. Late in the first half, Denver was threatening again. With about a minute left before intermission, the Broncos lined up for a 22-yard field goal attempt. It was a chip shot for Turner, who led the NFL in scoring twice and retired as the fifth-leading scorer in league history.

The ball was snapped to holder Norris Weese and Turner stepped toward the football. As his right leg swung forward, Weese sprung from his crouch and took off with the ball looking for a receiver. It was a fake field goal attempt. The Raiders were caught by surprise.

As the Oakland defenders tried to recover, Turner snuck out of the backfield and raced down the left sideline. There wasn't a Raider within sight. He was all alone and waved his arms wildly, hoping for Weese to spot him.

Weese, the Broncos' backup quarterback, saw Turner and fired a high spiral. It was a routine catch for the former wide receiver. Turner nabbed it unmolested and danced into the end zone. He then added the extra point to give Denver a 21-7 lead.

The Raiders were dumbfounded. The only thing that angered them more than losing a football game was being embarrassed, especially in front of their home fans. Being duped on a fake field goal and having a 37-year-old kicker catch a touchdown pass against them was a good way to arouse their hatred.

As the teams left the field at halftime, harsh words were exchanged between the opposing players. The Raiders made it clear that Turner was a marked man.

Early in the second half, Denver drove into field goal range and once again Turner and Weese trotted onto the field. This time the Raiders were ready.

As Turner lined up the kick, he was taunted unmercifully by the Oakland defenders. His masculinity was questioned as well as his mother's heritage. Former 6-foot-8, 280-pound defensive lineman John Matuszak was particularly vocal.

"Matuszak yelled, 'If you try to fake another one, we're going to break your (expletive) legs,'" Turner recalled. "We decided to kick it."

Turner's 37-yard field goal attempt split the uprights and Denver went on to win 30-7.

But the seed was planted. And the animosity between the two clubs still exists.

JIM TURNER

During his 16-year career, Turner was one of the league's most accurate kickers. He made 96 percent of his 544 extra point attempts and 62 percent of his 488 field goal attempts. He was pro football's leading scorer in 1968 with 145 points and in 1969 with 125.

Turner retired as the fifth highest scorer of all time with 1,439 points.

PLAYING HISTORY:
New York Jets 1964-1970
Denver Broncos 1971-1979

Jim Turner's three field goals in Super Bowl III proved to be the difference as the New York Jets became the first AFL team to win a Super Bowl, shocking the Baltimore Colts 16-7.

JETS FACT: Punter Steve O'Neal got off a 98-yard boomer against Denver in 1969, a league record.

JETS FACT: The New York Jets were originally called the Titans and wore blue and gold uniforms. They were renamed the Jets prior to the 1963 season and changed their colors to green and white.

Looking back on his early years with the New York Jets, when Broadway Joe Namath and the rest of the club were well-known for their late-night antics and postgame parties, Hall of Fame running back John Riggins (44) said, "I thought you had to be hung over to play in the NFL."

BROADWAY JOE'S GUARANTEE

"**D**id we really think we could win?" The full rounded features of Weeb Ewbank, former head coach of the 1968 American Football League champion New York Jets, relaxed into a knowing smile. "Yes, we thought so right from day one."

He referred, of course, to the Jets 16-7 upset of the heavily favored NFL champion Baltimore Colts in Super Bowl III, a victory which did much to hasten the merger of the two leagues.

"As you'll recall, we won the AFL crown in a cliffhanger with the Oakland Raiders 27-23." Ewbank reminisced. "But there wasn't any letdown with the players. Early the next week, we began preparing in earnest for the Colts. The coaches and the team looked at a lot of film for several days. Finally, (linebacker) Larry Grantham, I believe it was him, stood up and said, 'We've seen enough, Coach. These guys aren't all that much. We can beat them.' And that was our attitude right up to the game."

There were a number of "trash talkers" on the Jets club such as defensive back Johnny Sample, kicker Jim Turner and defensive end Gerry Philbin. But none of them triggered the Colts' ire quite so much as quarterback "Broadway Joe" Namath, who was as quick with his lip as with the release of a pass.

"I'm a pretty confident guy," Namath said at the time. "I know what my abilities are. I know that if you add up all the things a quarterback needs—the ability to throw, to read defenses, to call plays, to lead the team—nobody has ever played the quarterback position any better than I do."

The Colts snorted with disdain. Namath didn't compare to their own Johnny Unitas. Soon angry

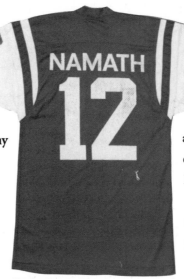

Photo from Richard Wolffers Auctions, Inc., San Francisco

rebuttals and threatening sounds began emanating from the Baltimore players. The Jets responded in kind and the media war was on. When both teams switched their training sites to Miami the week preceding the matchup in the Orange Bowl, the verbal fusillade further intensified. And then Namath dropped the bomb.

In response to reporters' questions, he said, "Sure, I think we can win. In fact, I absolutely guarantee it."

A few nights later Namath, Turner and company were enjoying several after-hours refreshments when they encountered Colts defensive end Lou Michaels and his party.

"Michaels was for having it out right there," Namath said. "He had a mind to force feed me some knuckles to shut my mouth. But cooler heads prevailed and we sat down to a few drinks. We ended up driving him and his buddies to their hotel. They were feeling pretty good."

"I didn't try to control what the players told the media," Ewbank said. "The coaches merely cautioned them to think before speaking. I did tell them not to pay attention to what I was saying publicly."

For the benefit of the masses, Ewbank properly extolled the many strengths of the Colts and wondered aloud how his club might hope to fare against such an armada of might.

"Our coaching staff studied films until the day of the game," Ewbank said. "I can't remember ever spending so much time in the dark. One night, while a few of us were out for a walk, this guy comes up and says, 'Hey, do you want to see some filthy films?' I said, 'No thanks. We've been looking at them for weeks.' He

didn't know what to make of that."

But the long hours spent sitting beside a projector were well spent.

"We caught them off guard," Ewbank said. "Instead of going downfield to George Sauer and Don Maynard, we opted for a ball-control attack. Fullback Matt Snell ran mostly through their right side for 121 yards and we threw just enough to keep them off balance. And our defense did a great job of stopping whatever they tried."

At the final gun, Turner, who had kicked three field goals, raised his arms in a triumphant gesture and shouted to the vanquished foe, "Welcome to the AFL."

For Namath, it was the turning point in a legendary career. Although he was in his fourth season with the Jets, he was known more for his wild bachelor living than his quick release and cannon-like arm. Super Bowl III made him a national celebrity. In the biggest game of his career, Namath completed 17 of 28 passes for 206 yards and was named the MVP.

Joe Namath (12) scrambles in a vain attempt to elude an Oakland Raider defender.

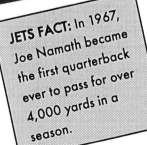

JETS FACT: In 1967, Joe Namath became the first quarterback ever to pass for over 4,000 yards in a season.

JOE NAMATH

Namath continued to lead the Jets until 1976, despite suffering a string of injuries. He retired in 1977. During his career, he completed 1,886 passes for 27,663 yards and 173 touchdowns. In 1969, he was named to the AFL's all-time team.

Namath was elected to the Pro Football Hall of Fame in 1985.

PLAYING HISTORY:
New York Jets 1965-1976
Los Angeles Rams 1977

199

The Jets were 18-point underdogs to the Baltimore Colts in Super Bowl III, but Joe Namath (12) completed 17 of 28 passes for 206 yards in the game and New York stunned the Colts, 16-7. Here, Colts defensive lineman Bubba Smith (78) tries to knock down one of Namath's passes.

In 1971, the Oakland Raiders finished out
of first place for the first time in five years.

Los Angeles Rams programs
from games with the
Washington Redskins and
New York Yanks.

An artist captures the intensity of Oakland Raiders quarterback Ken Stabler. He was named AFC Player of the Year in
1974 and 1976.

Tom Harmon, old number 88, is
shown on the cover of Sport
magazine with his wife. Harmon
won the Heisman Trophy at
University of Michigan in 1940.
After serving in the armed forces
during World War II, Harmon
joined the Los Angeles Rams in
1946 but played just two seasons
of pro football.

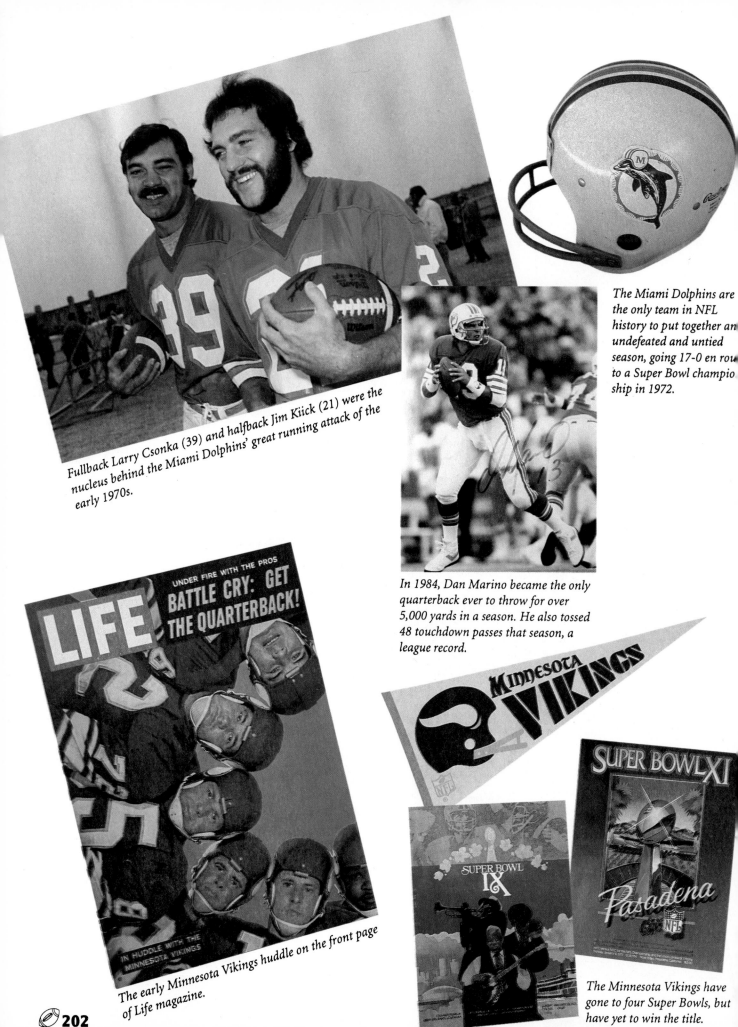

Fullback Larry Csonka (39) and halfback Jim Kiick (21) were the nucleus behind the Miami Dolphins' great running attack of the early 1970s.

The Miami Dolphins are the only team in NFL history to put together an undefeated and untied season, going 17-0 en rou to a Super Bowl champio ship in 1972.

In 1984, Dan Marino became the only quarterback ever to throw for over 5,000 yards in a season. He also tossed 48 touchdown passes that season, a league record.

UNDER FIRE WITH THE PROS

BATTLE CRY: GET THE QUARTERBACK!

LIFE

IN HUDDLE WITH THE MINNESOTA VIKINGS

The early Minnesota Vikings huddle on the front page of Life magazine.

MINNESOTA VIKINGS

SUPER BOWL IX

SUPER BOWL XI

Pasadena

The Minnesota Vikings have gone to four Super Bowls, but have yet to win the title.

NEW YORK GIANTS

Beginning his career with the New York Giants in 1956, Sam Huff became one of the most feared middle linebackers in the game.

Sam Huff

The Giants -our team

The New York Giants of the late 1950s, pictured here, included defensive linemen Andy Robustelli (81), Rosey Grier (76), Dick Modzelewski (77) and Jim Katcavage (75), quarterback George Shaw (15), halfback Frank Gifford (16), safety Jim Patton (20), halfback Dick Lynch (22), halfback Alex Webster (29) and fullback Mel Triplett (33).

A New York Giants helmet, signed by the Super Bowl XXV champions.

Frank Gifford

During his stint as a halfback with the New York Giants in the 1950s, Frank Gifford was almost as famous for his matinee-idol good looks as his football playing ability.

The Biggest Upset: New York Jets quarterback Joe Namath (12) gets off a pass while under pressure from the Baltimore Colts in Super Bowl III. Namath guaranteed his Jets would beat the heavily-favored Colts and they did, 16-7.

During his career, Joe Namath completed 1,886 passes for 27,663 yards and 173 touchdowns.

Photo from Richard Wolffers Auctions, Inc., San Francisco

A program and ticket from Super Bowl III at Miami's Orange Bowl. Admission was only $12 and fans got their money's worth.

Los Angeles Rams flanker Elroy "Crazy Legs" Hirsch stretches to grab a Bob Waterfield pass while Ray Pelfrey defends during a game against the Green Bay Packers in 1951.

Sammy Baugh was a great quarterback and also one of the top punters in NFL history. His 45.1-yard career punting average ranks as the best ever.

The Los Angeles Rams pass-catching duo of Tom Fears (99) and Elroy "Crazy Legs" Hirsch (40) was the best in the NFL in the late 1940s and early 1950s.

One-Hit Wonder

In 1960, the Eagles enjoyed their last championship season. En route to the league title, they met the New York Giants in an important Eastern Conference contest on a windswept November afternoon at Yankee Stadium. The Giants were only a half game behind Philadelphia in the standings and boasted a potent scoring attack featuring versatile running back and receiver Frank Gifford.

Chuck Bednarik was one of the last pro players still playing on both sides of the ball. Offensively, he held forth at center as perhaps the best blocking pivot man in the NFL. When the defensive unit took the field, he simply switched to the left linebacker spot.

"We had a 17-10 lead in the fourth quarter, but the Giants were moving the ball with the clock winding down," Bednarik said. "Gifford was lined up outside. And at the snap he took the handoff and ran a little down-and-in pattern. When he cut over, I came up fast from the left side."

The result was one of the most controversial hits in the history of pro football.

"We met head-on," Bednarik said. "I don't believe he ever saw me. I think of that situation being like a one-way street with a Mack truck hitting a Volkswagen. I knocked out Gifford and preserved a 17-10 win."

In a wild surge of emotion at having saved the Eagles' victory, Bednarik thrust his arms skyward and danced happily.

The following morning, sports pages across the country ran a news wire photograph of Bednarik standing over the prostrate Gifford with arms raised in a gesture of celebration. The picture made it look as though he was elated at having seriously injured the Giants' star performer.

"Nothing could be further from the truth," Bednarik said. "I was excited because Gifford had fumbled and we made the recovery to ensure victory. I didn't know he was badly hurt. Not until a few days later did I learn that he had suffered a fractured skull."

Gifford missed all of the 1961 league schedule due to complications from that vicious tackle. Through the years more than a few media types have persisted in referring to it as a "cheap shot."

"Even today, people still insist that I blindsided Frank," Bednarik said. "I hit Gifford a clean, legitimate shot. The films show that. But I guess there'll always be someone to claim otherwise."

At least one former Giant disputes the cheap-shot theory.

"Linebackers dream about that kind of tackle," said former New York Giants Hall of Famer Sam Huff. "A good, clean shot that takes out the opponent's star. And Chuck got one."

Ironically, Bednarik retired after the 1959 season, thinking the Eagles had no title hopes in the near future. He changed his mind just before the start of the 1960 season and reported to play for them.

CHUCK BEDNARIK

*T*he son of a steelworker, Bednarik was an All-American at the University of Pennsylvania and received the Maxwell Award as the College Player of the Year in 1948. The Philadelphia Eagles made him the first collegiate player drafted that year.

During his 13 seasons with Philadelphia, Bednarik played in eight Pro Bowls and was a member of two NFL championship teams. He intercepted 20 passes during his career and returned one for a touchdown. Bednarik was named the All-NFL center for the league's 50th anniversary.

In 1967, Bednarik was named to the Pro Football Hall of Fame.

PLAYING HISTORY:
Philadelphia Eagles 1949-1961

Chuck Bednarik of the Philadelphia Eagles was one of the last men in NFL history to play on both sides of the ball. He was a center on offense and linebacker on defense.

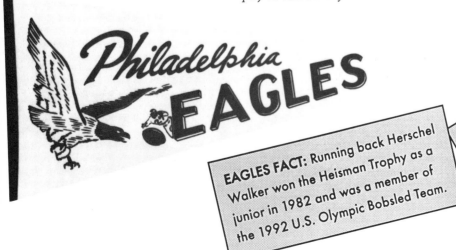

EAGLES FACT: Running back Herschel Walker won the Heisman Trophy as a junior in 1982 and was a member of the 1992 U.S. Olympic Bobsled Team.

EAGLES FACT: Former Pro Bowl running back Tim Brown tied an NFL record against the Dallas Cowboys in 1966 by returning two kickoffs 93 yards and 90 yards for touchdowns in the same game.

On a Clear Day, You Can See the End Zone

Bright and sunny with patchy fog. That was the weather forecast at Chicago's Soldier Field on New Year's Eve, 1988 for a playoff game between the Philadelphia Eagles and the Chicago Bears.

"I remember it was clear and warm when we started," said Eagles quarterback Randall Cunningham, who completed 54 percent of his 560 passes that season. "Then all of a sudden I remember coming from the sideline to the field and looking to one end of the stadium. Players were pointing that way and I looked up and saw a huge cloud. I thought the stadium was on fire. A few minutes later, I realized what it was— fog—and I could barely see anything."

The thick fog rendered reporters, broadcasters and both teams nearly helpless. Like an eerie scene from a horror film, the fog rolled off Lake Michigan and poured over the rim of the stadium.

Nevertheless, Chicago was able to take an early lead, when Mike Tomczak hit Dennis McKinnon on a 64-yard touchdown pass and Neal Anderson added a four-yard run.

By halftime, as both teams left the field with Chicago leading 17-9, the entire field was smothered in a thick gray mist.

In the second half, visibility from the stadium press box was nearly zero, so newspaper reporters were permitted onto the sidelines to view the game. Radio and television accounts of the contest were now sketchy at best. And the players themselves were incredulous.

"A pass would literally come shooting out of the fog at you," said Philadelphia running back Keith Byars, who managed to top all receivers that day with nine pass receptions for 103 yards. "You'd go out for a pass, not more than 10 to 15 yards because that's all you could see. Then you'd look up and all of a sudden the ball would come out of nowhere. It was like batting against a pitching machine, where the ball just squirts out at you."

"It was wild," said Eagles center David Alexander, who was in his second year with the club. "You could see only half the field. Guys would just disappear. I didn't know where the sidelines were. It was definitely the strangest thing I've ever encountered."

Lack of visibility stymied both clubs in the second half as they were unable to move the ball. Each team settled for a field goal and the Bears went on to win the game, 20-12.

Cunningham supplied the bulk of the Eagles offense, passing for 407 yards, most of it to the backs and tight ends. All of Philadelphia's points came on Luis Zendejas' field goals.

"The weather wasn't an excuse," said Cunningham, "but why did we even play the game? People couldn't see it on television. We couldn't even see each other on the field. It was just a bizarre day."

KEITH BYARS

*I*n the 1988 "Fog Bowl," Keith Byars was the Eagles leading receiver and rusher. Besides grabbing nine passes, he carried the ball seven times for 34 yards.

Since that game, Byars has established himself as one of the league's most versatile players, having seen action as a halfback, fullback, wide receiver and tight end. He joined the Eagles in 1986 as a first-round draft pick from Ohio State.

EAGLES FACT: Al Nelson returned a Dallas Cowboys field goal attempt 101 yards for a touchdown, a league record, in 1971.

BELOW: Philadelphia Eagles running back Keith Byars (41) scrambles over Washington Redskins defensive tackle Darryl Grant for a touchdown.

ZANY ANTICS, SURREALIST DIVISION

Physically, Tim Rossovich had it all. He stood 6-foot-4, tipped the scale at 245 pounds and was blessed with good speed for a middle linebacker. He also filled in admirably at defensive end. Color him tough, durable, determined.

Psychologically, Tim Rossovich was in a different world. Some said he had room for rent between his ears. In reality, he possessed plenty of smarts. Eagles teammate Tom Woodeshick said it best: "All of Rossy's lights go on upstairs. It's just that some of them don't connect with anything." Succinctly put, he could be a grade-A weirdo.

When the Eagles selected Rossovich out of USC with their number-one pick in 1968, they knew what they were getting. At USC, he had a propensity for trashing lockers with his head, eating lit cigarettes, chewing glass beer mugs and hailing passing motorists clad only in a thin film of shaving cream. But they figured he would change in the pros. They figured wrong.

During his rookie year, the club took him to task for his hedgehog hairdo, a Viva Zapata mustache and his odd practice of sleeping naked on motel room floors with a compass at his head. The latter aberration didn't go over very big with the cleaning service ladies.

"The compass is so I can sleep with my head pointing due north," Rossovich once said. "That way magnetic waves can flow through my body and revitalize me."

On one occasion, Rossovich was seen walking through downtown Philly clothed in a wizard's outfit that consisted of a long flowing cape and pointed slippers with jingling bells. He also had an affinity for Daniel Boone-style clothing and psychedelic ensembles.

Another time, a young fan approached him during training camp while he was sunning himself between workouts. She was startled to see painted across his chest the words, "Unidentified Frying Object."

When he entered the Eagles locker room, a chorus of voices would intone, "H-e-e-e-r-e's Timbo!" More often than not he would regale his teammates with such histrionics as diving headlong into the whirlpool tank, even though it was occupied, or opening bottles with his teeth.

"Timbo totally disrupted a meeting just before an important game with the New York Giants once," recalled Bill Bradley, a former Eagles safety. "He stood up to speak and a sparrow flew out of his mouth. The coaching staff just

about lost it."

During road trips, Rossovich was not above doing headstands in airport lobbies or spooking hotel patrons with his Dracula disguise.

But his most memorable and dangerous escapade was at a party hosted by Steve Sabol, head of NFL Films. Rossovich came to the door completely aflame. As the guests screamed in horror, two men threw him to the floor and smothered the fire. Still smoldering, he got to his feet and, looking around, said, "Sorry, I must have the wrong apartment." Then he calmly made his exit.

"Rossovich had it all down pat," Sabol said. "He knew the flames would burn up to 40 seconds without injuring him. At about 30 seconds, two of his friends put them out."

"I can't explain what I do beyond the fact I live my life to enjoy myself," Rossovich said. "I have more energy than I know what to do with. I can't just sit around. I get bored."

TIM ROSSOVICH

*T*im Rossovich was a first-round draft pick of the Philadelphia Eagles in 1968 out of University of Southern California, where he was an all-league defensive end. He was converted to linebacker by the Eagles and was selected to the Pro Bowl in 1970. In 1971, Rossovich was traded to the San Diego Chargers in exchange for a first-round draft pick.

PLAYING HISTORY:

Philadelphia Eagles 1968-1971
San Diego Chargers 1972-1973

BELOW: A poster advertising an early 1930s Eagles-Packers game.

PHILADELPHIA

Eagles

PHILADELPHIA
Eagles

Photo from Richard Wolffers Auctions, Inc. San Francisco

NATIONAL LEAGUE FOOTBALL
CITY STADIUM - GREEN BAY

RECORD OF GAMES		
1925 - Packers	7 --- Philadelphia	13
1926 - Packers	14 --- Philadelphia	19
1927 - Packers	17 --- Philadelphia	9
1928 - Packers	9 --- Philadelphia	19
1928 - Packers	0 --- Philadelphia	2
1929 - Packers	14 --- Philadelphia	2
1929 - Packers	0 --- Philadelphia	0
1930 - Packers	27 --- Philadelphia	12
1930 - Packers	25 --- Philadelphia	7

SUNDAY OCT. 18

PHILADELPHIA VS. GREEN BAY PACKERS

Packers' Line Faces Crucial Test

The Packers' great line which has swept all before it this season faces a crucial test in the Philadelphia game as the Easterners have a front wall which they claim is the best in the country. Such stars as Bull Behman, Nate Barrager, Frank Racis, Bill Fleckenstein, Art Jones, Ray Tackwell and Pat Leary should make things interesting for Dilweg, Stahlman, Michalske & Co.

Every Seat in Park Reserved

Kickoff 2 o'clock Admission Prices: $1, 1.25, 1.50, $2 Buy Your Tickets Early and Be Sure of a Seat

Fly Like an Eagle

Even now, so long after it happened, All-Pro cornerback Eric Allen is breathless when he talks about "The Play."

It was a play that saved the day for the Eagles in the fourth game of the 1993 season. With time running out in the fourth quarter and the Eagles trailing the New York Jets, quarterback Boomer Esiason was at the controls of

Philadelphia Eagles cornerback Eric Allen (21) races into the end zone after intercepting a pass against New Orleans. Allen has become a fixture in the Pro Bowl after seven NFL seasons.

another New York drive. A touchdown would put the game out of reach. A long, time-consuming drive would kill the clock.

Esiason dropped back and unleashed a pass to Jets' wide receiver Chris Burkett at the Philadelphia Eagles six-yard line. Eagles All-Pro cornerback Eric Allen anticipated the play perfectly. He stepped in front of Burkett, made the interception, then embarked on the run of his life.

The speedy defensive back bounced off one Jet at the 10-yard line, cut inside at the 15, hopped over a groping Esiason at the 25, then zigged left up the sideline, eluding one last Jets player before hitting the afterburners.

Allen's return measured 94 yards in football distance, about 175 yards in reality. The touchdown put the Eagles in front and capped a miraculous 21-point comeback by Philadelphia. It was a lead they would not let slip away as the Eagles came away with a dramatic victory.

In the end zone, a jubilant Allen spotted injured quarterback Randall Cunningham. Just an hour earlier, Cunningham had left the game after suffering a broken left fibula. In an emotional moment, Allen handed the Eagles quarterback the football.

"All I wanted to do was catch my breath, but then I saw Randall," Allen said. "It had been such a rotten day for us until then. I wanted to make something happen on that play. It was like that game you play as a kid when you have the ball and try to stay alive. That's how it felt. It's something I'll never forget."

The Money Game

Randall Cunningham spent the early morning hours shaking and trying to keep his cool as the Eagles prepared to take on the Washington Redskins in the second game of the 1989 season.

But it wasn't the Redskins that had Cunningham worried. He had been summoned to the office of Philadelphia Eagles owner Norman Braman, who wanted to make his star quarterback a very rich man. He wanted Cunningham to sign a contract extension worth $15 million over five years.

"It was scary," Cunningham said. "All that money. And then I was supposed to keep my head on straight for the game."

Signing a new contract turned out to be the easy part of Cunningham's day as the Redskins dominated the game in the early going, building a 20-point halftime lead. Cunningham tried to rally the Eagles while Washington varied its blitz scheme, shifted zone coverages, and kept a linebacker in to spy the shifty quarterback and limit his running and scrambling. The result? Washington sacked Cunningham four times and held him to six yards on seven rushes.

The Redskins were unable to nullify Cunningham's arm, though, and in the second half he came to life. He turned a 20-point deficit into a victory with the best game of his career. The Philadelphia quarterback blistered the Redskins by completing 34 of 46 passes for a franchise-record 447 yards and five touchdowns. Three of his touchdown passes came in the fourth quarter as the Eagles rallied to win 42-37. Cunningham's performance earned him NFL Player of the Week honors.

"I think this was probably as good as I could play a game," Cunningham said after the contest. "Now I think I'm going to go to sleep for a year. I've been through a lot."

"It doesn't matter what you do against Cunningham," said former Washington defensive end Dexter Manley. "The playbook doesn't matter. He does things that don't exist in playbooks. He had a great day."

But Manley didn't realize the magnitude of Number 12's day. To understand its significance he would have needed access to Cunningham's checkbook.

"I don't know how many of those kinds of days I can take," said Cunningham, who threw his fifth touchdown pass with 52 seconds remaining to win the game. "By the end of the day, I was exhausted."

The Immaculate Reception

Franco Harris, Jack Tatum and Frenchy Fuqua will be linked forever with one of pro football's magical moments. The "Immaculate Reception" was a play so unbelievable, so miraculous, religious terminology is needed to describe it.

It happened in 1972 when the Oakland Raiders were on the verge of beating the Pittsburgh Steelers in the first round of the AFC playoffs. Oakland took a slim 7-6 lead late in the fourth quarter after a 30-yard touchdown run by quarterback Ken Stabler.

After the ensuing kickoff, Pittsburgh quarterback Terry Bradshaw took over with less than a minute on the clock. He quickly moved the Steelers to the 40-yard line and, with time left for one last play, took the snap and dropped back to pass.

"I saw Bradshaw scrambling around," former Raiders safety Jack Tatum said. "I was covering the tight end on that play and I saw Frenchy Fuqua out of the corner of my eye."

Fuqua swung out of the backfield and ran a curl pattern toward the middle of the field. Bradshaw spotted him and released the pass just as he was decked by a squadron of Raider linemen.

"Once the pass was in the air, I made a break on the ball," Tatum continued. "I just didn't want Frenchy to catch it. I wasn't thinking about an interception or anything. I just wanted to lay a good hit on him and knock the ball loose."

Tatum, Fuqua and the football simultaneously converged in midair. Tatum knocked Fuqua senseless and the ball bounced off the men high into the darkening sky.

"When I made the hit, I figured the game was

Photo from Richard Wolffers Auctions, Inc., San Francisco

over," Tatum said. "I didn't really see the ball after that. I remember a couple of us jumping around in celebration for a second. Then I saw Franco (Harris) running down the sideline. My first thought was, 'Boy, he's in a hurry to get to the locker room.' Then I saw (Raider defensive back) Jimmy Warren chasing him and it clicked that Franco had the football."

Tatum's ferocious hit sent the football floating in the direction of Harris, who was running an outlet pattern near the sideline. The Steelers running back made the catch just inches off the turf and raced 60 yards for the winning score.

"I knew the game was over if I didn't make something happen," Harris said. "The ball was just hanging there and I was lucky enough to be in the right place at the right time."

There was one problem. According to the NFL rules of that time, a receiver could not make a legal catch if the ball was deflected or touched by one of his own men. The stunned Raiders argued vehemently that the football bounced off Fuqua, making Harris' catch illegal. They wanted the touchdown nullified. After a long discussion, the officials ruled in favor of Pittsburgh and the touchdown stood.

"After the score, Tatum grabbed me by the shoulder pads and shook me and said, 'You touched that football, didn't you, Frenchy? You touched that football. Go tell them,'" Fuqua said. "I was so shook up I almost did."

"I've seen Frenchy a few times since then and asked him if that ball touched him, but he won't say," Tatum said with a chuckle. "He'll take that secret to his grave."

FRANCO HARRIS

For Harris, the "Immaculate Reception" marked the beginning of a long and celebrated career. In 1972, the Steelers first-round draft pick had the first of his eight 1,000-yard rushing seasons.

Harris was an important part of Pittsburgh's four Super Bowl winning teams during the 1970s. He holds the Super Bowl record for most career rushing yards at 354.

During his 13 years in the NFL, Harris carried 2,949 times for 12,120 yards and 91 touchdowns. In addition, he caught 307 passes for 2,287 yards. He appeared in nine Pro Bowls.

In 1990, Harris was elected to the Pro Football Hall of Fame.

PLAYING HISTORY:
Pittsburgh Steelers 1972-1983
Seattle Seahawks 1984

STEELERS FACT: Art Rooney paid $2,500 in 1933 for an NFL franchise in Pittsburgh. The 32-year-old Rooney named his club the Pirates, after the baseball team, then changed it to the Steelers in 1941. The Steelers did not win a championship until 1972, the club's 40th anniversary.

STEELERS FACT: The Steelers' "Steel Curtain" of the 1970s was one of the best defensive units in history. In the final nine games of the 1976 season, it held opponents to just 28 points. The Steelers shut out five teams and gave up only two touchdowns.

JOHN "FRENCHY" FUQUA

Originally signed by the New York Giants in 1969 out of Morgan State, Fuqua joined the Piitsburgh Steelers in 1970 and was the club's leading rusher in 1970 and 1971.

During his eight-year career, he carried 719 times for 3,031 yards and 21 touchdowns. Fuqua was also an excellent receiver and hauled in 135 passes for 1,247 yards.

PLAYING HISTORY:
New York Giants 1969
Pittsburgh Steelers 1970-1976

BELOW: Franco Harris takes off with the ball following the "Immaculate Reception" in the 1972 AFC divisional playoffs.

That's Mr. Cornerback to You

The Pittsburgh Steelers of the 1970s defined the word intimidation. They not only beat teams before the game began, they had young players questioning whether they even wanted to take the field.

Pittsburgh cast a spell over a young and wildly unsuccessful San Francisco 49ers team in 1978. The 49ers went through two coaches and a pair of general managers that year on its way to winning just two games.

The Steelers had already won two Super Bowls. They would win two more before the decade was over.

Late in the season, the 49ers were content just to play out the remainder of a horrible campaign. But this game was on Monday Night Football. The entire country was watching during prime time.

Mike Shumann was a rookie wide receiver for the 49ers that year and remembers the wind-swept night better than his own name. Early in the game, the 49ers broke the huddle and hurried to the line of scrimmage.

"When we got to the line of scrimmage, the Steelers were still in the huddle," Shumann said. "But we were so intimidated we waited for them to get to the line and get ready."

Shumann was split wide on the play and saw future Hall of Fame defensive back Mel Blount creep out his way. Blount was a master at the bump-and-run, before the NFL outlawed such pass coverage, and routinely mauled wideouts on their way downfield. At 6-foot-3 and 210 pounds, he had the strength of a nose tackle.

"He was the biggest cornerback I'd ever seen," Shumann said. "As he was coming toward me, he just keep getting bigger and bigger. By the time he lined up in front of me, he looked more like 6-foot-9."

Blount's glare was enough to melt the black bars of Shumann's face mask. In a voice so deep it seemed to come from beneath Candlestick Park, he said, "Where are you going, son?"

"I was so intimidated I didn't know what to say," Shumann said. "I just looked back at him and said, 'Wherever you want me to go, Mr. Blount.'"

The ball was snapped and Shumann skimmed past Blount to run a crossing pattern. He was momentarily open, but quarterback Steve DeBerg never saw him. DeBerg rifled a pass over the middle where Steelers linebacker Jack Ham snatched it for an interception.

After the pass theft, middle linebacker Jack Lambert raced over to Ham. Lambert, who was once described as "Count Dracula in cleats," grabbed Ham by the shoulder pads and violently hoisted him to his feet.

The 49ers receiver heard a clatter as Lambert forced his face mask into Ham's. Shumann could see a mist of sweat and spit flying from Lambert's face and mouth into the chilly night air. Lambert was missing two front teeth and his open mouth looked like a monstrous black hole. He was yelling wildly at Ham.

"I though he was going to congratulate Ham," Shumann said. "Then I hear him yelling, 'Hey, that was my damn interception, you son of a bitch. Stay in your own zone!' I couldn't believe it."

The Steelers went on to wax San Francisco 24-7. After the game, Shumann trudged down the tunnel lost in thought.

"I was making about 25 grand at the time and I remember thinking, 'I can make more money bartending. Do I really want to play in this league with those psychos?'"

STEELERS FACT: Steelers middle linebacker Jack Lambert was one of the most ferocious players in NFL history. A native of Ohio and a graduate of Kent State University, Lambert always had a special place in his heart for games against the Cleveland Browns.

The Browns had lost every game they ever played at Pittsburgh's Three Rivers Stadium—the streak was 10 and counting—but Cleveland was in the midst of a fine season behind the quarterbacking of Brian Sipe.

In the first half, Sipe was flushed out of the pocket and was rolling to his right as he looked downfield for a receiver. About two yards from the sideline, Lambert came out of nowhere and drilled Sipe with a wicked shot that was brutal but within the rules. Lambert was thrown out of the game anyway and the fans at Three Rivers Stadium went wild.

After the game, Lambert was asked if he knew why he had been ejected.

"The official said I hit Sipe too hard," Lambert said.

"Did you hit him hard?" a reporter asked.

"I hit him as hard as I could."

JACK LAMBERT

Although he played middle linebacker at just 215 pounds, Jack Lambert was the anchor of the Steelers' great defensive units of the 1970s. He was named the NFL's Defensive Rookie of the Year in 1974 and the league's Defensive Player of the Year in 1976.

Lambert was the spark that ignited the Steelers to four Super Bowl wins between 1975 and 1980. He played for the Steelers from 1974 to 1984.

STEELERS FACT: "Bullet Bill" Dudley, a halfback and defensive back with the Steelers during the 1940s, won football's rare "triple crown." In 1946, he led the league in rushing with 604 yards, punt returns with a 14.2-yard average, and interceptions with 10.

Ironically, Dudley did not get along with Steelers coach Jock Sutherland and quit the team at the end of the year.

Only two other players in pro football history have led the league in three completely different categories in a single season. Sammy Baugh led the NFL in punting, passing and interceptions in 1943 and Steve Van Buren topped the league in rushing, scoring and kickoff returns in 1945.

Scout's Honor

Dynasties are built through hard work, persistence and a little bit of luck.

One of the reasons for the Pittsburgh Steelers' great success through the 1970s, when they won four Super Bowls over a six-year period, was the club's ability to find and draft outstanding talent from the small black colleges of the South.

But every once in a while the Steelers found diamonds where others saw coal.

Bill Nunn was the Steelers' chief scout throughout the Super Bowl years. His mission was to personally search the small Southern campuses and locate potential talent.

In those days, certain NFL scouts often traveled as a group from college to college. Underpaid and overworked, they banded together to share expenses and information. Together they put professional prospects through a workout, then compared numbers and evaluations.

Pittsburgh's John Stallworth (82) juggles the ball as he is hit by Atlanta Falcons Kenny Johnson and Bobby Butler (23).

In 1973, Nunn accompanied several scouts as they made a call on a wide receiver named John Stallworth at Alabama A&M. At 6-foot-2 and 200 pounds, he had the size to be successful in the NFL, but they needed to test his agility.

They had Stallworth go through various running, jumping and catching exercises in an effort to assess his potential. Stallworth did well in all the drills except the 40-yard dash, where he was timed in the 4.8s, considered too slow for an NFL wide receiver. He was quickly dismissed as a prospect and the assembled group of scouts packed their stopwatches and called it a day.

But Steelers scout Bill Nunn was not convinced. He noticed the testing conditions were not ideal. Stallworth was running the 40-yard dash on thick grass made soft by several days of rain.

Nunn decided to act on a hunch.

The next morning, as the scouts were preparing to leave for another college destination, Nunn claimed he was ill. He told the rest of the scouting party he planned to rest up and would catch the group later.

Instead, Nunn returned to the Alabama A&M campus. He found Stallworth, took him to a dry field and ran him through the 40-yard dash all over again. This time Stallworth ran a 4.6.

On draft day in 1974, the Steelers made Stallworth their fourth-round pick. It proved to be a shrewd selection.

Teamed with quarterback Terry Bradshaw and wideout Lynn Swann, the Steelers put together one of the most dangerous passing attacks in the NFL during the 1970s. Stallworth emerged as the league's consummate deep threat.

LYNN SWANN

*L*ynn Swann's finest moment came in Super Bowl X, which capped the 1975 season. Swann caught four passes in the game for 161 yards and a touchdown as Pittsburgh defeated the Dallas Cowboys, 21-17. Swann was named the game's MVP.

"Swann was brilliant in that game," said Cowboys coach Tom Landry. "He made the difference with those two big catches when he was well covered."

Swann played in three Pro Bowls and caught 336 passes during his nine-year career for 5,462 yards and 51 touchdowns.

But it was in Super Bowl games that Swann excelled. In addition to being named MVP of Super Bowl X, Swann held career Super Bowl records for receptions with 16, and receiving yardage with 364 when he retired. He played his entire career with the Pittsburgh Steelers, from 1974 to 1982.

Lynn Swann scores a touchdown on a pass from Terry Bradshaw in the fourth period of Super Bowl X.

JOHN STALLWORTH

*I*n 14 seasons with Pittsburgh, John Stallworth caught 537 passes for 8,723 yards and 63 touchdowns. On four occasions, he was selected for the Pro Bowl.

Stallworth was at his best in the clutch. He holds the league record with 12 touchdown receptions in 18 playoff games.

He was also a key member of four Steelers Super Bowl wins. Against Dallas in Super Bowl XIII, Stallworth had three receptions for 115 yards and two touchdowns, including a 75-yard scoring reception. In Super Bowl XIV against the Rams, Stallworth scored the winning touchdown on a 73-yard reception in the fourth quarter. He played with the Steelers from 1974 to 1987.

The Making of a Quarterback

Terry Bradshaw reported to the Pittsburgh Steelers as the prototypical NFL quarterback. He had size, strength, confidence and, above all, a cannon for an arm.

The Steelers were looking for a savior after finishing 1-13 in 1969. They noted Bradshaw's physical tools and made him the first player chosen in the 1970 NFL draft. But in the early days of his career, he found the transition to the money game to be a humbling experience.

In the first regular season game of his career, Bradshaw completed just four of 16 passes against the Houston Oilers. And as his rookie season progressed, he had seven different games in which he threw at least three interceptions.

"I can laugh now," Bradshaw said, "but back then I had no idea what it meant to be a number-one draft choice in the NFL. I was an outsider who didn't mingle well. The other players looked at me as a Li'l Abner type.

"I was totally unprepared for pro football. I had no schooling on reading defenses. I never studied game films the way a quarterback should. In college (Louisiana Tech), I simply overpowered the opposition."

With all that firepower packed into his right arm, Bradshaw enjoyed making use of it. Frequently he did so to his own detriment.

"I always wanted to go downfield with the ball at every opportunity," he admitted with a grin. "And sometimes I tried to make things happen when it wasn't the percentage thing to do. I never really did develop that feather touch, that light touch, especially

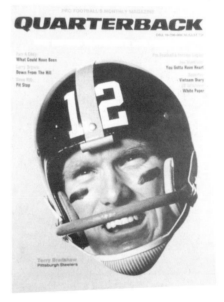

QUARTERBACK

over the middle. My inclination was always to put something on it."

Bradshaw obviously had the athletic ability to be a success in the NFL, but during that rookie season denizens of the press corps questioned his mental approach to the game.

"A lot of that had to do with my making mistakes," he said. "Particularly when I was a rookie. I did things like scrambling all over the field, then throwing it up for an interception. Some people wrote about me being dumb. When things didn't go right, they just tapped a finger to their head and figured I was dumb. And I had nobody to defend me. When I tried to defend myself, I only dug a deeper hole. Finally, I said the heck with it and kept my mouth shut."

Bradshaw couldn't be sure how much credence Steelers head coach Chuck Noll gave to these slurs. But he had plenty of time to mull over the matter while watching other quarterbacks play his position. Then, six games into the 1974 season, Noll summoned him.

"Go make your mistakes," Noll said. "We're going to win with you."

"When Noll told me that, that's when I became a quarterback," Bradshaw said, reflecting on the turning point in his career. "Before that, I wasn't making any progress. I knew that when I made a mistake, I was going to be yanked."

With the monkey off his back, Bradshaw led the Steelers to the Super Bowl in 1974, where they defeated the Minnesota Vikings 16-6.

TERRY BRADSHAW

*B*radshaw's 1974 triumph was the first of his four Super Bowl victories in as many attempts. His best performances came in Super Bowls XIII and XIV. He was named Most Valuable Player in both games.

During Bradshaw's 14-year NFL career, he completed 2,105 of 3,901 passes for 27,989 yards and 212 touchdowns. In 1989, he was selected to the Pro Football Hall of Fame. Bradshaw played with the Pittsburgh Steelers from 1970 to 1983.

ABOVE: Pittsburgh's Terry Bradshaw (12) is flushed out of the pocket by Minnesota Vikings Mark Mullaney (77) and Randy Holloway (75). The Steelers signal-caller was also an excellent runner.

STEELERS FACT: The longest pass of Terry Bradshaw's career was an 88-yard completion to backup quarterback Mark Malone, who had lined up as a receiver on the play.

STEELERS SUPER BOWL CHAMPIONS
SUPER BOWL IX — 1975

1974 PITTSBURGH STEELERS — AFL CHAMPIONS

STEELERS SUPER BOWL CHAMPIONS
SUPER BOWL X — 1976

Beyond the Call of Duty

It was a calm and humid day in Miami, temperature about 85 degrees, when the San Diego Chargers met the Dolphins in the first round of the 1981 playoffs.

Then the Chargers exploded like a Caribbean hurricane.

In just 15 minutes of football, San Diego put on a spectacular offensive performance. The Chargers scored every way imaginable, on a pass, a run, a punt return and a field goal, building a 24-0 lead at the end of the first quarter. They appeared to be running like a well-tuned Lamborghini and had complete control of the football game.

But that was just the beginning of one of the greatest football games ever played, a game in which Chargers tight end Kellen Winslow played a heroic role.

Winslow began his extraordinary afternoon early in the contest as he teamed with Chargers quarterback Dan Fouts to give the Dolphins a clinic on the medium-range passing game. Before the half, they hooked up on six passes for nearly 90 yards.

But Miami had an offensive attack of its own. Under the leadership of quarterback Don Strock, the Dolphins came storming back. They scored 17 unanswered points in the second quarter as Strock fired a pair of touchdown passes.

Miami tied the game at 24 early in the third period on Strock's third scoring pass of the day.

The shell-shocked Chargers could have wilted and folded up in the sweltering Miami heat. Instead, Fouts and Winslow put their enormous talents to work.

"In the second half, the humidity was getting to several of our players," Fouts said. "Kellen was having some physical problems with dehydration which caused him to have leg cramps. Then, at one point, he took a good shot across the head and had to leave the game to get his lip stitched back together."

Winslow returned to the field in time to put San Diego back in front 31-24 midway through the third quarter. This time, the elusive tight end hauled in a 25-yard scoring pass from Fouts. It was his ninth catch of the day.

But Strock engineered more comebacks than Richard Nixon on this particular afternoon. Once again, he rallied the Dolphins. He fired a 50-yard touchdown pass to tie the game, his fourth scoring heave of the game.

On the Dolphins' next possession, Strock put together a 62-yard touchdown drive. Midway through the fourth quarter, the Dolphins took the lead for the first time, 38-31.

As the clock continued to tick away, it was time for Winslow's heroics once again. After being helped from the field with a shoulder injury, Winslow returned to make a critical third down catch, keeping the Chargers' late drive alive. Fouts then drilled a nine-yard touchdown pass to James Brooks, tying the score at 38.

"Kellen Winslow put on one of the greatest individual performances I've ever seen," said Dolphins coach Don Shula. "When you think about everything he did in that game, you think about Superman."

Winslow set a playoff record with 13 catches for 166 yards, despite having a badly bruised shoulder, a stitched lip, leg cramps, dehydration and shoulder pads that were broken twice because of the constant pounding he took.

But Winslow still wasn't finished. He saved the best for last. The most important play he made came in the closing seconds of regulation time.

The Dolphins took the ensuing kickoff and Strock quickly moved them into field goal range. After a timeout, kicker Uwe von Schamann lined up to attempt a game-winning field goal for Miami. But Winslow wouldn't allow it to happen. He stormed through the line and blocked the kick. It was the only blocked kick of his career.

San Diego went on to win the game in overtime, 41-38. The people who witnessed Winslow's performance will never forget it.

"At the end of the game, we needed a couple of people to carry Kellen into the locker room," Fouts said. "He was completely exhausted and beat up. He lost something like 12 pounds in the game. I can't imagine anybody doing more for his team than he did that day."

CHARGERS FACT: Running back Chuck Muncie scored 19 rushing touchdowns in the 1981 season, a club record.

CHARGERS FACT: The Chargers set a professional football record in 1961 by intercepting 49 passes. Defensive back Charley McNeil led the club with nine interceptions while Bob Zeman had eight, Dick Harris had seven and Chuck Allen, Bob Laraba and Claude Gibson had five thefts each.

CHARGERS FACT: Dan Fouts passed for 4,802 yards in 1981, the second highest single-season total in NFL history. He led the Chargers to the AFC Western Division crown that season.

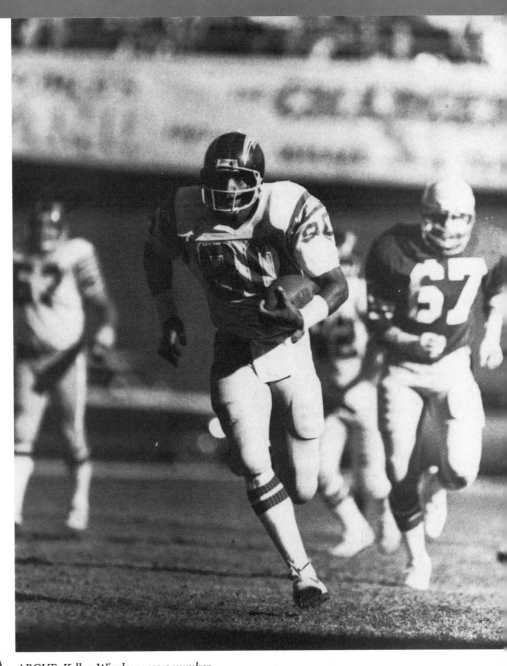

ABOVE: Kellen Winslow was a number-one draft choice from Missouri in 1979.

KELLEN WINSLOW

During his nine-year career playing for the Chargers, tight end Winslow caught 541 passes for 6,741 yards and 45 touchdowns, more than any other tight end in NFL history. Winslow played with the Chargers from 1979 to 1987.

Outsmarting the Blitz

It was late on a Friday evening when Sid Gillman put the final touch on his game plan. In two days, his San Diego Chargers would take on the Boston Patriots for the 1963 American Football League crown. He felt a wave of satisfaction, the feeling only an offensive coordinator or army field general could grasp from knowing his plan of attack was too good to be thwarted.

The 53-year-old Gillman had been around pro football a long time and had coached the 1955 Los Angeles Rams to the NFL Western Conference title. His life had been dominated by X's and O's. They were his passion, musical notes that translated into acts of violence. He was hailed as an offensive genius, one of the fathers of the modern passing game.

Boston had the league's top defense, led by linebacker Nick Buoniconti. He was the lifeblood of a blitzing, kamikaze unit that was liable to attack the quarterback from any angle on any down.

"I watched film after film of Boston and had never seen any team go after the quarterback quite like that," Gillman said. "The all-out blitz was a relatively new idea in football then. Our goal was to throw them off balance."

Gillman had a pair of anti-blitzing weapons on his side in running backs Paul Lowe and Keith Lincoln. Both men were blessed with exceptional speed and Gillman planned to use it.

"You don't want to change your entire offense or anything like that," Gillman said. "What you do is give your offense a different look, put guys in motion, line up a back in the slot, anything to make the defense back off and think for a second."

Gillman wasted no time in putting his plan to work. On the Chargers second play from scrimmage, he put Lowe in motion. Quarterback John Hadl faked a quick toss to Lowe, then handed the ball to Lincoln who sprinted off-tackle, bounced off a defender and

raced 56 yards to the Boston four-yard line. Lincoln promptly picked himself up, walked to the sideline and vomited.

"I think he was overly excited," Gillman said.

The Chargers scored two plays later and the rout was on.

On the Chargers' second offensive possession, they took just two plays to find the end zone again, and on their third possession just four plays. San Diego ended the day with 610 yards of total offense and averaged 10 yards per play as they destroyed the Patriots 51-10 to capture the AFL title.

Lincoln gained 206 yards rushing on 13 carries and caught seven passes for 123 yards.

"It's rare to have your game plan work that well," Gillman said when it was all over. "After scoring the first time we knew it would work, though, and things just snowballed from there."

In his first season as a head coach in 1955, **SID GILLMAN** guided the Los Angeles Rams to the NFL Western Conference title. He became the first coach of the AFL's Los Angeles Chargers in 1960, then relocated with the club to San Diego in 1961. With the Chargers he won four division crowns and the 1963 AFL Championship.

Gillman retired because of illness after the 1969 season but returned to the Chargers in 1971. In 1973, he took over the Houston Oilers and was named AFC Coach of the Year in 1974.

During his 18 years as a pro football coach, Gillman posted a 123-104-7 record. Acknowledged as the guru of the modern pro passing game, Gillman tutored numerous coaching assistants in its intricacies. Among the coaches who worked and studied under Gillman are Bill Walsh, Dick Vermeil, Chuck Noll, Bum Phillips and Al Davis.

Gillman was elected to the Pro Football Hall of Fame in 1983.

CHARGERS

CHARGERS FACT: The Chargers won the AFL Western Division title in five of their first six seasons. The club's only AFL Championship came in 1963 when they routed the Boston Patriots, 51-10.

CHARGERS FACT: In the Chargers' first preseason game ever in 1960, Paul Lowe returned the opening kickoff 105 yards for a touchdown and San Diego went on to defeat the New York Titans 27-7. Lowe is the Chargers' all-time leading rusher with 4,963 yards between 1960 and 1967. He averaged 4.9 yards per carry.

CHARGERS FACT: Lance Alworth averaged over 1,000 yards in receptions every season for nine years with the Chargers and earned the nickname "Bambi" for his speed and grace.

CHARGERS FACT: Quarterback Jack Kemp's 91-yard touchdown pass to Keith Lincoln against the Denver Broncos in 1961 is the longest play from scrimmage in club history.

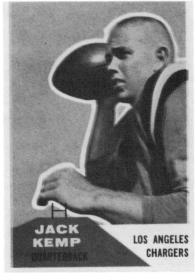

JACK KEMP
QUARTERBACK

LOS ANGELES CHARGERS

San Diego CHARGERS

THE SAN DIEGO CHARGERS

SAN DIEGO CHARGERS ™

CHARGERS FACT: Junior Seau spent his early years in American Samoa and did not learn to speak English until he was seven years old.

RIGHT: San Diego Chargers linebacker Junior Seau sacks Los Angeles Raiders quarterback Jay Schroeder in 1992. Seau was named NFL Defensive Player of the Year that season.

Money Where Your Mouth Is

Even before Super Bowl XXIV began, Denver's rugged safeties Steve Atwater and Dennis Smith began badgering San Francisco 49ers wide receiver Jerry Rice. Taking trash talk to a new level, Atwater and Smith suggested that Rice and fellow receiver John Taylor were not tough enough to make any catches against the Denver secondary.

Smith and Atwater weren't issuing empty threats. Both men were over 200 pounds with numerous Pro Bowl visits between them. And they had undressed their share of unsuspecting receivers venturing over the middle.

But Rice has never been one to back down from a challenge. The challenge of making a game-turning play is what makes Rice train six hours a day during the offseason. It's what makes him run sprints in the rain all alone while his teammates warm themselves in the locker room.

"Their comments got me all fired up," Rice recalled. "They acted as if we were rookies just coming into the league."

Rice set the game's tone on San Francisco's opening drive. The 49ers advanced to Denver's 20-yard line, when quarterback Joe Montana sent Rice over the middle. Atwater was tracking Rice on the play and when he made the catch, the 217-pound safety made a vicious hit on Rice. He had visions of leaving Rice sprawled in pain on the turf.

"He really tried to just unload on me," Rice said. "But when you're trying to hit somebody that hard, you don't wrap up."

Instead of leaving Rice dazed, confused and demoralized, Atwater only knocked him slightly off course. The 49ers wideout bounced off Atwater's big hit and waltzed into the end zone, further insulting the Denver safety.

Once again, Rice's play spoke volumes. He didn't need to respond verbally to the Denver safeties' taunting.

"Scoring a touchdown, that's painful to them," Rice said.

And Denver experienced quite a bit of pain that day because it was the first of eight touchdowns San Francisco scored, three of them by Rice.

San Francisco clobbered the Broncos, 55-10.

JERRY RICE

Rice's football career is chock full of memorable moments and challenges met.

He rang up 204 yards in pass receptions against the Washington Redskins in 1986. He snared a game-winning 25-yard touchdown pass against Cincinnati as time expired in 1987. He was named NFL Player of the Year in 1987 after making a league-record 22 touchdown catches. He broke off a 78-yard touchdown with 42 seconds left that beat the New York Giants in 1988. He had 13 receptions and five touchdowns against Atlanta in 1990. He caught 11 passes for 215 yards in Super Bowl XXIII and was named the game's MVP.

He is pro football's all-time touchdown leader, having broken Jim Brown's mark of 126 scores early in the 1994 season. Rice joined the 49ers as a first-round draft pick in 1985.

Photo from Richard Wolffers Auctions, Inc., San Francisco

49ERS FACT: Rifle-armed quarterback Y.A. Tittle and springlegged wide receiver R.C. Owens teamed up in the 1950s to create the Alley-Oop pass. Tittle would unload a high looping spiral and Owens would use his great jumping ability to outleap the defenders and grab the football.

"The Alley-Oop was developed by accident," Tittle recalled. "R.C. could really jump, so he wanted to try it out. We practiced it a few times, but I never thought we'd use it in a game.

"In 1957, we won five games in the last couple minutes using the Alley-Oop. What made it work was R.C.'s jumping ability. The defenses knew it was coming. They would put extra defensive backs on R.C. It didn't help, though. They just got in the way of each other.

"I guess you could say it was the same as a Hail Mary pass, except we didn't pray," Owens said.

The Catch

When the two-minute warning sounded, wide receiver Dwight Clark could barely breathe. The 49ers were trailing Dallas 27-21 in the 1981 NFC Championship Game. Standing between them and San Francisco's first NFC crown was 50 yards of chewed-up Candlestick sod and the vaunted Cowboys defense.

While CBS television cut to a commercial, assistant trainer Hal Wyatt raced into the 49ers huddle toting water bottles. There was no energy for words. Wyatt dutifully squirted water into the dry mouths of nervous players. After he finished, he spun around in the huddle and said, "We're going to win."

He turned to Clark and said, "And you're going to catch the winning touchdown pass."

Then Wyatt disappeared.

On the next play, wide receiver Freddie Solomon bolted 14 yards on a reverse. Solomon and Clark combined for another 23 yards on a pair of receptions. At the 12-yard line, quarterback Joe Montana hoisted an end zone pass for Solomon that fell incomplete. Then running back Lenvil Elliot darted seven yards to the Dallas six.

With 56 seconds remaining, Montana called a "red right" formation, Solomon slotted inside of Clark on the right side. Solomon went downfield and darted quickly to the right and looked for the ball. He had scored the game's first touchdown on the same play, but this time he was covered. Montana checked off and looked at Clark. He was double-covered.

A pack of Cowboys broke through the 49ers offensive line and were breathing fire down Montana's neck. He fled the pocket.

Meanwhile, Clark had snuck to the back of the end zone and was running toward the right corner. Montana saw him, pump-faked and then unleashed a high pass toward Clark as he was decked by Larry Bethea and Ed "Too Tall" Jones. The ball sailed and Clark leaped high to snare it with his fingertips while cornerback Everson Walls looked on in amazement. The 62,000 fans in attendance at Candlestick Park exploded in ecstasy. The 49ers were about to win their first NFC title.

"A lot of people think Joe was just throwing the ball away," Clark said. "Nothing could be further from the truth. It's a planned play. If I'm not open on the hook route, I'm supposed to go to the back of the end zone. Joe's supposed to throw high. I think Everson thought Joe was throwing the ball away, because I know for a fact he can jump higher than I can. It was just a perfect pass."

While Clark spiked the ball, "Too Tall" Jones was climbing off Montana's back at the 15-yard line. Jones said, "You just beat America's team."

"Now you can watch us on television with the rest of America," Montana replied.

It wouldn't have been possible if Clark hadn't made what will forever be remembered in pro football annals as "The Catch."

"It wasn't a hard catch to make," Clark said. "I was in the back of the end zone, so I knew there was no one behind me. If I had been in the middle of the field it would have been tough. Any catch over your head is. But when you're in the end zone every catch is easy. You get that instant gratification."

DWIGHT CLARK joined the 49ers in 1979 as an unknown tenth-round draft choice out of Clemson. A year later, he was the club's starting wide receiver and grabbed 82 passes for 991 yards and eight touchdowns.

In 1982, he led the league in receptions and was named Sports Illustrated's Player of the Year. He also played in the first of two Pro Bowls that year.

Clark retired in 1987 as the 49ers' all-time leading receiver (a record since eclipsed by Jerry Rice) with 506 catches, good for 6,750 yards and 48 touchdowns.

Grace Under Pressure

The Super Bowl annually separates the champions from the also-rans. Few players in any sport have performed with such confidence and cool under big-game pressure as former San Francisco 49ers quarterback Joe Montana.

Although Montana has won three Super Bowl MVP awards, his finest moment may have been in Super Bowl XXIII at Miami's Joe Robbie Stadium. Ironically, it is the only Super Bowl game he has appeared in and not been named MVP.

There was just 3:10 left to play when Montana lead his club onto the field, trailing the Cincinnati Bengals 16-13. The ball was spotted on San Francisco's eight-yard line. Montana knew it was do-or-die as he huddled his teammates in the end zone.

"When we came onto the field," Montana said. "I was thinking to myself, 'We have done this before. We've driven the length of the field to win games before.' I was thinking of the NFC Championship Game in 1981 when we drove down the field to beat Dallas."

Before Montana could break the huddle, a television time out was called and the players got an unwanted breather.

"The extra time out made us all a little nervous," recalled center Randy Cross. "We wanted to get the game going. Then Joe points over to the stands and says, 'Hey, guys, look over there. It's (comedian) John Candy.' Joe did not seem bothered by the pressure. It put us all at ease."

If some Bengals felt they had the 49ers right where they wanted them, Bengals receiver Cris Collinsworth was not among them.

"Montana is not human," Collinsworth said. "I don't want to call him a god, but he's definitely somewhere in between. I've never seen a guy who, every time the chips are down and people are counting him out, is able to come back. I knew we were in trouble when he walked out there. I'd seen him do it before."

Montana started the drive by hitting on three short passes, then running back Roger Craig picked up eight rushing yards to move the 49ers to the 35-yard line. From there, the 49ers called a timeout with 1:54 remaining.

On the Bengals' sideline, Cincinnati coach Sam Wyche, Montana's former tutor as the 49ers quarterback coach in the early 1980s, reviewed strategy that could stop his former pupil.

When play resumed, Montana picked up the tempo. He hit Jerry Rice for 17 yards and Craig for 13, moving the 49ers to the Bengals' 35-yard line and almost within range of a game-tying field goal. It was then that the excitement momentarily got to Montana.

"I was starting to hyperventilate," Montana said. "I'd never experienced that before. I threw a pass out of bounds to stop the clock and slow things down."

A penalty moved the ball back to the 45 and out of field goal range, but Montana looked for Rice again. Although he was double-covered, Montana connected for a 27-yard pickup to the 18-yard line.

"That's when I started thinking touchdown," Montana said. He hit Craig with an eight-yard pass to the 10. The clock showed 39 seconds. Montana called for a timeout.

On the sideline, Montana conferred with Bill Walsh, appearing in his final game as the 49ers head coach. They decided to go with "20 halfback curl x-up." Rice would go in motion to freeze the defense and Craig would be the primary receiver over the middle.

As the play unfolded, Craig drew double coverage, but Montana spotted secondary receiver John Taylor slicing across the end zone. He fired a pass between two defenders. Taylor made the scoring catch, his only reception of the day, giving San Francisco a 20-16 lead with 34 seconds left. It clinched another Super Bowl victory for San Francisco.

With a Super Bowl hanging in the balance, Montana took complete control. He connected on eight of nine passes for 97 yards. Because of a penalty, Montana's passing yardage actually accounted for more yardage than the 92-yard drive. For Montana, it was just another day at work.

49ERS FACT: Linebacker Hardy Brown, one of the most vicious tacklers in football history, knocked unconscious 21 opponents during the 1951 season, according to former 49er teammates. Against the Washington Redskins he used his famous shoulder tackle to knock out every member of the starting backfield during one game.

"We called him 'Hardy the Hatchet,'" Y.A. Tittle said. "He may be the hardest hitter that ever played. Hardy just exploded through people."

49ERS FACT: The 49ers Alphabet Backfield of the late 1950s consisted of quarterback Y.A. Tittle, flanker R.C. Owens, halfback J.D. Smith and fullback C.R. Roberts.

Photo from Richard Wolffers Auctions, Inc., San Francisco

JOE MONTANA

Montana was chosen by the San Francisco 49ers in the third round of the 1979 draft. The former Notre Dame star won the 49ers starting quarterback job in 1981 and promptly led the 49ers that season to the first of four Super Bowls victories. On three occasions, Montana was named Super Bowl MVP. In 1993, Montana was traded to the Kansas City Chiefs. He is the highest-rated quarterback of all-time with a 93.5 mark, according to the NFL rating system, and has participated in five Pro Bowls.

PLAYING HISTORY:
San Francisco 49ers 1979-1992
Kansas City Chiefs 1993-

Beginner's Luck

Steve Young was nervous. He was finally getting his chance.

After struggling for two seasons with the hideous Tampa Bay Buccaneers, a draft-week trade brought him to the San Francisco 49ers in 1987. San Francisco had already socked away two Super Bowl championships and were making perennial appearances in the playoffs.

Young loved the Bill Walsh offense, the multiple formations, the timed pass patterns. Now, after spending the first two months of the 1987 season on the bench, Young was getting the call. Starting quarterback Joe Montana had injured his hand and Young was summoned to continue the game against the division-rival New Orleans Saints.

Young's first play was a handoff to Roger Craig on a simple running formation. He hunched over center and heard a voice say, "Get out of it. Get out of it." He looked down and saw veteran guard Randy Cross issuing the command.

"Randy's been on a few Super Bowl winners," Young thought. "He's probably spotted something."

Immediately, Young called an audible.

"Red 22 Seattle," Young bellowed. "Red 22 Seattle."

It was a hot call, a pass play called at the line of scrimmage. It was designed to go to tight end Russ Francis running a 15-yard out pattern.

Young could feel the adrenaline surge through him as he took the snap and dropped into the pocket. Francis turned out of his break and headed for the sideline. Young's pass whistled far above his head. Miraculously, it landed in the hands of wide receiver Jerry Rice, who was streaking down the sideline.

Rice was supposed to be a decoy on the play. Instead, he caught the errant pass and raced 46 yards into the end zone. It was Young's first touchdown toss as a 49er.

Afterward, Young jogged to the 49ers sideline and was accosted by Bill Walsh. The coach was dumbfounded.

"How did you know to change the play?" Walsh asked. "How did you know Rice would be open?"

"Just a hunch," Young shrugged.

Young then searched out Cross on the bench.

"Why did you tell me to change the play?" Young asked.

"I didn't," Cross answered. "I was talking to the tackle."

49ERS FACT: Vince Lombardi was in his first year as the Green Bay Packers coach in 1958 when the 49ers traveled to Milwaukee to play them in ice-cold conditions. The 49ers won the game, 33-12, but the postgame party got an unexpectedly early start.

"In Milwaukee, the stands were real close to the bench," recalled former 49ers defensive back Abe Woodson. "In those days, there was just a bucket and dipper for water. Well, somehow one of the fans got on the field and poured some scotch into our water bucket.

"It was a real cold day so you really weren't getting dehydrated where you needed a lot of water. But our players knew what was in there and they would run off the field and take a big swig from the water bucket.

"Before long, we were all giggling and having a good time over at the water bucket and the coaches began to wonder what we were doing over there."

San Francisco quarterback Steve Young pulls the ball down and scrambles to elude Keith Hamilton (75) of the New York Giants in a 1993 playoff game. Young took over as the 49ers starting quarterback in 1991 when Joe Montana was injured. He went on to win the NFL passing title that year.

STEVE YOUNG

Young's first touchdown pass with the 49ers may have been a fluke, but his rapid development into one of the NFL's premier quarterbacks has not been accidental.

For four seasons, Young waited on the sidelines as the highest-paid clipboard holder in the NFL. He watched patiently as Joe Montana guided the 49ers to consecutive Super Bowl wins in 1988 and 1989. Then in 1991, Montana, the 49ers' three-time Super Bowl MVP,

was sidelined after elbow surgery. Young was tossed into the fire.

San Francisco's new signal-caller got off to a rocky start as Montana's heir, but he hit his groove by the fourth game of the season. Although he missed several late season games with a knee injury, Young ended the year with a 101.3 quarterback rating and won the league passing title.

In 1992, Young put together his most impressive season. He started every game and ended the

year with a 107 quarterback rating to win his second straight passing title. He became the first quarterback in NFL history to have a rating of over 100 in back-to-back seasons. Young also was named the league's MVP.

PLAYING HISTORY:
Los Angeles Express (USFL)
1984-1985
Tampa Bay Buccaneers 1985-1986
San Francisco 49ers 1987-

A Moment of Truth

The San Francisco 49ers went into the final game of the 1970 season with a 9-3-1 record. The club's first-ever NFC Western Division Championship loomed before them. For San Francisco to clinch the title, the New York Giants had to beat the Los Angeles Rams or else the 49ers needed a win over the Raiders at the Oakland Coliseum.

"Right before the game started, we heard the Rams had won," former 49ers All-Pro wide receiver Gene Washington said. "So that meant it was all up to us. If we wanted to go to the playoffs, we would have to do it ourselves. And I'm glad that's the way it worked out."

Beating the Raiders at Oakland was no easy task in 1970. In fact, the Raiders were undefeated on their home turf going into the final game. A capacity crowd of over 55,000 partisan Raider rooters waited in a steady drizzle for the contest to get underway.

"Not only were we traveling into the lion's den at the Oakland Coliseum," Washington said, "but the Raiders were in their heyday then. They were stacked with future Hall of Famers. Their secondary was among the best in football. And to top it off, Ben Davidson, their big defensive end, guaranteed a Raiders victory."

Art Shell, Gene Upshaw, Jim Otto, Willie Brown, George Blanda and Fred Biletnikoff were among the Raiders on the field that day who would later be enshrined at Canton, Ohio. They were led by Daryle Lamonica, the league's top-rated passer, and head coach John Madden. In addition, Oakland's defense was among the most rugged in the NFL.

"We always had problems with the Raiders," Washington said. "They beat us in preseason games all the time and a tremendous rivalry had grown between the two teams and between the fans. We knew we had our hands full if we expected to win the division title."

The first half belonged to the 49ers. Quarterback John Brodie, who was named the league's MVP that season, hit tight end Ted Kwalick on a 26-yard touchdown pass early in the game. He followed that up with a three-yard scoring toss to Washington as the 49ers built a 24-7 halftime lead.

"At halftime, Coach (Dick) Nolan reminded us that no lead was safe at the Oakland Coliseum," Washington said. "So we knew the game wasn't over yet. There was too much at stake for us."

With that in mind, the 49ers continued to pour it on. Brodie threw another touchdown pass and San Francisco went on to defeat the Raiders 38-7.

"Personally, I had a good day," said Washington, who led the league that season with 1,100 receiving yards and averaged 21 yards per catch. "But that was overshadowed by the win. It was just a real emotional moment for the team because it was the first time the 49ers ever won a title. I remember the atmosphere in the locker room afterward was just euphoric. I guess what was so special for me and the rest of the team was that we were in a situation where we had to beat a great team to clinch the title and we did it."

49ERS FACT: Leo Nomellini is the only member of the Pro Football Hall of Fame to have been born in Italy. Nomellini, who was born in Lucca, Italy, began playing football in the U.S. Marines and never saw a live professional football game until he was playing in one with the San Francisco 49ers. A two-way star at offensive and defensive tackle, Nomellini played in 10 Pro Bowls.

ABOVE: *San Francisco 49ers wide receiver Gene Washington (18) jumps in anger after an official ruled he had trapped a pass during a game against the Minnesota Vikings in 1977. Minnesota defensive back Tom Hannon (45) looks on.*

GENE WASHINGTON

*W*ashington went on to a stellar career with the 49ers. Between 1969 and 1977, he was the club's leading deep receiver and played in four Pro Bowls. He closed out his career in 1979 with the Detroit Lions. Washington retired with 385 catches for 6,856 yards and 60 touchdowns. He averaged nearly 18 yards per catch.

PLAYING HISTORY:
San Francisco 49ers 1969-1977
Detroit Lions 1978-1979

49ERS FACT: The 49ers summer training camp often found club veterans performing pranks on unsuspecting teammates. Charlie Krueger, a fixture at defensive tackle from 1959 to 1973, was one of the club's stunt leaders.

"(Guard) Howard Mudd used to chew Copenhagen," recalled Dave Wilcox, a seven-time Pro Bowl linebacker for the 49ers between 1964 and 1974. "Somehow, Charlie Krueger found a little, tiny tree frog and put it in Howard's Copenhagen before practice. Everyone knew about it but Howard. So we were all waiting to see Howard put it in his mouth."

Finally Mudd reached for the snuff in his locker and put a copious amount between his cheek and gum.

"As soon as he did, he knew something was up," Wilcox said. "But he wouldn't let on. He just went about his business and wouldn't spit it out. He didn't want to give everyone the satisfaction of seeing that. Howard never said anything about it."

Instead, he went through the practice session with a minuscule frog hopping about in his mouth.

Pass It To Whatsisname

Hugh McElhenny began to make his presence known to the San Francisco 49ers barely 24 hours after reporting to training camp as a first-round draft choice in 1952.

"I played in the College All-Star Game on a Friday night," McElhenny said. "Then I reported to camp on Saturday. On Sunday, we had an exhibition game against the Chicago Cardinals. (Head coach) Buck Shaw told me to suit up, so I did."

The spectacular running back out of the University of Washington hadn't even had time to learn the names of his teammates when he found himself in the 49er backfield against the Cardinals.

"(Quarterback) Frankie Albert had called a time out and asked Buck Shaw to put me in the game," McElhenny said. "Buck told him I didn't know the plays yet. At that time, Frankie pretty much had his way with Buck, so Buck went along with him. In the huddle, Frankie drew a play on the ground and told everybody what to do. It was completely improvised. He threw me a pitchout and I ran 42 yards for a touchdown."

It was the first of many touchdowns for the elusive McElhenny.

Crowning Achievement

One of Hurryin' Hugh McElhenny's most memorable touchdowns occurred during the fourth league game of his rookie season against the always dangerous Chicago Bears.

McElhenny knew he was breaking a cardinal rule when he fielded a punt on the four-yard line, juked a couple of Bears and took off on a 96-yard scamper for a touchdown. A veteran would have allowed the punt to go into the end zone. McElhenny's rookie mistake was ignored, but his running ability wasn't overlooked.

"After the game in the locker room," McElhenny said, "Frankie Albert gave me the game ball and said, 'You're now the king.' Then he turned to Joe Perry, who was part of the Million Dollar Backfield and said, 'Joe, you're just the Jet.'"

That's when the legend of Hugh McElhenny was born. The king was coronated. McElhenny was named Rookie of the Year at the end of his inaugural season and played in his first Pro Bowl where he continued his spectacular play by scoring two touchdowns.

After nine great seasons with the 49ers, the Minnesota Vikings selected **HUGH McELHENNY** in 1961 as an expansion-draft pick. He continued his fine play with Minnesota that season, rushing for 570 yards, catching 37 passes and returning punts and kickoffs.

When he retired after the 1964 season, McElhenny was one of just three players to accumulate more than 11,000 all-purpose yards. In 13 NFL seasons, he rushed for 5,281 yards and caught 264 passes for 3,247 yards. McElhenny scored 60 touchdowns, 38 rushing, 20 on receptions and two on punt returns.

In 1970, McElhenny was elected to the Pro Football Hall of Fame in his first year of eligibility.

PLAYING HISTORY:
San Francisco 49ers 1952-1960
Minnesota Vikings 1961-1962
New York Giants 1963
Detroit Lions 1964

RIGHT: Hugh McElhenny cuts up field against the Los Angeles Rams at San Francisco's Kezar Stadium. McElhenny was a first-round draft pick of the 49ers in 1952. He ran 42 yards for a touchdown on his first play in a 49er uniform and was named Rookie of the Year and Player of the Year.

49ERS FACT: Red Hickey was the first coach to successfully use the shotgun formation in the pro ranks. He unveiled the shotgun in 1960 against the Baltimore Colts using John Brodie as his quarterback. The 49ers beat Baltimore 30-22. Hickey used the formation through 1960 and part of 1961, then scrapped it after the Chicago Bears defeated the 49ers 31-0.

SOMEBODY ADDED WRONG

During the 1950s, the 49ers backfield consisted of quarterback Y.A. Tittle, halfbacks John Henry Johnson and Hugh McElhenny, and fullback Joe Perry in what was called the Million Dollar Backfield.

In 1954, their first season together with San Francisco, Perry led the NFL in rushing with 1,049 yards, Johnson was second in the league with 681 yards and McElhenny was ninth with 515 yards and a league-leading eight yards per carry. They scored 23 touchdowns between them.

Tittle completed nearly 60 percent of his passes that season for 2,205 yards and was the second-ranked passer in the league.

All four men are in the Pro Football Hall of Fame, the only complete backfield that can claim that distinction. But Perry still wonders how they got their catchy nickname.

"I don't know why we were called the Million Dollar Backfield," Perry said. "The four of us together didn't make anything close to a million dollars."

In fact, the four of them together didn't make close to $100,000 that season. But their skill level made them NFL royalty.

The $5,000 Hit

It was just another pass route over the middle, one that Steve Largent had run hundreds of times in his record-setting NFL career. But this one, in the third quarter of the Seattle Seahawks' 1988 season opener at Denver, ended very differently.

Thanks to a forceful forearm from Broncos free safety Mike Harden, Largent was knocked unconscious and lay motionless on the field at Mile High Stadium for five minutes. Teammates said Largent was so far gone he was snoring.

"I was out before I hit the ground," Largent recalled after regaining his senses. "It was instant lights out. So there's absolutely no fear of going back across the middle again because I don't remember how bad it hurt."

The damage report was a subtle reminder. It included: one concussion, two broken teeth, one very tender cheek, a twisted left knee and one mangled facemask.

The impact actually bent the space bars of Largent's old-style, two-bar facemask. One was popped out over the top bar, the other shoved back behind the lower bar.

"It was a pretty severe collision," Largent said.

And it cost Harden $5,000. He was fined by the league office for an illegal blow to the head.

Still, the issue wasn't quite settled.

SEAHAWKS FACT: The Seahawks originally played in the NFC Western Division during 1976, their inaugural season. The next year they were moved to the AFC Western Division.

Fast forward to week 15 of the 1988 season, a rematch between the Seahawks and the Broncos at the Kingdome on Monday Night Football.

With the Seahawks holding a 14-7 lead midway through the second quarter, Harden intercepted a Dave Krieg pass in the end zone and returned it 26 torturous yards. Seemingly from out of nowhere, a blue-jerseyed blur drove Harden out of the picture and out of bounds. The dazed look on Harden's face asked, "Did anyone get the license of that runaway truck?" It was Number 80, Steve Largent.

Tight end Mike Tice recalled hearing the impact. The sound of the collision was almost as frightening as the sight of it.

"I was down," Tice said, "but I heard it. He hit him as good as any linebacker since Dick Butkus."

"It wasn't a matter of who it was," Largent later admitted. "It's just funny it worked out that way. It couldn't have happened more perfectly. It obviously wasn't premeditated. It was just kind of a Walt Disney type of situation—storybook.

"But I was definitely trying to hit him as hard as I could."

The 5-foot-11, 190-pound Largent accomplished his mission.

Reminded that Harden had been fined $5,000 for his earlier hit, Largent was all smiles.

"For that hit today," he said at the time, "I'd be happy to send him his $5,000."

OPPOSITE: Steve Largent (80) races around Minnesota Vikings cornerback David Evans (40) after hauling in a pass from quarterback Dave Krieg.

SEAHAWKS

STEVE LARGENT

Drafted in the fourth round out of Tulsa by the Houston Oilers in 1976, Largent was traded to the expansion Seattle Seahawks prior to the start of their first NFL season. He led the club in receptions that year, grabbing 54 passes from quarterback Jim Zorn. Two years later, he was the NFL's top receiver with 71 receptions.

During his 14 NFL seasons, he developed into one of the most reliable, consistent and productive wideouts in pro football history. He caught more than 50 passes in 10 seasons and had more than 1,000 receiving yards eight times.

In 1989, Largent retired with several NFL receiving records. Since then, many have been

broken. He caught 819 passes in his career for 13,089 yards and 100 touchdowns. He also had receptions in 177 consecutive games.

Largent was selected to play in seven Pro Bowls. In 1988, he was awarded the Bart Starr Trophy as the NFL Man of the Year. Largent played with the Seahawks from 1976 to 1989.

Doctor, Do You Need a Doctor?

*I*t was the last game of the 1980 season and the Seahawks prepared to host the Denver Broncos. The Seahawks' dream of making the playoffs for the first time was long over. The game had no meaning in the final standings.

In the first half, Seahawks quarterback Jim Zorn was racing from the pocket, a common sight in the Seahawks' early years when the passing pocket was as porous as a colander.

As Zorn turned the corner, he found Broncos All-Pro linebacker Tom Jackson waiting for him. Jackson unloaded. Zorn crumpled, his rib cage collapsing like a spent accordion.

Zorn was helped from the sideline and ushered into the locker room where X-rays were taken. Team doctors informed Zorn there were no broken bones or damaged ribs. Trainer Jim Whitesel and an attending physician advised Zorn to have a pain-killing injection to ease the discomfort. It wouldn't cause the injury to become any worse, they said.

That was all Zorn needed to hear. He wanted to go back into the game. He was ready for the needle.

It was not a simple injection, however. He was advised that if the needle was inserted in the wrong location or at the wrong angle, it could puncture a lung and cause it to collapse.

After the first injection, Zorn was still feeling pain. The doctor then loaded up and tried again. This time, Zorn let out a slow "Aaaagh" and passed out on the trainer's table.

The physician took one look at the unconscious Zorn and began to panic, thinking one of Zorn's lungs must have collapsed. Suddenly, he began to hyperventilate and passed out beside the star quarterback.

Whitesel then entered the trainer's room to see how everything was going. To his surprise, he found Zorn out cold. The attending doctor was on one knee trying to regain his composure.

Whitesel helped steady the doctor and then revived the patient. As Zorn started to come around, he discovered he could breathe. The lung was fine. But he was still feeling discomfort. The doctor loaded up his needle one more time.

On the third try, the doctor hit the troubled area. The pain was numbed. Zorn was ready to return to action.

Unfortunately, Zorn could not revive the Seahawks' sagging offense that day. Seattle lost to the Broncos 25-17 to finish the season at 4-12.

JIM ZORN served as the Seahawk's quarterback from 1976, the club's inaugural season, to 1984. In 1976, Zorn was named AFC Offensive Rookie of the Year and was named the club's Most Valuable Player for the first time. He also received the Seahawks' MVP award in 1978.

But his most memorable season with the Seahawks came in 1983 when he helped direct the club to the AFC Championship Game. There, Seattle was knocked off by the Los Angeles Raiders 30-14. Zorn was 14 for 27 in the game, earning 134 yards and two touchdowns.

The Seahawks honored Zorn in 1991 by inducting him into the club's Ring of Honor alongside wide receiver Steve Largent. Zorn and Largent hooked up often during their nine years together at Seattle. Largent retired as the NFL's all-time leading receiver.

In his career, Zorn completed 1,669 of 3,149 passes for 21,115 yards and 111 touchdowns.

PLAYING HISTORY:
Seattle Seahawks 1976-1984
Green Bay Packers 1985
Tampa Bay Buccaneers 1987

LONG RIVALRY

In the late 1980s, Bryan Millard ranked among the AFC's top offensive guards. But during his six seasons with the Seattle Seahawks from 1986 to 1991, there was one man he hated to face.

Although he excelled against most of his NFL opponents, Millard had become the personal punching bag of Los Angeles Raiders defensive lineman Howie Long.

Twice a season for six years, as Millard prepared to face Los Angeles, he would dip into his bag of tricks, searching for the equalizer he needed against the Raiders' eight-time Pro Bowl player.

And every time the game was over, he straggled off the field with the realization that he had been treated like just another stiff by the Raiders' rampaging defensive lineman.

Although Long had his way with Millard for years, he may have saved his best for their last encounter. It occurred November 17, 1991 at Los Angeles Memorial Coliseum. Millard lost his personal battle with Long that day and the Seahawks lost the war, 31-7.

"It was a pass-rush drill for those guys," Millard said. "They brought out everything they had and pretty much everything worked. It was a whippin', no question about it."

Millard's assignment was to stop Long from getting to Seattle quarterback Dave Krieg. Although Long was credited with just one sack in the contest, he recovered two fumbles and applied considerable quarterback pressure throughout the afternoon. Krieg's abused body and Millard's bruised ego were testimony to the damage Long inflicted.

"I know what I did yesterday," Millard said following a film review of the game in which Los Angeles ravaged the Seahawks offensive line for seven sacks. "I played against, by far, the best defensive lineman in the National Football League, Number 75. At least I think that's what his number was. I caught him from behind most of the time. The S.O.B. is still the best and there won't be anybody better."

While Long created havoc for Millard, his teammates on the Raiders defensive line also benefited.

"Some of the other guys picked up garbage sacks that Long caused," Millard said. "He's so fast, so strong and he gets at such an angle to where a lot of times he doesn't give you a whole lot to hit.

"I've met him a lot of years and a lot of times. I certainly don't remember him playing that well. It was a super-human effort, as opposed to my sub-human effort."

At the end of the season as the Pro Bowl balloting rolled around to the players, Millard had little trouble filling out the defensive line spots.

"Pro Bowl?" Millard snorted about Long's chances. "Hell, I'm voting for him for President."

Millard suffered a back injury prior to the 1992 season which shortened his career and prevented him from ever getting the best of Long.

———— 🏈 ————

After finishing his college playing days at the University of Texas where he was the team co-captain, **BRYAN MILLARD** signed with the New Jersey Generals of the USFL in 1983.

He joined the Seahawks in 1984 as a free agent and started at three different line positions during his pro career, playing right guard, left tackle and right tackle. He is the only Seattle offensive lineman ever to be named to the Pro Bowl.

Prior to his back injury, Millard had played in 121 games, the second highest for offensive linemen in club history.

One of his biggest thrills was catching a deflected pass against Denver in 1987. It was good for negative five yards.

PLAYING HISTORY:
New Jersey Generals (USFL)
1983-1984
Seattle Seahawks 1984-1991

Big Bark, No Bite

Since joining the Seahawks as a highly touted first-round draft pick in 1987, linebacker Brian Bosworth's much talked about matchups with John Elway, the elusive quarterback of the Denver Broncos, were played out with more ferocity in the press than they ever were on the field.

In their first encounter at Mile High Stadium, during Bosworth's regular-season debut in 1987, his only lick against Elway came when he pushed the Denver quarterback out of bounds at the end of a scramble. But the former University of Oklahoma star reacted as if he scored a last-minute sack producing a one-point win in the Super Bowl. He stood over the fallen Elway and bellowed like a wounded cow.

"He didn't say anything really. He just yelled," Elway said. "He screamed, 'Aaaaaaaaahhhh.' I couldn't decipher any English language coming out of him."

Bosworth claims he did utter something decipherable. He said to Elway, "I'm your worst nightmare, (expletive)."

Bosworth had set the stage for this semi-dramatic confrontation earlier in the week by telling a Denver reporter exactly what he was planning for Elway.

"You rarely get a chance to get a shot on somebody like that, and when you do, you want to take your best shot. I'm going to do that— take as many shots as hard as I can," Bosworth said.

The threats became banner headlines in Denver. But Elway nonchalantly replied, "Any time you hear that, it's something that goes in one ear and right out the other. I take it with a grain of salt."

So, when the Seahawks opened the 1988 season at Denver's Mile High Stadium, the Bronco faithfuls were ready for Bosworth. But like most of the over-priced linebacker's talk, he backed it with very little action on the field.

"There were no gutteral sounds today," Bosworth said after the confrontation. "It was a situation where I didn't need to say anything." Truer words were never spoken.

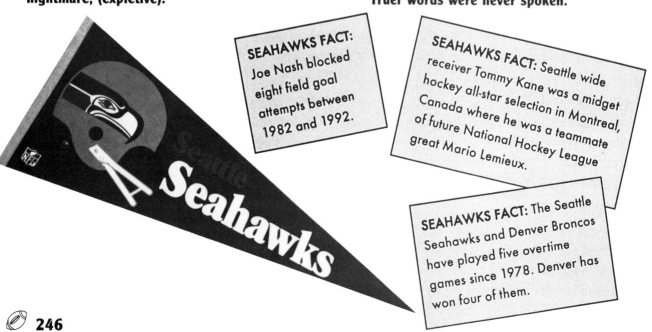

SEAHAWKS FACT: Joe Nash blocked eight field goal attempts between 1982 and 1992.

SEAHAWKS FACT: Seattle wide receiver Tommy Kane was a midget hockey all-star selection in Montreal, Canada where he was a teammate of future National Hockey League great Mario Lemieux.

SEAHAWKS FACT: The Seattle Seahawks and Denver Broncos have played five overtime games since 1978. Denver has won four of them.

BO GOES SOLO

Bosworth's bark was always worse than his bite, as the Los Angeles Raiders could also attest. During the 1987 season, Seattle took on the Raiders in a classic Monday Night Football matchup of the game's most glamorous rookies. It was billed as Boz versus Bo. Once again, there was no contest.

Raider running back Bo Jackson put on a solo performance rarely seen in modern times, rushing for 221 yards on 18 carries and scoring three touchdowns. On his first score, Jackson raced untouched around left end, then took off up the sideline like he'd been shot out of a cannon for a 91-yard touchdown.

But it was Jackson's last score of the night that proved most telling. It was then that he came face-to-face with Bosworth.

With the Raiders facing a third-and-goal from the two-yard line, Jackson got the call on an off-tackle play. Bosworth responded quickly from his linebacker spot and came up to meet him. He never had a chance. Jackson lowered a shoulder and blew right through Bosworth, knocking him three yards into the end zone.

Not long after, Bosworth's career came to an end just three years after it started. He suffered through a series of injuries that racked his 24-year-old body and hindered his performance. Then, in 1989, he packed his bags and moved to Hollywood where he tried his hand as an actor.

Bosworth played with the Seahawks from 1987 to 1989.

Seattle linebacker Brian Bosworth tackles Green Bay running back Kenneth Davis. Seattle used their first-round draft pick to select Bosworth in the 1987 supplemental draft. Bosworth played in just 24 games over three seasons before heading to Hollywood.

Nothing to Lose

Dave Krieg was still a bit awed by life in the National Football League when Seattle Seahawks starting quarterback Jim Zorn went down with a broken ankle. Suddenly, the little-known second-year man from tiny Milton College in Wisconsin was thrown into the fray against the New York Jets.

With three games left in the 1981 season, Seattle had just four wins under its belt and was assured of another season under .500. The Jets were gearing up for the playoffs.

New York's defense was among the league's leaders in sacks and turnovers. The sight of a greenhorn like Krieg strolling onto the field had Jets defensive linemen Mark Gastineau and Joe Klecko drooling and chomping at the bit.

"I wasn't really nervous," Krieg said. "I didn't have anything to lose."

Indeed, just a year earlier, Krieg was surprised to get a tryout with the Seahawks. After finishing his senior year at Milton College, which had a grand total of 230 students during Krieg's tenure, he had his football coach write a letter to the Seahawks on his behalf. He knew the chance of an invitation was a longshot. But as a courtesy to Krieg's old coach, he was invited to Seattle's 1980 training camp as an undrafted free agent.

"I wasn't sure I would last," Krieg said. "I just wanted the chance to try."

He impressed coach Jack Patera with his intelligence and accuracy, winning a spot behind starting quarterback Jim Zorn.

"Suddenly I was an NFL quarterback," Krieg said. "It was a little hard to believe at first, but I didn't have time to look at everything in wonder. I had to learn the system and about NFL defenses. It was a little overwhelming at first, but it's really the same game you play in high school and college. The pass routes are the same. The yardage is the same. Things are just speeded up a little more."

Unbeknownst to the Jets that day, Krieg was prepared to win. He completed 20 of 26 passes with two touchdowns in his first NFL start. Under his leadership, the Seahawks upset New York 27-23. After the contest, Krieg was surprised at the media attention his performance attracted.

"There were dozens of people around my locker," Krieg said. "That was probably a bigger crowd then we generally had for football games in college."

The media would continue to have reason to pay attention to Krieg. Midway through the 1983 season, he won the starting job from Zorn and a new era began in Seattle. Under Krieg's guidance, the Seahawks posted a 12-4 record in 1984, the best finish in the club's history.

DAVE KRIEG

Krieg's spectacular 1984 season ended disappointingly. After beating the Raiders in the 1984 wildcard playoff game, Seattle was sent home for the winter by the Miami Dolphins. But Krieg continued to perform as one of the league's finest quarterbacks with the Seahawks. During his 12 seasons with Seattle, Krieg teamed with Steve Largent while his star receiver quietly chased pro football's all-time records for receptions, yardage, touchdowns and consecutive games with a reception.

In 1992, Krieg signed with the Kansas City Chiefs. In his inaugural season with the Chiefs, he was the AFC's sixth-ranked quarterback and led the club to a 10-6 record. But Kansas City was bounced out of the playoffs in the first round by the San Diego Chargers.

By the 1993 season, when Krieg served as Joe Montana's backup at Kansas City, he had passed for just over 30,000 yards in his pro career, completing 59 percent of his 4,000 passes.

Dave Krieg went undrafted in 1980 after his senior season at tiny Milton College in Wisconsin. He earned a tryout with Seattle after he persuaded a college coach to contact the Seahawks on his behalf. After 15 seasons, he has developed into one of the NFL's most productive quarterbacks.

PLAYING HISTORY:
Seattle Seahawks 1980-1991
Kansas City Chiefs 1992-1993
Detroit Lions 1994-

SEAHAWKS FACT: The Seahawks' Rick Tuten was forced to punt 108 times in 1992, the third highest total in NFL history.

SEAHAWKS FACT: Michael Bates, Seattle's sixth-round draft pick in 1992 won the bronze medal in the 200-meter race at the 1992 Olympics.

SEAHAWKS FACT: The Seahawks have had seven players named Green on their roster since 1976: Boyce, Jacob, Jessie, Paul, Sammy and Tony Green, as well as Danny Greene.

Any Last Requests?

The Tampa Bay Buccaneers' first head coach, John McKay, had a marvelous sense of humor, a vital asset to a coach whose team would lose 26 games in a row before getting a victory, in the process becoming the laughing-stock of the NFL.

McKay endured the franchise's darkest days. In the club's first season of play, it suffered through five shutouts. In its second year, it was shut out six more times and, on two other occasions, it was held to just a field goal. During its first two seasons, Tampa Bay averaged only seven points per game.

So in the midst of the Bucs' nearly two-year losing streak, a Tampa reporter once opened a post-game press conference by asking McKay, "How do you feel about your team's execution?"

McKay had a simple reply.

"Personally, I'm all for it," he said. "Go ahead."

I'll Be There

One of the seemingly hundreds of prospects who tried out for a spot with McKay's Bucs was a young rookie kicker named Pete Ryjecki. The youngster foolishly mentioned to a journalist one day, "When Coach McKay watches me, I get really nervous."

The remark was passed along to the coach, who suggested, "You might inform Mr. Ryjecki that I plan to attend all the games."

No Sweat

After registering another defeat in the Bucs' 26-game losing streak, Coach McKay was feeling rather unsatisfied with his club's effort. He gave a succinct, if stinging, postgame address.

"Okay, if anyone needs a shower, take one," McKay was heard to say before retiring to his office.

Saints Preserve Us

Coach McKay finally squeezed a victory out of his Bucs in 1977 after 26 straight losses. Every team in the NFL had nightmares about being the first to lose to Tampa Bay. It was not the type of recognition any team wanted. The club's first victim was the hapless New Orleans Saints.

The Saints weren't much better than Tampa Bay. They had won just three games in 1977 and two of them were one-point victories. Fans began attending Saints games with paper bags over their heads and calling themselves the "Ain'ts."

But in Tampa Bay, beating New Orleans was akin to winning the Super Bowl. After capturing a 33-14 victory, the first win in club history, the Bucs returned home to a raucous crowd.

When the club's three chartered buses arrived at team headquarters, they were surrounded by nearly 10,000 screaming fans. The players could barely disembark. The fans finally agreed to move back after Coach McKay agreed to say a few words. No one could hear a thing he said, however, and the party lasted into the early morning hours.

JOHN McKAY

John McKay had won four national collegiate championships at USC before leaving to try his hand at the professional game.

During his nine seasons as the Buccaneer's head coach (1976-1984), the team compiled a 44-88 record and won two NFC Central Division titles.

> **BUCCANEERS FACT:**
> Buccaneer linebacker Broderick Thomas learned a few things about the pro game from his uncle, former Chicago Bears great Mike Singletary.

> **BUCCANEERS FACT:** In 1976, Tampa Bay became the first team in NFL history to finish 0-14.

John McKay was named head coach of the expansion Tampa Bay Buccaneers in 1976 after leading the USC Trojans to four national championships. Tampa Bay lost its first 26 games, but in 1979 McKay guided the Bucs to the NFC Championship Game.

POISON PEN

*L*ate in his career at Tampa, McKay had a falling out with local sports columnist Tom McEwen, whose work had been instrumental in bringing pro football to Tampa. It was an acrimonious feud that lasted well into McKay's retirement.

Years later, the Tampa Sports Authority, which operates Tampa Stadium, elected to honor McEwen's contributions by naming the stadium press box after him. When McKay caught wind of the honor, he cracked, "I figure so much bad writing came out of that press box, they ought to make him take the blame."

Beating the Heat

The Tampa Bay Buccaneers couldn't have asked for a more stifling hot opening day than the one they got at Tampa Stadium in 1979.

For All-Pro defensive end Lee Roy Selmon, the heat and humidity were particularly trying. Selmon had undergone offseason knee surgery and was testing the knee for the first time in game conditions. More importantly, he had not yet worked himself into top shape. By the second half of the contest against the Detroit Lions, Selmon was just about worn out.

"All I could think of was how to get the game over with and get off the field with a win, so I could enjoy a cold shower," said Selmon, the very first pick of the 1976 draft and the cornerstone of the Tampa Bay defensive unit for nine seasons.

Before the game was over, Selmon would experience the dream of a lifetime—and neither the heat, his weariness or a Detroit Lion would stop him.

"(Defensive end) Wally Chambers forced a fumble that came bouncing toward me," Selmon said. "I just scooped it up and began to ramble. It was only 30 yards or so to the end zone, but I felt like I was running in the Boston Marathon. I can still remember Jeris White, one of our defensive backs, running alongside of me, hollering, 'Gimme the ball! Gimme the ball!'"

But Selmon could smell the goal line. The thought of lateraling the ball to White never crossed his mind. The four-time All-Pro, who suffered through the expansion Bucs' 26-game losing streak in 1976 and 1977, would let nothing, not even his own teammate, get in the way of his moment in the sun.

"I kept it myself and it turned out to be my only NFL touchdown," Selmon said. "But if it happened again on the same kind of sweltering day, I'd probably give it up."

Selmon's touchdown was a catalyst in the Bucs 31-16 win over the Lions. It also provided Selmon with legitimate proof that he'd recovered from knee surgery. The 1979 season proved to be the best of his career, as he recorded 117 tackles, 11 sacks, 60 quarterback pressures and two fumble recoveries.

BUCCANEERS FACT: Nothing could keep quarterback Steve DeBerg out of a game.

While playing with the Tampa Bay Buccaneers, he contracted laryngitis. The Bucs equipment manager rigged a device that fit to DeBerg's helmet and shoulder pads and allowed him to amplify his voice as he called signals.

But the device worked too well.

In the huddle while calling a play, DeBerg accidently keyed the microphone while asking one of his wideouts if he could beat the defensive back playing him. DeBerg then called an "X go." As the conversation echoed through the stadium, the defense looked on in surprised amusement and DeBerg's teammates began to laugh in the huddle.

"I think you better call another play," wide receiver Mike Shumann said. "They might be on to that one."

LEE ROY SELMON

*S*elmon joined the Buccaneers in 1976 as the club's first-ever pick. The 6-foot-3, 250-pound defensive end from the University of Oklahoma recorded 79 sacks and 390 quarterback pressures during his nine seasons with the club.

Selmon played in six Pro Bowls and was the NFL's Defensive Player of the Year in 1979. He played with the Tampa Bay Buccaneers from 1976 to 1984.

Lee Roy Selmon (63) was the first player ever drafted by Tampa Bay in 1976. In the second round, the Bucs selected Lee Roy's brother, defensive tackle Dewey Selmon. They became the first pair of brothers ever drafted in consecutive rounds by an NFL team.

TAMPA BAY

Don't Jump the Gun, Coach

Quarterback Doug Williams stepped from the spotlight at Grambling University into a virtual firestorm as a Tampa Bay Buccaneer rookie.

Tampa Bay fans were still smarting from the team's first two seasons, which had produced only two wins in 28 games. Then coach John McKay used the club's first-round draft pick in 1978 to choose Williams, a generally unheralded kid out of a Division II NCAA all-black college. The fans were outraged.

It was one thing, many felt, to make a black tackle or black running back the club's number-one choice. But choosing a black quarterback was simply preposterous!

The hate mail and the anonymous phone calls appeared almost immediately. The Bucs beefed up security to protect their prize rookie from any physical ugliness, but they couldn't shield him from the letters that appeared in newspapers or the comments by callers to radio talk shows. There were threats and slurs from loud-mouthed, anti-black rednecks who said they'd "never pay good money to watch a black kid play quarterback."

On Opening Day 1978, the Bucs were at home against the New York Giants in a game Tampa Bay would eventually lose, 19-13.

"I remember early in the game being hit really hard by Gary Jeter," Williams said. "It was a real welcome to the NFL and I knew I was hurt. I should have come out right away. But I guess I thought that would make me look bad or something, so I stayed in. I called a play in the huddle—I don't remember what it was, I was so dizzy—and went to the line of scrimmage.

"By the time I got under center, though, it all caught up to me and I just crumpled, falling to the ground in pain. I can remember it to this day, though, because the stadium got kind of quiet while people tried to figure out what was going on. Then I heard Coach McKay shout from the sideline, 'Oh, my Lord! They've shot him!'"

They hadn't, of course. Williams had suffered a slight shoulder separation, and after missing the rest of the game and all of the next one, he came back to finish the season.

BUCCANEERS FACT: The Bucs traveled to bitterly cold Green Bay in 1986 to meet the Packers in a blizzard. Green Bay won the game 21-7 and afterward the Tampa players were eager to escape the frozen field.

Later, as the club boarded a plane at Green Bay airport, they noticed their charter jet covered in snow and ice. Then, the players learned that the airport had been closed to incoming traffic. Several players expressed fear of flying in the horrible weather and were ready to walk off the plane.

That's when the plane's pilot appeared and showed offensive lineman Sean Farrell a wallet full of pictures of his wife and children. The pilot said to Farrell, "I've got a family of my own. Do you think I'd risk going up if I thought there was a chance I'd never see them again?"

It was enough to convince Farrell, who then persuaded the rest of the nervous Bucs to take their seats for the ride home to Tampa Bay.

DOUG WILLIAMS

*I*n his second year with the Bucs, Williams led Tampa Bay to its first NFC Central Division title. The Bucs then rolled over Philadelphia in the playoffs and were one game away from the Super Bowl. But against Los Angeles in the NFC Championship Game, Williams suffered an arm injury in the third period and the Bucs went down to defeat, 9-0.

Williams left the Bucs after the 1982 season, largely because of a contract dispute with team owner Hugh Culverhouse. He played in the United States Football League for two seasons. When it folded, he signed with the Washington Redskins.

In 1987, Williams had his finest moment as a professional. He led the Redskins to the NFC Championship and a date in Super Bowl XXII against Denver.

Early in the first quarter of the Super Bowl, Williams fell while dropping back to pass and hyperextended his left knee. He was replaced by backup quarterback Jay Schroeder. Denver jumped out to a 10-0 first quarter lead and Redskins coach Joe Gibbs went back to Williams to start the second quarter.

On his first play from scrimmage, Williams found Ricky Sanders with an 80-yard touchdown pass. On five consecutive

Minnesota Vikings defensive end Mark Mullaney (77) chases Tampa Bay quarterback Doug Williams in a 1980 contest. Williams completed 30 of 55 passes in the game for 485 yards.

possessions in the second quarter, Williams led touchdown drives of 80, 64, 74, 60 and 79 yards. It was the most lopsided quarter in Super Bowl history. He completed nine of 11 passes in the quarter for 228 yards and touchdowns of 80, 27, 50 and eight yards. At halftime, the Redskins had a 35-10 lead.

Williams finished the day with a Super Bowl-record 340 yards passing and was named the game's Most Valuable Player.

PLAYING HISTORY:
Tampa Bay Buccaneers 1978-1982
Oklahoma Outlaws (USFL)
1983-1984
Washington Redskins 1986-1989

255

Gentlemen's Agreement

As a 6-foot-7, 315-pound defensive tackle with the Washington Redskins, Dave Butz was regularly accorded special attention when opposing teams devised their game plans. He uniformly drew double-team blocking and enemy backs rarely attempted to pass through or around his position. It was mute testimony to his prowess as a run-stuffer.

But Butz also excelled as a pass rusher. He would advance on the quarterback with short, choppy steps, his oaken arms upraised, the pure bulk of his person wedging back laboring blockers like a barge forging through troubled waters.

"It would have been easier to throw the ball over a tree," said Tommy Kramer, a signal caller with the Minnesota Vikings.

Off the field, Butz displayed a somewhat dispassionate nature complete with a bland expression. They served as a blind, behind which hid a dry wit. In the bedlam of a victorious locker room, he would quietly expound with professorial eloquence upon the mundanities of the turf war recently concluded.

"The gentleman was persistently holding me," he explained. "I brought the matter to the attention of the officials, but they chose to ignore it. So I spoke to the gentleman directly. I said, 'You don't hold me and I won't hit you in the head.' On that basis, we were able to reach an accommodation."

REDSKINS FACT: Mark Moseley made 23 field goals in a row over the 1981-82 seasons, a league record.

On the Road(kill) Again

Butz's only notable idiosyncrasy was an odd pregame ritual which often included kicker Mark Moseley and tight end Don Warren.

"Before home games, Mark, Don and I would get in my van and we'd go out looking for roadkill to run over," he said. "When the wheels hit the remains of a dead squirrel, rabbit or whatever, there was a dull thunking sound along with a slight jarring motion. That combination of sound and sense perception kind of put us in the right mindset for the rest of the day."

Prior to away games, the hunt for roadkill required an understanding cab driver and no lack of patience on the part of all concerned.

"One Sunday, we were in Cleveland and got a late start searching for roadkill," Butz said. "It was one of those times we just couldn't seem to find anything to hit.

"After about a half hour of cruising, the driver was really antsy. The poor fella must have thought he had some bona fide nuts on his hands who might go bonkers if they didn't get their fix. Finally, Donny Warren spots a bunch of birds gathered in a side street. He lets out a whoop and yells, 'Go for it!' Then the cab rolled over what appeared to be the carcass of a cat. We exchanged high fives and shouted, 'Awwrigght!'

"Back at the motel the driver said, 'I think you guys are sick in the head.' Maybe, but we beat the Browns 14-7. The defense rests."

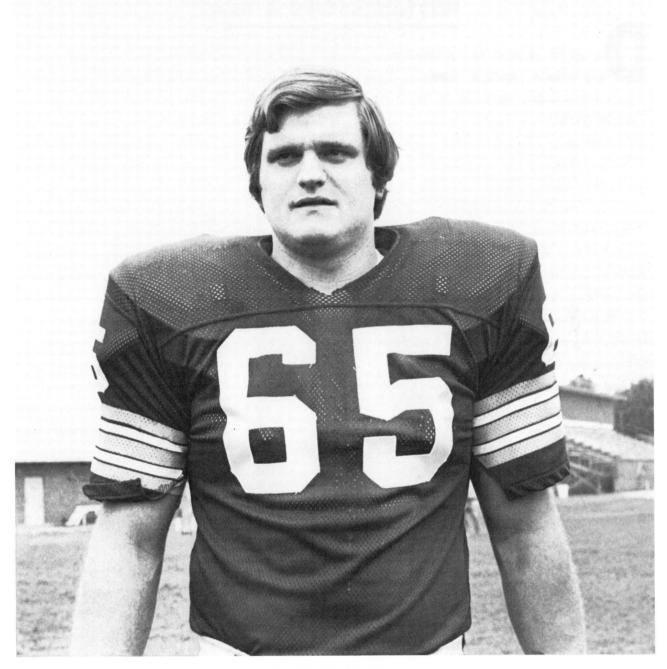

DAVE BUTZ

*B*utz was the fifth player chosen in the 1973 draft by the St. Louis Cardinals after being named All-American at Purdue. He signed with the Redskins in 1975 as a free agent.

Butz had his best NFL season in 1983 when he made 69 tackles, piled up 11-and-a-half sacks, forced five fumbles and recovered one. He was the anchor of the Redskins defense that allowed just 80 rushing yards per game. Butz was named All-Pro that season and played in his second Pro Bowl. He retired in 1988 with two Super Bowl rings.

PLAYING HISTORY:
St. Louis Cardinals 1973-1974
Washington Redskins 1975-1988

Never Deceive a Bear

During his 18 years as a professional quarterback, Christian "Sonny" Jurgensen was widely touted as the best pure passer in the NFL.

No less an authority on the subject than the Baltimore Colts' storied quarterback Johnny Unitas had this to say of his free-flinging contemporary: "If I threw as much as Jurgensen, my arm would fall off. And if I could throw as well, my head would swell up too big to get into a helmet."

Praise from Caesar is praise indeed.

But there was an occasion when Jurgensen's ability to propel a pigskin did not find an appreciative audience.

"We (Redskins) were playing the Bears in Washington in 1964," he recalled. "As I remember, it was just before the end of the first half. We had a slight lead and the ball was just past midfield. They were expecting us to simply kill the clock. So I waste a couple of plays with runs into the line. Then right before the gun, I stand up and throw one deep in their end zone and we get a touchdown."

Pleased with the success of his deception, Jurgensen turned and trotted for the Washington sideline. En route, he became aware of a considerable presence at his elbow. A cautious, over-the-shoulder glance determined it to be Chicago's 6-foot-8, 275-pound defensive end Doug Atkins, one of the money game's more pitiless purveyors of pain and distress.

"His expression told me he was not happy," Jurgensen said. "Then he grabs my arm. 'I don't like what you did, Jurgensen,' he says. I just keep trotting. Now, he gets close to my ear and says, 'Jurgensen, I could come right into your huddle and maim you, end your career. And all they'd do is penalize me 15 yards, or maybe throw me out of the game. Think about it.'"

Jurgensen did.

"That second half I spent a lot of time handing the ball off to somebody else," he said. "I was going to live to throw another day."

That he also did. Jurgensen's career, which began in 1957 after he was drafted by the Philadelphia Eagles out of Duke University, lasted 10 more illustrious seasons.

SONNY JURGENSEN

Jurgensen's rise to prominence began in 1961, his first year as a starter in Philadelphia. That season he turned heads by setting NFL records for completions and yards and throwing 32 touchdown passes. But he was surrounded by ineptitude with the Eagles. In 1966, he was dealt to the Washington Redskins.

With the Redskins in 1967 he set NFL standards for pass attempts, completions and yards, and was the league's top-rated quarterback.

Jurgensen closed out his career in 1974 at the age of 40 with 2,433 completions for 32,224 yards and 255 touchdowns. Only three quarterbacks have thrown more touchdown passes in NFL history.

He led the NFL in passing in 1967 and 1969 and played in three Pro Bowls. His 82.6 career quarterback rating is the fifth highest of all time.

Jurgensen was selected to the Pro Football Hall of Fame in 1983.

PLAYING HISTORY:
Philadelphia Eagles 1957-1963
Washington Redskins 1964-1974

Sonny Jurgensen (9) eludes Philadelphia Eagles defensive end Mel Tom (58) to make a throw downfield in 1969. Jurgensen threw for 32,224 yards and 255 touchdowns during his 18-year career with the Washington Redskins and Philadelphia Eagles.

Go Deep and Catch Your Flight

One of the more memorable games of Redskins quarterback Eddie LeBaron's career occurred during the 1955 season. The Redskins were playing in Cleveland against the Browns in their opening game. But it was a contest LeBaron almost missed.

"We were getting ready to leave on a plane from the National Airport," said LeBaron. "Dale Atkeson and I had arrived three hours before the charter was to leave. We got into some heavy discussions and before we knew it we heard an announcement over the loud-speaker. Then I looked up and realized the plane was gone.

"The plane was already at the end of the runway. Thankfully, the control tower explained our situation to the pilot, who turned the plane around and came back to pick us up."

In the end, it was the Browns' fans in Cleveland who probably wished that LeBaron had been left on the runway. LeBaron had one of those days that many quarterbacks can only dream about.

"I called a pass play to Ralph Thomas," said LeBaron. "I threw it too deep. But Leo Elter had run a pattern and was there to catch the pass, instead. It went for 70 yards. Vic Janowicz ran the ball into the end zone one play later and we were ahead, 6-0."

The Redskins increased their lead to 13-0 when John Carson caught a 24-yard pass from LeBaron and ran into the end zone. Carson would catch another touchdown pass from LeBaron in the third quarter to increase the Washington lead to 20-17.

LeBaron finished off the Browns in the closing minutes, scoring on a 13-yard run.

"But I probably ran 40 or more yards to do it," LeBaron said. "It seemed as though every Brown on the field had a shot at me and missed. I was never so glad to score a touchdown in my life."

Nor were the Redskins, who went on to beat the defending NFL champion Browns, 27-17.

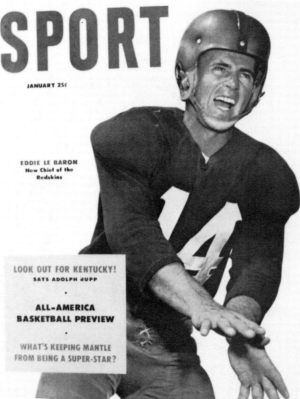

SPORT
JANUARY 25¢
EDDIE LE BARON
New Chief of the Redskins
LOOK OUT FOR KENTUCKY!
SAYS ADOLPH RUPP
ALL-AMERICA BASKETBALL PREVIEW
WHAT'S KEEPING MANTLE FROM BEING A SUPER-STAR?

EDDIE LeBARON

After joining the Redskins as a rookie, LeBaron played two seasons with the Redskins in 1952-1953 before heading north for a campaign in the Canadian Football League with the Calgary Stampeders. But LeBaron would return to Washington a year later. During the year he was gone, the Redskins had finished 3-9.

But 1955 proved to be a different story for the team and LeBaron. Washington improved to 8-4, good enough for second place in the NFC's Eastern Conference behind the powerful Cleveland Browns.

During his 11 NFL seasons, LeBaron completed 897 of 1,796 passing attempts for 104 touchdowns and 13,399 yards. He had one of his finest seasons in 1958, completing 54 percent of his passes and averaging 9.5 yards per attempt. The former University of the Pacific star was also one of the league's top punters, averaging 41 yards per kick. LeBaron was named to the Pro Bowl as a quarterback four times.

PLAYING HISTORY:
Washington Redskins 1952-1953
Calgary Stampeders (CFL) 1954
Washington Redskins 1955-1959
Dallas Cowboys 1960-1963

REDSKINS FACT: Great football coaches like Vince Lombardi, Don Shula, Bill Walsh and Jimmy Johnson have all been labeled a genius at some time in their career. But former Washington Redskins quarterback Joe Theismann thought the genius label was thrown around too loosely.

"The word genius isn't applicable in football," Theismann once said. "A genius is a guy like Norman Einstein."

261

I Am Not a Coach...Er, Crook

*F*ormer President Richard M. Nixon made his name in politics as a tough decision maker. But he also was an avid sports fan who had punted the pigskin as a backup player at Whittier College.

Nixon often tried to meld his passion for athletics with his gift for decision-making by calling the coaches of his favorite clubs to chat or offer strategic advice. During his term as commander-in-chief, it was Nixon who began the presidential tradition of placing a phone call to the winners of the Super Bowl, World Series and other major sporting events. But he also was unafraid to ring a coach at night to suggest an offensive play he had drawn up.

While serving in the nation's capitol, Nixon followed the Washington Redskins religiously and became good friends with Redskins coach George Allen. It was a friendship that lasted long after Nixon hastily left the White House in 1974. Allen was the coach Nixon usually called with advice.

History says that Nixon telephoned Allen the week of Washington's 1971 playoff game against San Francisco and suggested the Redskins run an end-around with receiver Roy Jefferson carrying against the 49ers. At least that's the story that was reported by the media.

The Redskins had a 10-3 lead near the close of the first half and were facing a second-and-six at the 49ers eight-yard line. Allen decided it was time for the play. But the 49ers stuffed it before it even got started. San Francisco defensive end Cedrick Hardman ambushed Jefferson in the backfield for a 13-yard loss. The drive stalled and the Redskins' subsequent field goal attempt was blocked.

San Francisco staged a furious second-half comeback, eventually winning 24-20, as quarterback John Brodie tossed a pair of touchdown passes. Although there was mourning on Capitol Hill, Nixon's play calling became a major topic of discussion.

Years later, Redskins players swear they knew the play wasn't going to work from the moment they first practiced it. They were amazed when the play was called, and shocked when they discovered after the game it was Nixon who designed the strategy.

Only he didn't! That was just the story.

What really happened was that Allen knew his friend in the Oval Office enjoyed being considered a football insider with a knack for play calling. He realized that Nixon was a closet football coach.

Being a bit of a politician himself, Allen called the White House one day and informed the president he thought the 49ers were vulnerable to an end-around near their goal line. He told Nixon he was going to use the maneuver, but that he would give credit publicly to the president. It would be good publicity for America's leader.

Of course, Nixon was delighted with the plan.

And Allen was so confident that his strategy would succeed that he put out word to the Redskins press corps during the week that Nixon had telephoned and "suggested" an end-around.

But when the play blew up in Allen's face, there was no way he could go back to the press corps and tell the truth. No one would have believed him. The nation's sports fans would think he was trying to take the heat off his friend in the White House. Jefferson's 13-yard loss became known as Nixon's play.

Redskins coach George Allen pleads with one of his Washington players on the sideline during a 1972 game. During his 12 years as an NFL head coach, Allen never experienced a losing season.

GEORGE ALLEN

George Allen spent 12 years as a head coach in the NFL, compiling a 116-47-5 record. He never had a losing season and his .705 winning percentage is fourth best of all time.

Allen had an innate ability to turn losing teams into winners with his infectious positive spirit. His motto was "The future is now" and, therefore, he was willing to trade future draft choices for veteran players capable of helping his club immediately.

In 1967, Allen was named NFL Coach of the Year after leading the Los Angeles Rams to an 11-1-2 record. In 1971, he took over the Washington Redskins and directed them to the playoffs five times in seven years. After beating Dallas for the NFC Championship in 1972, Allen got his only shot at a Super Bowl ring. The Redskins lost to Miami in Super Bowl VII, 14-7.

For more about George Allen, see the Los Angeles Rams chapter, pages 148-149.

COACHING HISTORY:
Los Angeles Rams 1966-1970
Washington Redskins 1971-1977

REDSKINS FACT: During his seven years as coach of the Washington Redskins, George Allen made a whopping 81 trades.

FIRST IMPRESSIONS

*I*f there was a category for off-the-wall personalities at the Pro Football Hall of Fame, former Redskins and Jets fullback John Riggins would command a special wing.

From his very first day in the professional game, Riggins caused a stir. When he signed with the New York Jets as the club's first-round draft choice in 1971, head coach Weeb Ewbank couldn't believe his eyes when the prize rookie showed up at the team's headquarters.

"John rides up to our training camp office on a motorcycle," Ewbank recalled. "He's wearing an outsized derby with a big red feather stuck in it, no shirt, a vest, baggy pants and storm trooper boots. When he took off the derby his head was shaved except for a strip of hair up the middle. I said to myself, 'Oh, no.' And that was only the beginning."

Russ Grimm, a standout member of the Redskins offensive lines of the 1980s, had this to say about his ball-carrying buddy: "Some guys march to the beat of a different drummer. John had his own band."

OUT OF WHEATIES

*R*iggins served the Jets for five seasons, his best year coming in 1975 when he rushed for 1,005 yards. But New York was on a downward slide and unable to compete for a championship. In 1976, Riggins left the Jets and became a free agent. He sought his fortune with the Washington Redskins.

Redskins head coach Joe Gibbs once decided to make an unannounced visit to see Riggins at his Kansas home.

"I found John sitting in a rocking chair on his front porch," Gibbs said. "He wore only undershorts and had a can of beer in each hand."

Recalling the meeting, Riggins said, "I don't think Joe was pleased about all that. Especially since it was just nine o'clock in the morning."

WAGON RIGGINS

*P*laying for the Redskins, Riggins became the centerpiece for Gibbs' one-back offensive attack. He helped guide the team to the NFL's Eastern Division title in 1982, then went to Gibbs with an unusual request.

"I was getting goose bumps just thinking about the Super Bowl," Riggins said. "I needed something to ease the pressure. I wanted the ball. So I went to Gibbs and said, 'I'm ready. I want the ball. Just hitch the wagon to me and I'll take you to the big hoedown.' Joe looked at me kind of funny for a moment before he finally said, 'Okay, you got it.' The rest is history."

Washington defeated Miami 27-17 in Super Bowl XVII, but it was Riggins' 43-yard touchdown run in the fourth quarter that put the Redskins ahead for the first time in the game. He finished the day with 166 yards rushing and was named the game's Most Valuable Player.

LIFE OF THE PARTY

*D*uring his 14-year career Riggins rushed for over 1,000 yards five times and always remained the life of the party. And in Washington, D.C., there was a party almost every night.

In the wake of the 1985 season, his last in the NFL, he made headlines on the social circuit. The occasion was a white tie and tux political bash in the nation's capital that included U.S. Supreme Court justices, foreign dignitaries and several of the country's most prominent politicians. But Riggins was unfazed by the glamour, glitz and power that surrounded him. Nursing a bad back, he lay on the floor to alleviate the pain, then proceeded to fall asleep under a table.

JOHN RIGGINS

Given an over-the-shoulder perspective of his days in the football sun, John Riggins has said, "For sure there were times I got too rich a mix in the old engine block. But I was in it for the crowds, the money and the good times. So I have no regrets."

Riggins will be remembered as one of the best short-yardage backs in the history of the game. He set a league record for rushing touchdowns in a single season with 24 during the 1983 campaign as he led the Redskins to their second straight Super Bowl appearance.

In the course of his 14-year career, he ran for 11,352 yards, fifth best in NFL history, and tallied 116 touchdowns, a mark topped only by Jim Brown and Walter Payton.

In 1992, Riggins was enshrined in the Pro Football Hall of Fame.

PLAYING HISTORY:
New York Jets 1971-1975
Washington Redskins 1976-1979;1981-1985

Special edition Gameday program from July of 1992 that featured John Riggins, Lem Barney, John Mackey and Al Davis on their induction into the Pro Football Hall of Fame.

REDSKINS FACT: Linebacker Rusty Tillman was a menace on the football field, but during his eight-year stint with the Washington Redskins, from 1970 to 1977, he also made a name for himself off of it. Tillman spent many of his off-duty hours with a hearty crew that included Redskins quarterback Billy Kilmer, safety Jake Scott and defensive tackle Diron Talbert. In the midst of his playing days, Tillman began dating Susan Ford, the daughter of then President Gerald Ford. When Ms. Ford hit the town with her Redskin friends, she was always accompanied by a pair of Secret Service men, who had a sobering affect on the group. One night, they all got together to celebrate Ms. Ford's birthday at a well-known restaurant near the capital. After a few drinks, Kilmer, Scott, Talbert and Tillman decided to test the patience and reflexes of the Secret Service men. They showered the stoic-faced agents with edibles in a classic food fight. The Secret Service men remained calm during the barrage and later that night reported back to the White House, covered with handfuls of birthday cake.

King Four-a-Day

During his 16 seasons with the Washington Redskins, Slingin' Sammy Baugh set a slew of passing records. But his finest day as a pro came when he made his mark as much on defense as with his throwing arm.

The Redskins were taking on the Detroit Lions at home in November, 1943. It was before unlimited substitution, an era when 11 men stayed on the field for 60 minutes. Star quarterback Sammy Baugh was no different.

"I liked playing defense," Baugh said. "But I was probably a liability on defense, the weakest link out there. The other team knew that. They worked on me and that gave me a chance to intercept some passes."

Against the Lions that day, Baugh intercepted four passes, a Redskins single-game record. But his work was only half done. When Baugh lined up at quarterback on offense, he threw four touchdown passes. He is the only man in NFL history to intercept four passes and throw four scoring passes in the same game.

"Now that's a record I know will never be broken," Baugh said. "You're never going to find a quarterback throw for four touchdowns and have four interceptions in the same game. That's not the way they play today."

Baugh went on to lead the NFL in passing, punting and interceptions in 1943, a feat that will never be equalled in the present age of specialization. He finished with 11 interceptions and was the NFL's top-rated quarterback, completing 133 of 239 passes for 1,754 yards and 23 touchdowns. But Baugh's Redskins were defeated by the Chicago Bears in the 1943 Championship Game, 41-21.

SAMMY BAUGH

Baugh is considered by many to be the father of the modern passing game. He was one of the first quarterbacks to incorporate a short passing attack into his offensive scheme.

During the 1945 season, Baugh helped usher in the T-Formation which would revolutionize football. Baugh proved that it was effective when used with an accurate quarterback, as he completed nearly 71 percent of his passes, a single-season record that stood for 38 years before being broken.

"He would cock the ball," former New York Giants head coach Steve Owen, once wrote, "then bring it down, and drift off as if about to run, cock again, make a mock throw to one side, and shoot a touchdown to the other. He was never committed until he was flat on the ground and the ball with him. I have seen him make bullet-like throws with his tremendous wrist action as he was nailed by a hard tackle and falling."

Baugh broke into the NFL with a bang in 1937, leading the Redskins to an NFL title his rookie season and topping the league in passing. In the 1937 NFL Championship Game, Baugh passed for 354 yards against the Chicago Bears, including touchdown passes of 55, 78 and 35 yards. The Redskins came from behind to beat the Bears 28-21.

Baugh retired in 1952 with six league passing titles. Four times he was the league's top punter. His 45.1-yard career punting average is the best of all time.

During his career, he completed 1,693 of 2,995 passes for 21,886 yards and 186 touchdowns. He was named All-Pro six times.

In 1963, Baugh was made one of the charter members of the Pro Football Hall of Fame.

PLAYING HISTORY:
Washington Redskins 1937-1952
COACHING HISTORY:
New York Titans (AFL) 1960-1961
Houston Oilers 1964

REDSKINS

BELOW: Slingin' Sammy Baugh (33) gets set to fire a pass against the Chicago Bears during the 1942 season. Baugh won six individual passing titles during his 16 seasons with the Washington Redskins and was named All-Pro six times.

What Are You, Deaf?

During the summer of 1969, new Redskins coach Vince Lombardi was perplexed at the lackluster performance of his rookie running back from Kansas State.

Larry Brown was an eighth-round draft pick, but had all the tools Lombardi sought in a great ground gainer. At 5-foot-11 and 195 pounds, he was a power back with speed, toughness, vision and above all, desire. Yet something was missing. Brown was always just a second slow in drills and scrimmages. For all his talent, it appeared Lombardi might be forced to cut his young back.

One evening during training camp, Lombardi was showing his club films of a recent Redskins exhibition game. He ran it in slow motion. There it became even more evident that Brown was a split second later getting off the ball than the rest of his teammates. Lombardi asked Brown if something was wrong, if he suffered from any physical ailments.

"I'm having trouble recognizing the defensive alignments," Brown said, knowing he was giving the coach a stock excuse often used by rookies. "He bought it for all of a week."

One day, though, two men in long, white coats appeared at training camp. While teammates watched in wonder, they approached Brown in the locker room and took him out of the building.

"They had been ordered by Lombardi to give me a hearing test," Brown recalled.

The test revealed that Brown was deaf in his right ear, something he'd suspected since childhood but had never told anyone. When Lombardi received the diagnosis, he approached NFL commissioner Pete Rozelle and obtained permission to have a hearing aid installed in Brown's helmet.

After Brown received the hearing aid, Lombardi wanted to test it. He told Brown to stand in one corner of a room while he stood in the opposite corner.

"Larry, can you hear me?" Lombardi screamed.

"Coach, I've never had a problem hearing YOU," Brown replied.

The makeshift audio test proved inconclusive. Lombardi's players never had trouble recognizing their coach's loud, baritone voice. But there was no doubt about the hearing aid's effect on Brown's performance.

Lombardi's ability to recognize Brown's hearing problem saved the rookie's career. During his initial season with the Redskins, Brown was the club's workhorse. He gained 888 yards to lead the Redskins in rushing and averaged 4.4 yards per carry.

LARRY BROWN

The season after Brown's stunning 1969 rookie debut, he won the NFL rushing title with 1,125 yards. In 1972, Brown had his best season. He led the NFC in rushing with 1,216 yards, and averaged 4.3 yards per carry despite sitting out the final two games of the regular season with an injury. He was a unanimous choice for NFL Player of the Year.

During the 1976 season, Brown suffered a knee injury and he retired at the end of the campaign. He had career totals of 5,875 rushing yards and 2,485 receiving yards. Brown scored 55 touchdowns during his career and led the NFL with 14 touchdowns in 1973. He was All-Pro in 1970 and 1972 and played in four Pro Bowls. Brown played for the Washington Redskins from 1969 to 1976.

Photo from Richard Wolffers Auctions, Inc., San Francisco

Pete Pihos joined the Philadelphia Eagles in 1947 and helped lead the team to three divisional titles and NFL championships in 1948 and 1949.

During World War II numerous NFL players were on military duty. The Philadelphia Eagles and Pittsburgh Steelers solved their player shortage problem by merging in 1943 and competing as the "Steagles."

The 1977 San Diego Chargers featured a young quarterback named Dan Fouts who would eventually be selected to the Pro Football Hall of Fame.

Number 28 was worn by Seattle Seahawks running back Curt Warner from 1983 to 1989. He's the club's all-time leading rusher with 6,705 yards.

Photo from Richard Wolffers Auctions, Inc., San Francisco

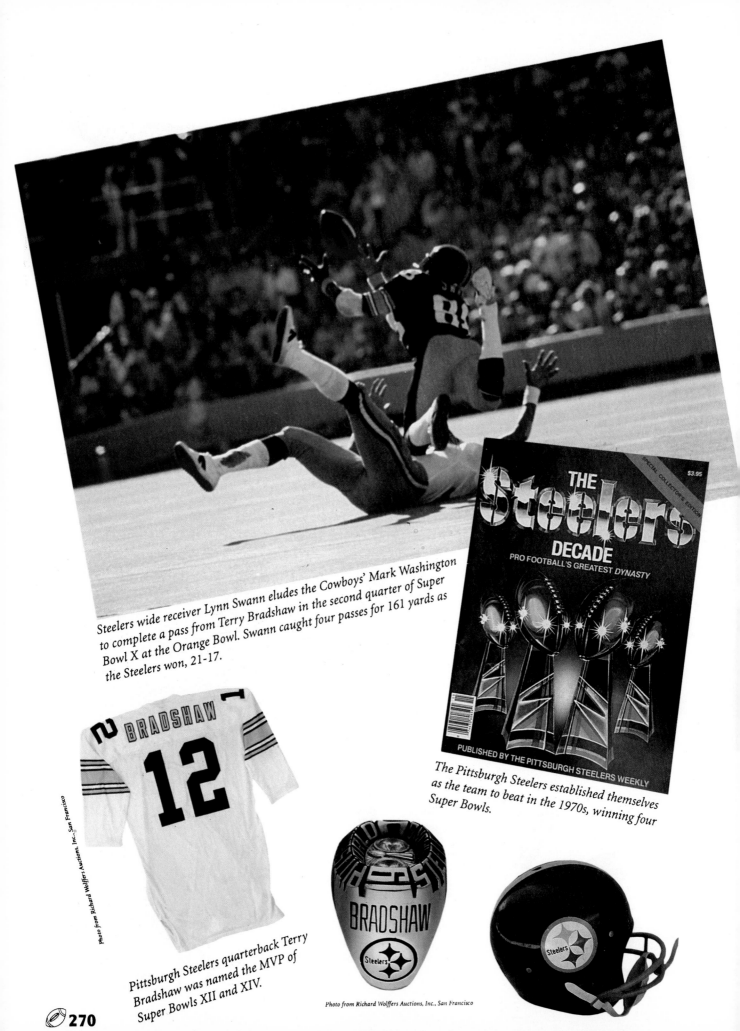

Steelers wide receiver Lynn Swann eludes the Cowboys' Mark Washington to complete a pass from Terry Bradshaw in the second quarter of Super Bowl X at the Orange Bowl. Swann caught four passes for 161 yards as the Steelers won, 21-17.

The Pittsburgh Steelers established themselves as the team to beat in the 1970s, winning four Super Bowls.

Pittsburgh Steelers quarterback Terry Bradshaw was named the MVP of Super Bowls XII and XIV.

The 49ers signed this helmet after they won Super Bowl XXIV.

Photo from Richard Wolffers Auctions, Inc., San Francisco

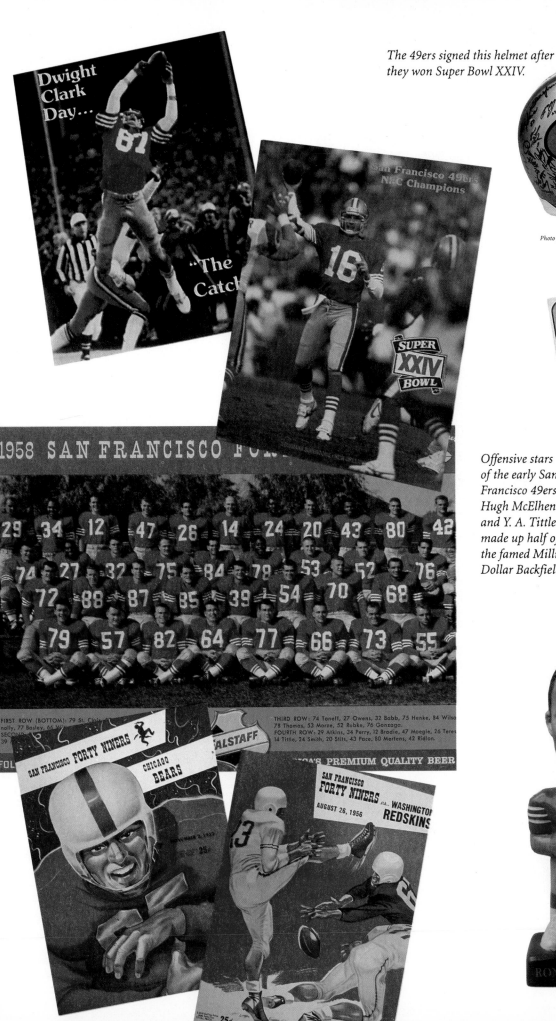

Dwight Clark Day…

"The Catch"

San Francisco 49ers NFC Champions

SUPER **XXIV** BOWL

1958 SAN FRANCISCO FO...

FIRST ROW (BOTTOM): 79 St. Cl...
...nolly, 77 Bosley, 66 W...
SECOND...
39...

THIRD ROW: 74 Toneff, 27 Owens, 32 Babb, 75 Henke, 84 Wilso...
78 Thomas, 53 Morze, 52 Rubke, 76 Gonzaga.
FOURTH ROW: 29 Atkins, 34 Perry, 12 Brodie, 47 Moegle, 26 Teres...
14 Tittle, 24 Smith, 20 Stits, 43 Pace, 80 Mertens, 42 Ridlon.

SAN FRANCISCO **FORTY NINERS** CHICAGO **BEARS**

...FF'S PREMIUM QUALITY BEER

SAN FRANCISCO **FORTY NINERS** vs. WASHINGTON **REDSKINS**
AUGUST 26, 1956

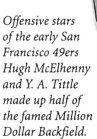

Offensive stars of the early San Francisco 49ers Hugh McElhenny and Y. A. Tittle made up half of the famed Million Dollar Backfield.

HUGH McELHENNY
SAN FRANCISCO 49ers

Y. A. TITTLE
SAN FRANCISCO 49ers

RONNIE LOTT

271

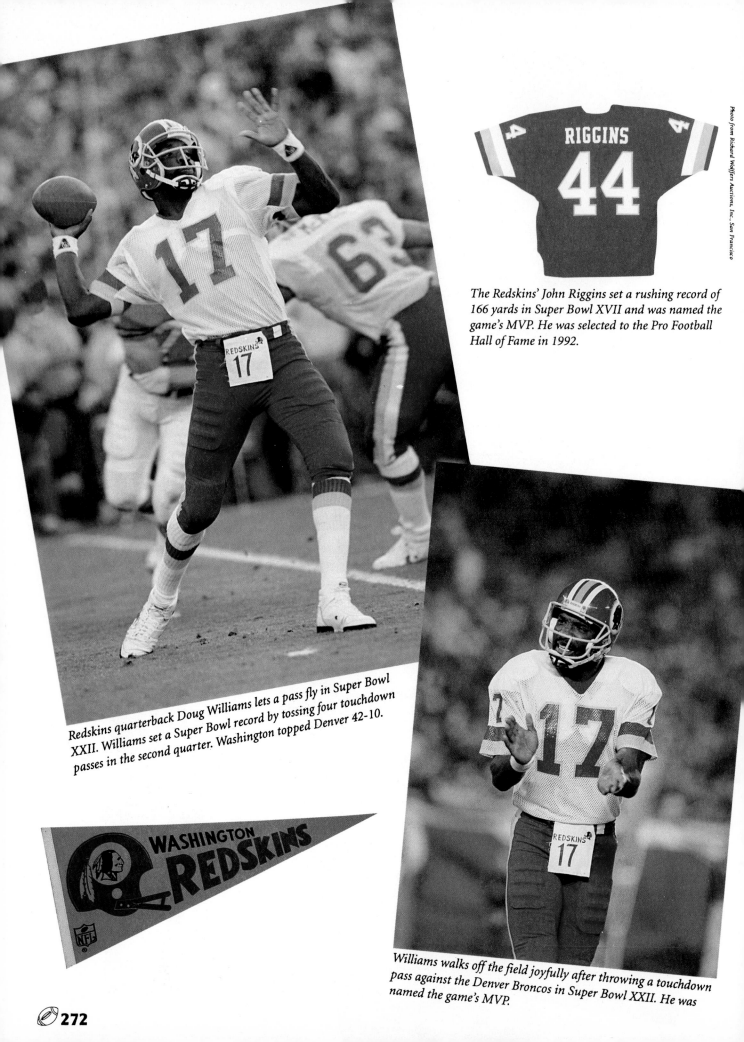

The Redskins' John Riggins set a rushing record of 166 yards in Super Bowl XVII and was named the game's MVP. He was selected to the Pro Football Hall of Fame in 1992.

Redskins quarterback Doug Williams lets a pass fly in Super Bowl XXII. Williams set a Super Bowl record by tossing four touchdown passes in the second quarter. Washington topped Denver 42-10.

Williams walks off the field joyfully after throwing a touchdown pass against the Denver Broncos in Super Bowl XXII. He was named the game's MVP.

INDEX

INDEX

INDEX

INDEX

INDEX

INDEX

INDEX

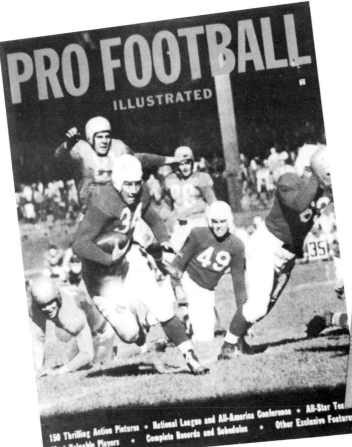

PRO FOOTBALL
ILLUSTRATED

150 Thrilling Action Pictures ★ National League and All-America Conference ★ All-Star Team
Most Valuable Players ★ Complete Records and Schedules ★ Other Exclusive Features

AFC-NFC
Pro Bowl
An Official Publication of the National Football League

The Eighth Meeting of
American Football Conference and
National Football Conference All-Stars

Tampa Stadium
Monday, January 23, 1978   9:00 P.M.
$1.25

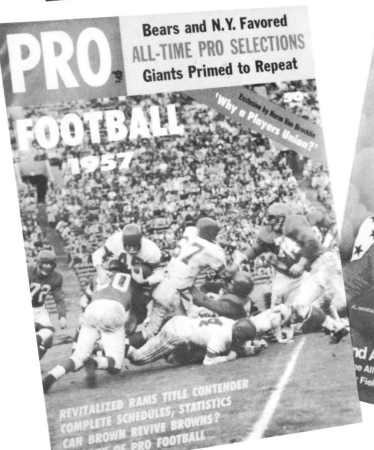

PRO

Bears and N.Y. Favored
ALL-TIME PRO SELECTIONS
Giants Primed to Repeat

FOOTBALL
1957

'Why a Players Union?'
Exclusive by Norm Van Brocklin

REVITALIZED RAMS TITLE CONTENDER
COMPLETE SCHEDULES, STATISTICS
CAN BROWN REVIVE BROWNS?
HISTORY OF PRO FOOTBALL

The Chicago Tribune Charities, Inc.

nd Annual All-Star Football Game
e All-Stars vs. World Champion Pittsburgh Steelers
Field August 1, 1975

OFFICIAL PROGRAM
AND RECORD BOOK
$1.00

285

National Football League Alumni

The National Football League Alumni is a non-profit service organization of former professional football players who work voluntarily on behalf of youth and charity. It was formed as an outgrowth of philanthropic and civic-minded impulses of men who have performed at the highest level of the nation's most popular spectator sport and have used that experience as a springboard to success in later life.

Founded in 1967 principally to deal with player welfare issues, the NFL Alumni was reorganized in 1977 as a tax-exempt charitable and educational organization. The NFL Alumni has national headquarters in Fort Lauderdale, Florida, and a network of local chapters across the country. It is a dues-paying membership association. Anyone ever employed by a major league football team qualifies as a professional member.

In their voluntary undertakings, members of the NFL Alumni are guided philosophically by the fundamental ideals expressed in their motto: "Caring for Kids."

One basic objective of the NFL Alumni is to render useful public service by raising funds for worthy causes, that, for the most part, are youth-oriented in nature.

A second major objective of the NFL Alumni is that of fostering development of "youth through sports and sports through youth."

Beyond helping disadvantaged children, the NFL Alumni members turn to a third prime objective—caring for their own. This is accomplished through funding the NFL Alumni Foundation in cooperation with the National Football League. Commonly called the "Dire Need Fund," the foundation provides financial assistance to former pros experiencing circumstances of hardship.

ALUMNI YOUTH OF AMERICA PROGRAMS

NFL Alumni Youth of America Programs give the Alumni players an opportunity to put their commitment to "Caring for Kids" into action. This is accomplished through both the NFL Alumni's Youth Scholarship Grants and Youth of America Week.

NFL Alumni Youth Scholarship Grants are given to outstanding high school scholar-athletes who otherwise would be unable to continue their education. Each grant is funded by corporate support and is given in memory of some of the game's most legendary figures. Thus far, two $5,000 grants have been given in memory of pro football legends Red Grange and Jack Christiansen. The students are selected by the National Football Foundation and the College Hall of Fame.

Although the Alumni and local chapters conduct charitable and educational programs year-round, the highlight is Youth of America Week, which culminates in seven days of concentrated youth work during the first week of the NFL season.

During Youth of America Week, Alumni members and supporters gather to reach out to the nation's youth through sports and service activities of all kinds, according to local needs. The underlying purpose of these and other Alumni activities is to present successful former professional athletes as role models for today's youth.

Activities range from visits to children's homes and hospitals to appearances at schools and juvenile detention facilities, hosting youth sports festivals, taking groups of inner-city kids to home-team games, hosting picnics and outings and holding Alumni Youth Football Clinics and seminars for coaches and parents.

After a modest beginning in 1982, the Youth of America concept has spread to each NFL city and beyond to wherever former professionals gather. Youth of America Week was proclaimed a national observance by President Reagan in 1983, received the blessings of Pope John Paul II in 1985, and shows promise of expanding into other sports as well as to other nations.

"DIRE NEED" FUND

With little fanfare, the Fort Lauderdale-based Alumni organization works closely with NFL Charities to lend a helping hand to former pros in financial straits who need assistance to support themselves.

Administered by the NFL Alumni Foundation, a body set up jointly by NFL Charities and the NFL Alumni to underwrite costs of the program, the Dire Need Fund provides eligible retirees with a measure of financial stability in times of hardship.

In order to qualify for Dire Need consideration, applicants must have played at least five years of professional football in the pre-1959 era. They and their spouses must have a total annual income of less than $12,000. The identities of recipients are not made public.

NFL Charities and the NFL Alumni are the foundation's only source of funding. Charities' grants accrue through the licensing of league and club trademarks, while Alumni contributions come primarily from its annual Charity Golf Classic Series.

Since its start in the early 1970s, the Dire Need Fund has received more than $1.8 million in total funding for its operations—$1,345,000 from NFL Charities and $517,000 from the NFL Alumni. From the perspective of both parties, it is money well spent.

Operations of the foundation are overseen by seven trustees. They are NFL Commissioner Paul J. Tagliabue, league appointees William V. Bidwell, Wellington T. Mara and Rankin Smith, Sr., and Alumni representatives William M. Dudley, John Panelli and John J. Rogers.